30 Essential Skills for the Qualitative Researcher

John W. Creswell
University of Nebraska–Lincoln

Los Angeles | London | New Delhi
Singapore | Washington DC

Los Angeles | London | New Delhi
Singapore | Washington DC

FOR INFORMATION:

SAGE Publications, Inc.
2455 Teller Road
Thousand Oaks, California 91320
E-mail: order@sagepub.com

SAGE Publications Ltd.
1 Oliver's Yard
55 City Road
London EC1Y 1SP
United Kingdom

SAGE Publications India Pvt. Ltd.
B 1/I 1 Mohan Cooperative Industrial Area
Mathura Road, New Delhi 110 044
India

SAGE Publications Asia-Pacific Pte. Ltd.
3 Church Street
#10-04 Samsung Hub
Singapore 049483

Printed in the United States of America

ISBN 978-1-4522-1686-7

Acquisitions Editor: Vicki Knight
eLearning Editor: Katie Bierach
Editorial Assistant: Yvonne McDuffee
Production Editor: Olivia Weber-Stenis
Copy Editor: Jim Kelly
Typesetter: C&M Digitals (P) Ltd.
Proofreader: Jennifer Grubba
Indexer: Molly Hall
Cover Designer: Anupama Krishnan
Marketing Manager: Nicole Elliott

This book is printed on acid-free paper.

SUSTAINABLE FORESTRY INITIATIVE
Certified Chain of Custody
Promoting Sustainable Forestry
www.sfiprogram.org
SFI-01268
SFI label applies to text stock

15 16 17 18 19 10 9 8 7 6 5 4 3 2 1

30 Essential Skills for the Qualitative Researcher

This book is dedicated to all of the students, faculty, and
staff at the University of Nebraska–Lincoln who helped me develop as
a writer and scholar in research methods over the past 30 years. Thanks for your support.

John W. Creswell, Lincoln, Nebraska

Table of Contents

14   Conducting a Good Observation   117

15   Designing and Administering an Interview Protocol   126

16   Collecting Data With Marginalized Populations   137

17   Being Culturally Aware in Global Qualitative Research   144

Part V Analyzing and Validating Data 151

18 Coding Text Data 152

19 Coding Images and Pictures 166

20 Developing Theme Passages 174

Part VII Evaluating a Study and Using Qualitative Designs   249

29   Selecting Quality Criteria for a Qualitative Study   250

30   Introducing Qualitative Designs   257

Preface

Purpose

As with most of the books I have written, I developed this book so that I would have a text for my course, in this case an introductory qualitative research course. As I reviewed existing introductory books, it seemed as if they adequately covered the general principles of doing qualitative research. Some of them relied heavily on specific qualitative studies and summarized the major elements of those studies. Others I found overly complex to a point where I could not in good conscience recommend them as texts for my students to read. What was needed, it seemed to me, was a text that spoke to the "practical" aspects of actually doing qualitative research. By "practical" I do not mean a lockstep or rigid approach to qualitative research, but a discussion of "how" one goes about actually conducting qualitative research. How does a person code qualitative data from transcriptions of text or from pictures drawn by participants? How does a person design a qualitative central question or engage in the steps of analyzing qualitative interview data? This is all practical "how-to" advice that is missing from the introductory literature on qualitative inquiry. Without this type of discussion, students or beginning qualitative researchers are left to figure out on their own how to conduct this form of research.

Moreover, I wanted to share some of the techniques and procedures I have learned over the past 30 years in conducting my own qualitative projects. My intent is not to say that "this is the only way" it can be done, but to at least share how it has worked for me. I offer these techniques and procedures here only as approaches that have worked well for me. So often qualitative book writers hide behind the views of others, and we do not learn about what has worked well for them. So, this book is my attempt to share with you many of my ideas about qualitative research, which I have learned from practice, teaching, and writing about the subject. Accordingly, I draw on a few examples from my prior texts on research design, qualitative inquiry, and mixed methods. I will cite some other authors, but when I do, it will be in the spirit of sharing their specific practical approaches and presenting a counterpoint to my ideas.

What you will find in this book are several innovative topics not traditionally addressed in "research methods" books. For example, you will find chapters on thinking like a qualitative researcher, dealing with the emotional side of doing qualitative research, engaging in intercoder agreement checks, coding pictures, writing conclusions, and scripting out passages to ensure the accurate inclusion of important elements.

So, the aim of this book is to present 30 essential skills I have used in conducting my own qualitative studies. Thirty is certainly an arbitrary number; the skills actually used in research may be much more extensive or even less extensive. But these 30 are the central ones I would use in conveying to beginning researchers what they need to know to get started with their qualitative projects. I realize that readers will not find all chapters or skills equally relevant. Because of time constraints in classes or areas of interest, readers may certainly choose certain chapters to read or to use.

I also recognize that a basic feature of qualitative research is to develop "understanding." But consistent with my practical approach, I see some definite "skills" beginning researchers need to master to have a rigorous, sophisticated qualitative project. A skill is a particular ability or type of expertise that can be developed, and once it is acquired, it can help a person conduct a thorough, rigorous qualitative study. You will see that I start each chapter with skills to be "developed" by studying the content of that chapter. Developing a skill set is important before creatively inventing your own approaches. In a similar way, a solid understanding of music theory is essential before you move on to composition; the basic skills of architecture provide a foundation before you move on to creative innovation in design. So, although I am a strong proponent of innovation and creativity in qualitative research, I feel that the beginning inquirer first needs to master the basic skills.

Audience

The audience for this book is individuals in the social, behavioral, and health sciences who hope to conduct qualitative research. It is especially aimed at the new researcher, an individual who is contemplating qualitative research for the first time. These individuals may be graduate students, faculty, or those who perform qualitative research outside of academia. For more experienced inquirers, this book provides a review of key skill areas and shares how I work as a qualitative researcher.

Organization of the Book

My writing style, as I hope you will find in most of my books, is straightforward, focusing on the key content to be learned. I also bring a "conversational" style to the writing, talking about my own experiences, using personal pronouns, and keeping the narrative as user-friendly as possible. I try to follow in the footsteps of one of my significant mentors, the late Harry Wolcott, who wrote in this conversational style while at the same time conveying important content about qualitative methods (see Wolcott, 2009, 2010). I also bring in exercises so that you can practice my ideas, and I keep the references to a minimum so as to not unduly interrupt the flow of ideas. The book contains seven parts with short chapters. I intentionally kept the chapters short so that each could be focused on a single skill.

Part I provides some initial remarks about what it takes to understand qualitative research. You will learn how to think as a researcher, how this thinking differs from that required for quantitative research, how to make a qualitative study conceptually and methodologically interesting, how to negotiate the emotions that arise when conducting qualitative research, and how to work with faculty research advisors and committees. Part II reflects on some core ideas necessary before beginning to design a qualitative study. I reflect on philosophical ideas and on theory as ideas that flow throughout a project. I also suggest that you anticipate ethical issues and develop a literature map in order to see how your study adds to existing knowledge. Finally, I suggest that you understand the macrostructure of a published qualitative study—the internal structure of a written project that provides a scaffold for your study. In Part III, I start with the beginning of a qualitative study and work through to the end of the study. I begin with ideas about writing a title, building a clear abstract, writing an introduction, and developing a clear purpose statement and research questions. You will see in this section "scripts" and "templates" I would recommend to add a clarity of presentation to your project. Armed with this introduction, in Part IV, I discuss collecting data by first assessing the types of data available, and then reviewing the specifics of conducting a good observation and a thoughtful interview. I also speak about collecting data with marginalized populations, and reaching out globally with your research to samples and audiences that differ in social identities, such as culture, gender, race, or socioeconomic status. Part V continues into the next phase of the research: analyzing and validating the results. This section begins with the important step of coding data, both text and pictures, and then moves into larger abstractions, called themes. I also take time to reflect on the use of qualitative software for analysis and then turn to validity checks and reliability assessment through intercoder agreement. In Part VI, I take up the important topic of compiling a written qualitative study through scholarly writing and the inclusion of important qualitative writing elements. I also address the qualitative concept of reflexivity and how to write it into your study, and how to write a good conclusion to a qualitative project. I end with some advice on how to publish a qualitative study in a scholarly journal. In the final section of book, Part VII, I turn to helping you decide how to evaluate the quality of your project, and I end the book by foreshadowing the next phase to build on this book—the use of specific types of qualitative research approaches or designs, such as ethnographies, case studies, and grounded theory projects—that will extend your skill set even further.

Writing Features

Please note several writing elements in this book that will hopefully serve to make it practical and conversational. I start each chapter by mentioning the skill (or skills) I hope to address and why this skill is important. I have written short, easily digestible chapters, used bullets to highlight key points, brought in activities to practice the content, and, most important, shared my approach to using the skill. As for disclaimers, this book is not intended to be a comprehensive assessment of qualitative research, to dwell at length on philosophical ideas, to rigidly convey "one approach" to inquiry, or to subject all phases of research to an analysis of ethical problems and issues. As is customary in all of my books, I try to present options for consideration and present enough information so that you can weigh the options as you consider how to practice qualitative research.

Acknowledgments

This book could not have been written without the use of the student examples of good and better models sprinkled throughout. I also profited from the expertise of Tim Guetterman, a doctoral student who spent extensive time on the book, its revisions, and review, and from Rachel Sinley, another doctoral student who helped shape several chapters. Both individuals have worked closely with me in my research office. I also acknowledge the contribution of my colleagues at SAGE Publications, who saw the need for this book and encouraged me to write it. My editor and publisher, Vicki Knight, has been a mainstay throughout my writing over the past half dozen years, and her thoughts, guidance, and wisdom helped bring this book to fruition. I also acknowledge the helpful comments provided by many reviewers employed by SAGE to give thoughtful, considered feedback on earlier drafts of the book: Ellen Barber, Massachusetts College of Liberal Arts; Jennifer M. Beller, Washington State University; Lori L. Britt, James Madison University; Erin Graybill Ellis, Texas Woman's University; Julie L. Guay, Immaculata University; Andrew W. Ishak, Santa Clara University; Clarena Larrotta, Texas State University; Brian McNely, University of Kentucky; Judith M. Meloy, Castleton State College; Tara L. Shepperson, Eastern Kentucky University; Kristen Hawley Turner, Fordham University; and David M. Yaskewich, Southeast Missouri State University.

Online Resources

The companion Web site at study.sagepub.com/30skills includes open-access resources for students and password-protected resources for instructors. Instructor resources include PowerPoint slides, lecture notes with discussion questions, and suggested exercises and assignments. Students who visit study.sagepub.com/30skills will find quizzes, eFlashcards, and SAGE journal articles for each module to deepen their understanding of qualitative research.

About the Author

 **John W. Creswell** is a professor of educational psychology at the University of Nebraska–Lincoln. He has authored numerous articles on mixed methods research, qualitative methodology, and general research design in 26 books (including new editions). He held the Clifton Institute Endowed Professor Chair for 5 years at the University of Nebraska–Lincoln. For the past 5 years, Dr. Creswell has served as a codirector in the Office of Qualitative and Mixed Methods Research at the University of Nebraska–Lincoln. He served as the founding coeditor of the SAGE publication *Journal of Mixed Methods Research*, and worked as an adjunct professor of family medicine at the University of Michigan. He also worked extensively as a consultant in the health services research area for the U.S. Department of Veterans Affairs. Dr. Creswell was a Senior Fulbright Scholar to South Africa in 2008 and to Thailand in 2012. In 2011 he served as a co-leader of a national working group at the National Institutes of Health developing "best practices" for mixed methods research in the health sciences. In spring 2013, Dr. Creswell was a visiting professor at Harvard's School of Public Health. In 2014, he was awarded an honorary doctorate from the University of Pretoria in South Africa. Recently, he has been elected president of the Mixed Methods International Research Association for 2014 to 2015. He has also assumed the role of director of the College of Education and Human Sciences Mixed Methods Training Academy at the University of Nebraska–Lincoln. His newest book *A Concise Introduction to Mixed Methods Research*, was published by SAGE Publications in April 2014.

Understanding the Landscape of Qualitative Research

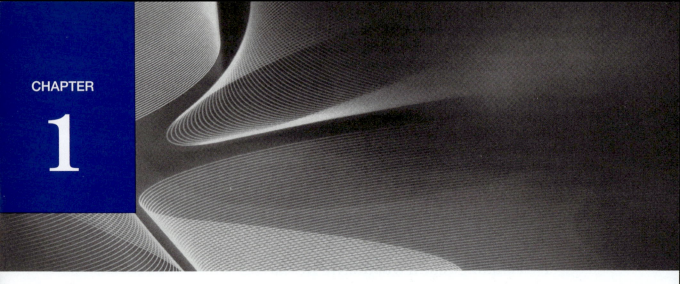

Thinking Like a Qualitative Researcher

Skill

Develop the skill of thinking like a qualitative researcher.

Why the Skill Is Important

Qualitative research requires that people approach research from a perspective that may be different than what they have previously learned. It requires thinking differently than the perspectives taken in quantitative research. The skill is also important because today there are many varieties of qualitative research. Some individuals take more of a philosophical approach, more of a theoretical or advocacy approach, or more of a specific focus on topics such as data analysis or validity. My approach is more of a strong methods approach in which I emphasize rigorous methods, good protocols for collection and analysis, multiple and extensive data collection, and multiple steps in data analysis. You will see my approach emerge as a structured way to conduct qualitative research (e.g., scripting the purpose statement and the use of computer software). Thus, understanding the skill is important both as you develop as a qualitative researcher and as you understand my approach to the topic.

The Research Process

Qualitative research is an approach to inquiry that follows the traditional ways of conducting social, behavioral, and health science research. In this **process of research**, the inquirer starts with a problem that needs to be solved, and then formulates a question that, if answered, will help address the problem. The question will be answered by collecting and analyzing data gathered from people who can help answer the question. Once this information is collected and analyzed, the inquirer then writes up a report of the study summarizing the findings. These conclusions are disseminated in many types of reports, such as doctoral dissertations, master's theses, journal articles, proposals for funding, and local organizational studies. This process may be familiar to many beginning researchers.

Different Approaches to This Research Process

We have three genres of research that follow this process of research: quantitative research, qualitative research, and mixed methods research. Not all people divide up the genres of research into these three types, but this is the way I think of them and have written about them. Both quantitative and qualitative research approaches have been around a long time. In the early 20th century, scientists developed our procedures for quantitative experiments and surveys and invented different ways to statistically analyze our data. Also in this early period, qualitative research was born out of the writing of anthropologists and then sociologists. Although qualitative research as an approach is largely ascribed to the mid-1900s, it developed rapidly during the late 1900s and has been extensively used in the social and behavioral sciences over the past 40 years. Mixed methods research is new, beginning about 25 years ago during the late 1980s, with several writers developing the features we know today.

How Qualitative Researchers Think

The entire idea of considering how qualitative researchers think and approach the social world they are in resulted from my composition of a "qualitative inquiry quiz" I gave a few times to students who entered my qualitative research courses. I told them that the intent of this 30-item quiz was to determine whether they would make good qualitative researchers, and the items were intended to elicit responses to these questions. These questions helped determine if students had characteristics I often associated with qualitative research. In my answers to this quiz, I said that the qualitative researcher

- Saw the big picture

- Made connections easily

- Liked to write

- Liked to draw pictures

- Organized diffuse information into categories

- Saw unusual things in everyday detail

- Was bored by the routine

- Saw many perspectives about things

- Loved to explore

- Liked to tinker

- Knew how to count, but liked words better

For example, one question in the quiz asked whether, if students were standing at the entrance to Rocky Mountain National Park and looking off into the distance, they saw the broad panorama of the entire series of peaks and valleys or the detail of individual trees. My thought was that the qualitative researcher often sought the "big picture" rather than focusing on individual elements (as the quantitative researcher might do). Needless to say, I did not administer this quiz very often. Students were concerned that they were failing as qualitative researchers in just the first class!

Unquestionably, this quiz focused on personal orientations of qualitative researchers. But the quiz did cause me to think that there is a way that qualitative researchers might look at the social world they are in, and my first skill would be to convey some sense of what this vision might be. So I changed the entrance activity for my qualitative research courses and shifted my focus to a single picture. Basically, I wanted to understand from the students what qualitative research meant to them. We often make qualitative research much too difficult to describe when essentially it can be reduced to a few key ideas. The sign of a good thinker is the ability to conceptualize in a simple way as well as in a complex way. There is a way to describe qualitative research simply, and that is to discuss how qualitative researchers think when they approach a research topic. So, instead of a quiz, I decided to give my students a picture to look at and to describe.

The Boat Picture

I provided a picture of boats on a lake. Most people are not familiar with this picture, and I asked my students to simply describe what they saw in the picture.

Furthermore, I asked them to write a short paragraph about what they saw in the picture. What they wrote tended to fall into groups of qualitative or quantitative observations. This provided an opportunity for me to explain how quantitative and qualitative researchers observe a scene.

Reaction From a Quantitative Researcher

Those who approach the picture in a more *quantitative* way have described in their paragraphs these features:

- They report measures such as water level or distance of the boats from shore.

- They describe the time of day on the basis of the sun's position.

- They describe the topography of the land.

- They describe the dimensions of things in the picture, such as the large hills, the small boats, and the small sticks in the water.

- They enumerate the types of colors they see, such as the oranges, the browns, and the blacks.

Reaction From a Qualitative Researcher

Other students in the class might describe the picture in more of a *qualitative* way—a less counting or numeric way. Perhaps these students come from the humanities or they have read something about qualitative research. Here are some ways these students describe the boat picture:

- They tell stories about people who were fishing during the day and are now resting at home with their families.

- They describe a hush over the lake as the boats rest for the night.

- They describe all aspects of the picture—the sun, the trees, the lake, the boats. A panorama unfolds.

- They discuss the contrasts of light and dark.

- They might create poems or songs about the lake.

- They might see themselves sitting on the shore looking at the calm boats and feeling at peace with themselves.

- They might place themselves on the boats, sitting there peacefully at sundown.

- They talk about what is not in the picture, such as people or children playing on the shore.

- They see the disturbance in the water—something unusual or unexpected.

The Nature of Qualitative Research

What is qualitative research, and when is it the best choice for a study? Various authors have enumerated the nature of this form of research, and I would like to present what I have used over the years as the major elements of this approach. At the heart of qualitative research is, I believe, a **central phenomenon** (or topic) we wish to explore. This is the one central idea you would like to learn about or study in your project (your focus may move beyond this one idea as your project proceeds). Around this central phenomenon are arrayed several elements of the nature of qualitative research (presented in no specific order). About the central phenomenon we hope to:

> You can identify the nature of a qualitative study by assessing whether it contains many of 11 different major elements.

Report the voices of participants. Qualitative research involves reporting how people talk about things, how they describe things, and how they see the world. This comes through in a qualitative study in terms of the quotations we see in published qualitative projects. It comes through individual perspectives. Through these quotations, we hear the voices of individuals—their personal views, their ways of talking, their takes on the situation.

Go out to the setting (or context) to collect data. Qualitative research involves going out to a setting and studying it firsthand. Thus, we are not only interested in how people talk about things, we are also interested in how their particular setting or context shapes what they have to say. We are interested in the boats, the hills, the sun, and the sky. The context may be their families, their friends, their homes, their work, or many other contexts in which they live, work, or interact. Context or setting is very important in qualitative research.

Look at how processes unfold. In qualitative research, inquirers often study processes or what unfolds over time. These processes have steps, and one step comes before another. This study of process has a time element as well, so we need to follow what unfolds over a long period of time. A person might reflect on what happened during the day on a boat and how the boat was put to rest in the evening.

Focus in on a small number of people or sites. In qualitative research we study a small number of people but go deep to develop the detail they provide to us. Rather than trying to apply conclusions from a small number of individuals to a large number, researchers study a small number of people who are, in and of themselves, of interest. If we studied a large number, we would lose the richness of learning from a few and lose the depth of understanding specific individuals. In the picture, we have one lake and a small number of boats.

Explore in an open-ended way. Qualitative research is exploratory research. We do not often know what questions to ask, what variables to measure, or what people to initially talk to. We are simply exploring a topic (later we will call it a central phenomenon) with some individuals (or organizations) we think will yield useful information. We are not trying to explain predetermined factors or specific relationships, because they may not hold true with the people we need to learn from. We might simply want to describe what it is like to sit and look at the boats in the evening.

Develop a complex understanding. The beauty of qualitative research is that it provides a complex understanding of a problem or situation. The more facets the researcher uncovers, the better; the more unpredictable aspects that surface, the better. We hear multiple voices from many participants, gather multiple perspectives, and develop multiple themes. In short, qualitative studies represent the complexity of a situation, a complexity that does often mirror that of real life. For example, in the boat picture, the glaring sun offsets the calm of the boats—a contrast that adds complexity.

Lift up the silenced voices of marginalized groups or populations. Qualitative research works best when studying people who have not often been studied. These may be individuals from diverse cultures, socioeconomic levels, racial groups, and gender orientations. For these groups, the traditional instruments, measures, and variables do not fit, because available research was developed on nonmarginalized groups of people. These groups often remain outside the mainstream of conventional research, and hence, we do not know much about them. The people who own and use the boats may be an understudied group.

Create multiple perspectives or views of the phenomenon. The best qualitative research shares information about themes drawn from **multiple perspectives**. I say, "report the good, the bad, and the ugly." So, qualitative research is not a "Pollyanna" perspective of hope and gratitude. Intermixed with these ideas would be the worries, concerns, setbacks, and dilemmas that are the very fabric of our lives. When a theme is presented in a qualitative study, we hear about the many perspectives of individuals, individuals from different walks of life, age groups, geographic regions, genders, and so forth, that provide a rich mosaic of life. One theme from the boat picture might include the multiple perspectives of the "transitions" of daily life for individuals, from busy fishing trips to the calm of the lake at night.

Contrast different views of the phenomenon. Qualitative research gives us the opportunity to contrast what is stated (e.g., organizational goals) with what is not stated (e.g., informal goals). When we talk to people we may obtain a different perspective than when we look at the formal structure of an organization. This contrast may lead to some useful observations or useful changes for organizations. This point again speaks to contrasts—the heat of the sun and the calm of the water, the one pole left unattended by a boat and fisherman.

Study sensitive topics. Qualitative research involves the study of emotionally charged topics that are hard to research. Because we talk directly to people and spend time in their settings, we may get them to talk about the "hard issues," the problems that typically do not surface in more conventional research. Qualitative research is known for addressing **sensitive topics**, hard-to-study topics, and topics close to the problems of individuals living in this complex world. Thus, it takes a brave person to engage in qualitative research, to go out and confront individuals directly in open-ended interviews, and to wrestle with difficult topics to understand and embrace. We can see the emotions of calm, the uncertainty as to what the next day will bring, and the hope for better fishing tomorrow in the boat picture.

Reflect on our own biases and experiences. Qualitative researchers are self-conscious researchers, always reflecting on what they personally bring to a study. They realize that they bring their own cultures and backgrounds and that this shapes how they view the social world they see. Moreover, they are willing to talk about their backgrounds and their influence on their writing and their conceptualizations of their qualitative studies. This is being reflexive, or positioning themselves in their studies. They are not passive observers of the study and in the background; instead, they are in the foreground and are present in the final writing product of a study.

Some Misconceptions About Qualitative Research

Now that I have talked about what qualitative research is to me, it might be helpful to review some of the misconceptions people have of qualitative research. Sometimes people characterize qualitative research by one method of data collection—"It means hanging out by the fountain and observing." Or someone might say that qualitative research is "holding focus groups." Instead, I view qualitative research as incorporating many methods of data collection, using multiple methods, and drawing on the strength of each method to understand the problem at hand. Sometimes people characterize qualitative research as not rigorous or systematic—indeed, as not having a structure to the steps in the process of research. Instead, qualitative research is a science in which we collect data to answer questions. It is also empirical in that we collect data. I see qualitative research as having steps in all phases of the research process, and qualitative researchers engage in these steps with as much systematic attention as in any other form of inquiry. The chapters in this book will hopefully attest to the rigor of qualitative research.

Some people think that qualitative research is too subjective and too interpretive. They are often referring to the open-ended nature of qualitative questions, which then permits the researcher to draw together the codes or themes that describe the responses. True, the qualitative researcher does need to make an interpretation of the data and to form themes in the data analysis steps. But then the accuracy of this interpretation can be examined through the many validity checks the researcher could put into place. In the end, the researcher's interpretation is often checked by the participants in a study and ultimately examined by the readers of the study.

Some people think that qualitative research is too expensive and too labor intensive to carry out. True, qualitative researchers stay in the "setting" for long periods of time, and conduct labor-intensive interviews and observations. To transcribe qualitative interviews, for instance, takes considerable time. To then analyze the transcriptions by going line for line again takes time. But the technology is now in place to help the qualitative researcher. Voice translation programs are available to use in addition to qualitative data analysis software programs. These tools will at least reduce the time required for the more labor-intensive phases of this form of research.

SUMMARY

So the skill I am writing about in this chapter is to know how qualitative researchers think and to be able to convey the essential characteristics of qualitative research. Knowing these characteristics will enable you to define qualitative research when you need to defend your choice of research methodology and to evaluate whether you have a good qualitative study. Knowing what characteristics you bring to qualitative research will give you confidence to engage in this form of inquiry and to assess your own personal readiness for conducting a qualitative study.

ACTIVITY

Do you now have a sense of how a qualitative researcher might think about the boat picture? One activity for follow-up would be to redraft your initial statement about the boat picture and try to incorporate as many of the characteristics of qualitative research as possible. Alternatively, you might choose another picture—something that has a panoramic view—and describe it from a qualitative way of thinking.

When someone asks you, "What is qualitative research?" you have a list of central characteristics you could tell them. Alternatively, you might pull out a picture and describe how a qualitative researcher might think about it.

FURTHER RESOURCES

Look at the core characteristics of qualitative research. Many introductory qualitative research books include their own lists, and there are many features common from book to book. Begin by looking at:

Marshall, C., & Rossman, G. B. (2015). *Designing qualitative research* (6th ed.). Thousand Oaks, CA: Sage.

Visit study.sagepub.com/30skills for quizzes, eFlashcards, and more!

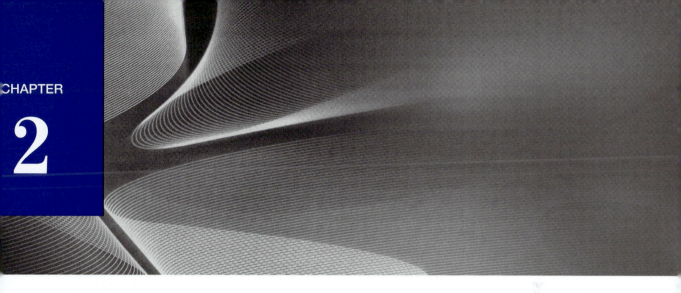

Building on Quantitative Research Knowledge to Implement Qualitative Research

Skill

Develop the skill of knowing how qualitative research differs from quantitative research.

Why the Skill Is Important

It is not enough to understand how qualitative researchers "think"; we also need to actually "see" how they practice research. There are two skills involved in learning the characteristics of qualitative research. The first is that researchers need to build or scaffold onto what they already know about research. This often means that they have some foundation in quantitative approaches, typically learned through their psychology classes. They then need to be "lifted over" into qualitative research in a way they can understand and add to their understanding. As one student said, "I had to retrain my brain to think as a qualitative researcher" (K. Doud, personal communication). The best way to do this is to develop a one-for-one comparison between the "parts" of quantitative research and the "parts" of qualitative research. Thus, the skill of learning the essential characteristics of qualitative research involves distinguishing it from quantitative research. Second, with this learning in mind, the next skill can be advanced—understanding the major characteristics of qualitative research and being able to "see" them in a published qualitative research study. In order to accomplish this, we can analyze a quantitative journal article and see how the authors incorporated the major characteristics of quantitative research. We can also look at a qualitative journal article, examine the elements of qualitative research that went into it, and then make comparisons between a qualitative and a quantitative study.

Characteristics of Quantitative Research in a Quantitative Journal Article

The characteristics of a good quantitative study can be seen through an examination of the aspects of the process of research that typically appear in a journal article, as shown in Table 2.1.

In a quantitative journal article, the design is set with hypotheses and research questions identified in advance, and the data collection (and analysis) organized before the project begins. These features do not change during the administration of a project. Before the study, the investigator specifies the hypotheses and questions, selects the constructs or variables to be measured, and identifies instruments (with good validity and reliability scores) to be used in the study. These hypotheses and questions, in turn, narrow the variables to be examined, and, although the variable list is small, the N, or number of participants in the study, is large because of the demands of specific statistical tests for certain sizes to meet test assumptions. The

TABLE 2.1   How Quantitative Characteristics Are Manifest in a Quantitative Journal Article

Quantitative Characteristics	How Characteristics Are Manifest in a Quantitative Journal Article (Look-Fors)
Fixed design	Hypotheses set in advance; design does not change in field; fidelity of procedures
Researcher's views	Researcher identifies questions, selects instruments, selects statistics
Narrowed picture	Reduced to specific variables; large N
Researcher bias absent	Researcher not mentioned; bias kept out of study
Contrived setting	Artificial laboratory setup; survey sent at distance
Closed-ended data collection	Specific instruments, scales, measures used
Structured writing format	Accepted structure: introduction, literature review, methods, results, conclusions

researcher is not usually mentioned personally in a quantitative study (e.g., his or her experiences and interpretations), and the investigator tries to keep bias that might influence the outcomes out of the project. Often quantitative studies are conducted in a laboratory setting under tight controls or administered through the mail, as in survey research. The questions on instruments administered are closed-ended, with forced-choice response categories and scales that are continuous or categorical. The data analysis procedure is then to enter the scores into a computer file and to analyze the data using statistical programs. In the end, we see a quantitative article that typically fits a prescribed structure, moving from the introduction (statement of the problem), through the literature review and the methods, and on to the results and the discussion.

Characteristics of Qualitative Research in a Qualitative Journal Article

What makes a journal article a qualitative study? Books and articles on qualitative research often present definitions of qualitative research, but those studying this form of research do not always know how to apply these definitions to actual qualitative articles to see how the key ideas in definitions manifest themselves in the articles and in specific research studies. I recall teaching a group of faculty the basics of qualitative research, and one individual, a hard-discipline scientist, came up to me at the end of the session and said that he saw no difference between quantitative and qualitative research. He obviously did not understand the key components of qualitative research and how they are manifest in an actual published study.

This discussion is an attempt to remedy this situation, and I believe that to get to a point of "seeing" the meaning of qualitative research unfold in a study, we need to go through several steps. As shown in Table 2.2, we can take the core characteristics of quantitative research and apply them now to what we hope to see in a published qualitative research journal article. In the table, I have put in parentheses the core characteristics of qualitative research as first introduced in Chapter 1. This discussion will expand on these core characteristics and also relate them to a published journal article.

As shown in Table 2.2, we would expect that the design of the study would change during the project. New questions become important to ask as researchers clarify what they seek to learn. New participants and sites may be studied to better understand the core learning to be gained. The original plan for analysis may change as new information becomes available that needs to be probed. In addition, when we read a qualitative article, we "hear" the participants' voices through quotations that may be entire paragraphs or single phrases or sentences. How participants speak and frame answers to questions is of upmost importance. What emerges from this qualitative analysis is a complex picture—not simply cause-and-effect thinking or group comparison thinking—but the complexity of human life. We will find multiple

TABLE 2.2   How Qualitative Characteristics Are Manifest in a Qualitative Journal Article

Qualitative Characteristics	How Characteristics Are Manifest in a Qualitative Journal Article (Look-Fors)
Emerging design (exploratory, process)	Changing research questions, changing data collection
Participants' views (voices of the people; multiple perspectives; small N; marginalized populations)	Quotations from participants
Complex picture (complex understanding; sensitive topics)	Multiple codes and themes
Researcher bias present (reflexivity)	Remarks by authors about their experiences and interpretations
Context/setting important (context or setting)	Data gathered on site; setting discussed
Open-ended data collection (exploring)	Open-ended interviews/observations
Inductive data analysis (exploring; contrasts)	Analysis from specific to general
Flexible writing structure	Structure may begin with authors; writing different than traditional approach of introduction, literature review, methods, results, conclusions

themes and codes that show this complexity. After reading a qualitative study we will say to ourselves, "This is really a complex subject with many moving parts." In reading the study, we will learn about the researchers—what their experiences were with the phenomena under study, and how their experiences shaped their interpretation of what they saw. The researchers will be present from the written work. We will also be given some detail about the setting or context in which the study took place. We should be able to visualize the setting, and know details about the people who interact in that setting. We will gain this knowledge from the interviews asking general, open-ended questions to solicit the wide range of views from participants. The analysis of these open-ended views will build "from the ground up," as they say. We see the quotations, which are embedded within larger codes, and the multiple codes providing evidence for larger themes. The larger themes are then spun into a story, and the story is presented often with an added visual picture. We are reading results from the raw data into broad conceptualization. This qualitative project may not fit into our traditional ways of seeing research presented. It may start with a personal story, or the methods may be described in a piecemeal fashion throughout the study rather than in one separate section, or the literature review segment may not exist. We need to be open to a creative writing project that may not fit the traditional way of staging the report of research.

Comparing Qualitative and Quantitative Characteristics on a Continuum

What can be said is that these characteristics might be seen as forming two ends of a continuum, with qualitative articles tending toward the qualitative end and quantitative articles leaning toward the quantitative end. Although a rigid dichotomy is not a useful heuristic to understand these two forms of research, their differences can be highlighted by a continuum. Studies tend to be weighted more heavily toward one end of the continuum than the other. How many end points of one approach (say qualitative) would result in calling a study qualitative is a debatable point. I tend to think that if all of the end points, to a certain extent, are represented by one approach (qualitative or quantitative), I would consider the study as lodging in that approach. Table 2.3 helps illustrate the two ends of this continuum of research, from the qualitative end on the left to the quantitative end on the right.

> Qualitative and quantitative research should not be seen as opposite approaches, but two different perspectives on a continuum.

Easy- and Hard-to-See Components

In terms of these continua, some are easy to spot in a qualitative or quantitative study, and some are difficult to identify. Let us start with the easy-to-see components that differentiate quantitative versus qualitative research in journal articles. We can easily see in the results sections of both types of journal articles a difference between the *report of numbers or statistics* and the *report of themes* that are discussed by authors in a results or findings section. Also, if we look closely at the

TABLE 2.3

Qualitative Research		Quantitative Research
Emerging design	<=======>	Fixed design
Participants' views	<=======>	Researchers' views
Complex picture	<=======>	Narrowed picture
Researchers bias present	<=======>	Researcher bias absent
Context/setting important	<=======>	Contrived setting
Open-ended data collection	<=======>	Closed-ended data collection
Inductive data analysis	<=======>	Deductive data analysis
Flexible writing structure	<=======>	Highly structured writing

research questions, we can see that the quantitative study contains hypotheses or questions that specify in a *closed way* the relationships among variables or, alternatively, a comparison of groups. In qualitative research we do not use variables and instead present a central phenomenon (or key idea) that we want to explore in an *open-ended way* by asking participants general questions about it. The writing style also differs. In quantitative research studies we see a literature review section that may contain a theory. The extensive literature and theory put a space (or *objective distance*) between the researcher and the reader and thus contrasts with the more *personal* style of qualitative research, where the researcher's experiences might be shared with the reader as well as his or her personal opinion (in the form of personal pronouns). Another easy-to-see aspect is in the writing structure. The typical quantitative project follows a *set structure* of introduction, literature review, methods, results, and discussion, while the qualitative structure may vary. It may *start with the personal views* of the author or interweave the methods with the results.

Some differences between the two approaches are harder to see. In quantitative research many decisions are made *before the study begins*: the identification of variables to study, the use of select instruments, and the types of statistical analysis, to list but a few. In qualitative research, the research questions are open ended, allowing the researcher to identify the relevant factors (such as the counterparts to variables) and thus allowing them to *emerge*. No set instrument is made in advance; indeed, the researcher is the instrument of data collection and poses general questions. These elements may not be made explicit, and therefore they are more difficult to see in a study.

The way the researcher analyzes the data, from the raw data to more general perspectives, may also not be evident. In quantitative research, the process of research often consists of advancing a theory, deductively testing it, and conducting this test by collecting and analyzing data. This is a *deductive* process of research. In qualitative research, the inquirer uses an **inductive** process of gathering data, and then making sense of it by grouping data segments into codes, and then themes, and finally larger perspectives. Although both quantitative and qualitative researchers may use deductive and inductive logic, this general difference typically holds for most studies. In most studies it is difficult to tell when deductive or inductive logic is being used because the researchers do not tell us what logic they are using.

In quantitative research, the investigator reports detailed results about the relationships among variables. This is a *detailed* and explicit analysis of variables. In qualitative research, the results often go in the opposite direction; rather than a focused attention on variables and their relationships, the qualitative findings address the *complexity* of the situation. Often the factors explored are interactive—they go back and forth rather than one way as in quantitative research. It may be hard for the reader to discern when cause-and-effect thinking is being used and when the complexity of a situation is being presented.

Also, in qualitative research complexity is presented through *multiple perspectives* introduced in the themes. Often these perspectives may not be easily seen in a theme discussion. Finally, in quantitative research the results are presented as the *view of the researcher*. It is the researcher who conducts the analysis and makes an interpretation. It is the researcher who selects the theory, selects the variables, and forms the hypotheses or research questions. Typically the researcher does not explicitly take ownership for this—it is assumed, and therefore it may be difficult to see. In qualitative research, on the other hand, the inquirer presents the *views of participants*. In most cases, this can be seen when researchers communicate the findings using direct quotations from study participants. But in some qualitative articles, few quotations are used, and the multiple perspectives of participants are simply reported. In these studies it is hard to see participants' views.

SUMMARY

To understand the unique characteristics of qualitative research, it is useful to have the skill of differentiating qualitative research from quantitative research. One way to easily see the difference is through a comparison of how the research appears in both quantitative and qualitative published journal articles. Unquestionably, some of the differences are easy to see and others more difficult.

ACTIVITY

Examine the following quantitative article:

Constantine, M. G., Wallace, B. C., & Kindaichi, M. M. (2005). Examining contextual factors in the career decision status of African American adolescents. *Journal of Career Assessment, 13*(3), 307–319.

Using Table 2.2, go through each characteristic of quantitative research and determine how each characteristic was used in the quantitative study. Then examine the following qualitative article:

Brown, J., Sorrell, J. H., McClaren, J., & Creswell, J. W. (2006). Waiting for a liver transplant. *Qualitative Health Research, 16*(1), 119–136.

Again using Table 2.2, go through each characteristic of qualitative research and determine how it was used in the qualitative study.

FURTHER RESOURCES

In my book on educational research, you will find an extended discussion of the differences between qualitative and quantitative research and how they differ on a continuum:

Creswell, J. W. (2015). *Educational research: Planning, conducting, and evaluating quantitative and qualitative research* (5th ed.). Upper Saddle River, NJ: Pearson.

Visit study.sagepub.com/30skills for quizzes, eFlashcards, and more!

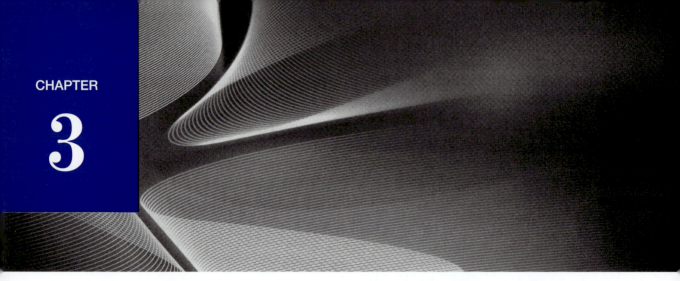

Making Your Qualitative Project Rigorous and Conceptually Interesting

Skill

Develop the skill of creating a qualitative project that has a rigorous and conceptually interesting element.

Why the Skill Is Important

Qualitative research is creative inquiry, and it permits the study of unusual groups or taking an unusual slant. The final study may attract attention for being out of the ordinary. A hallmark of qualitative research is also that it is interesting to read, as it often is written in a literary, persuasive way. Furthermore, you want to attract reader interest, potentially add to the literature, get your study published, win over your graduate committee, and perhaps ultimately get funded for your research. So, as a researcher you need to put those parts into your study. Simply put, qualitative inquirers study unusual problems, tackle difficult-to-access topics, and take perspectives that are often not anticipated in more traditional research.

Decide on Your Research Topic

Before you begin your research project, you will need to decide on the topic of your inquiry, or the central idea you want to learn about. *What is the topic of your study?* This is what we will call your *central phenomenon* and is the main subject of your study. It is the topic you would use if you were to conduct a computer search of databases on your topic. It is the idea that will catch the attention of readers when they see the title of your journal article in print. You might consider describing this phenomenon in a short phrase of two or three words.

Now, you need to ask yourself several questions about your topic. It is important to ask yourself whether this topic *can* be researched. Do you have access to participants? Do you have the resources to collect and analyze information? If not, you may need to rethink your study, or find a way to gain access to what you need. Moreover, is it an interesting topic to study? Will audiences find it of interest? The topic should be researched if *the research will add to the literature or to policy or to practice. Will scholars be interested in the topic?* Can you sell it to your research (thesis or dissertation) advisor or committee? Will you be able to publish this study? An interesting topic is a great start to any qualitative project. Will this study *advance your personal goals*? Are you interested in your topic? Can you build a thesis, a dissertation, or even a full research agenda out of it? Can you stay with the topic for a prolonged amount of time? Is it something you feel committed to, or passionate about? If so, this topic is well suited for you.

Refrain From Studying Your Own Backyard

One of the first things to be conscious of is what we call "studying your own backyard." This means that you need to be careful about conducting a study where you work, or with agencies or sites you are affiliated with, because of problems that may arise due to your role and the roles of people with whom you work. There are pros and cons of studying your own backyard (Marshall & Rossman, 2011), and basically I discourage this practice on political and ethical grounds.

One argument against studying your own backyard is that you have predetermined expectations of what you will find. Another is that the people you collect data from may see you as a colleague (and not answer truthfully), rather than as a researcher. Perhaps the most compelling case against studying your own backyard is that it raises ethical and power issues. Can you uncover and report damaging information without jeopardizing your job, your position, and your family? Will you feel comfortable reporting it? These are all serious issues and good reasons for staying away from your backyard as a place of study.

Of course, on the other side, in your backyard you will have easy access to data, and it will be convenient for you to collect data. In turn, this may reduce expenditures of time, effort, and money, which are all advantages to the busy student or researcher. You already have trusting relationships, so it may be easy to establish rapport and obtain information from people. Because it is your backyard and you are familiar with the situation, you may have more detailed and better data.

I agree that these are some useful advantages of studying a topic in your own backyard. But I see the disadvantages outweighing the advantages and would encourage you to not study your own backyard but to go to a location or meet with people who are not familiar to you. Go to the "strange" place, as ethnographers have been saying for years.

Make Your Topic Conceptually Interesting

The research site you choose for your study is just one of several important factors to help make your project interesting. Overall, any project undertaken by a qualitative researcher needs to be an insightful and rigorous study that someone would like to read. Here are some interesting elements that would make your study attractive to audiences:

- Study an unusual location (e.g., a small town in Alaska). The location in a qualitative study is called the *research site*. Is your site located in an unusual geographic location? Is it a place where people do not traditionally go or have not gone? Is it off the beaten path?

- Study an unusual group of participants. These participants may be individuals who are difficult to access, such as gang members, or they may be individuals relocated from some remote place who have not participated in a research study (e.g., Bhutanese refugees relocated to the Boston area).

- Take an angle or a perspective that may not be expected. It might well be the reverse side (the **shadow side**) of what *is* expected (e.g., in a distance learning class, rather than study-ing how students react when they are "on camera," look at them when they least expect to be filmed in the class). Qualitative researchers are good at flipping topics over, looking at their underside, exploring with this underside something that is unusual. Granted, whether an angle is unusual is a subjective assessment. What may be unusual to me may be ordinary for you. When a topic is flipped to look at the reverse side, it often becomes something quite unexpected—an unusual angle. For example, a student in my qualitative class, Michael Butchko, studied college-aged women who frequented pro-ana Web sites, where anorexia nervosa is viewed as *desirable* (the flip side), rather than what might be expected, Web sites that highlight the health dangers of anorexia nervosa (M. Butchko, personal communication, December 12, 2014).

- Collect data that are not typically expected in social science research (e.g., collect sounds; have participants take pictures; have participants look at relics that remind them of past experiences; interview people about the pictures they have taken; use Web sites' main pages, text messages, and so forth). For example, at a funeral of a leading educator who had spent years in one school district, the people organizing the funeral played sounds of children playing in a schoolyard for a full 20 minutes. The collection of sounds presented an unusual form of data to provide evidence for the closeness this educator felt to the students in his school district.

> Insert into your project one or more interesting elements mentioned in this chapter.

- Present your results or findings in an unusual way, such as through the creation of analogies (see Wolcott, 2010), maps, drawings, figures, or tables (e.g., include results that show geomapping of the incidence of substance use across a state). Move beyond simply reporting themes, and include an extensive array of data sources that characterize qualitative research.

- Study a timely topic that many individuals are discussing and one that is in the news media (e.g., write about campus violence and how a campus reacted to it). What topics are many people interested in right now (e.g., big data, the environment, immigration)?

Include an Interesting Element in Your Title

I suggest to my students that they begin with drafting titles for their projects and placing at least one interesting element in their titles. I recognize that authors often develop their titles at the end of their studies rather than at the beginning. However, drafting a title provides a placeholder at the beginning of your study that can be modified (even multiple times) during the course of a project.

So write down a draft title for your project. You might follow these guidelines to get started:

- Keep the title short, maybe no more than 10 words.

- Create a question within a title if this appeals to you.

- Start with a **gerund**, or "-ing" word, to convey action (e.g., "Waiting for a Liver Transplant").

- Create a two-part title if you wish. Usually, the second part of the two-part title conveys the type of design (e.g., "Returning to Vietnam: A Qualitative Study").

- Stay away from quantitative phrases, such as "impact of," "relationship between," "effect of," "correlation between," or "influence of."

- Include these elements in your title:
  - The topic (or central phenomenon)
  - The participants
  - The site

As my students write out their titles, I am looking for the aspects that would make their studies interesting, and I have them redraft their titles several times until the interesting angles, sites, data collection, and so on, become clear.

Here are some examples of titles that were rewritten to include an "interesting aspect":

Example 1

Draft #1, original: "Interconnectedness: Minority Students in a Community College"

Draft #2, improved: "When Minority Students Disconnect From Their Community College"

Draft #3, the best: "Do Minority Students Ever Become Connected to Their Community College? A Qualitative Study"

In this example, the final version poses the title as a question as well as a two-part title. Rather than studying the obvious angle of minority students' becoming disconnected, the author took the reverse approach and asked whether they ever become connected. The study of minority students presents an often underrepresented group as well as the setting of a community college, where one would expect the atmosphere to be friendly and open. So, there are several "unusual" aspects to this title that would make it appealing to scholars as well as practitioners.

Example 2

Draft #1, original: "Exploring Educators' Perspectives of Professional Learning Communities in the Public Schools"

Draft #2, better: "Exploring the Cultural Shifts of Educators When Teachers Participate in Professional Learning Communities in the Public Schools"

In Example 2, the author took the traditional "educators' perspectives" and shifted it to a more compelling angle: how the teachers potentially shifted their cultural understanding of the school when they participated in professional learning communities. Unquestionably, a new model of interacting would cause teachers to shift their views of the school as they reached out to diverse people within the school.

Example 3

Draft #1, original: "When a Vet Returned to Vietnam: A Qualitative Study"

Draft #2, better: "Never-Ending Racial Tension: A Vietnam Vet Returns to the Tragic Site"

In Example 3, the first draft conveys the site but does not specify the central phenomenon of interest. In the second draft, this is corrected, and we learn two new elements, that at the Vietnam site there was both racial tension and a killing. These insertions add conceptual interest to a study.

SUMMARY

In this chapter, I reflect on ways you can put an interesting idea into your qualitative study. Begin with a topic and make sure that it is researchable, especially at a site where you do not have a vested interest in the outcome. Then, consider several ways to make a qualitative study interesting, ranging from selecting people and sites to choosing an angle that conveys an unexpected turn of ideas. Whatever the interesting aspect, write it into the title. Start by inserting this element into your title and sharing it with others. Keep refining it until you have at least one interesting aspect in your title.

ACTIVITY

Find a published qualitative journal article and assess the factors that might make it interesting to you. Use these questions to make this assessment:

- Did the authors study an unusual location?

- Did the authors study an unusual group of participants?

- Did the authors take an unusual angle or perspective?

- Did the authors collect unusual forms of data?

- Did the authors present results or findings in an unusual way?

- Did the authors study a timely topic?

FURTHER RESOURCES

It was Glesne and Peshkin who first introduced the idea of the "backyard" study and the problems inherent in studying a site that was familiar to the researcher:

Glesne, C., & Peshkin, A. (1992). *Becoming qualitative researchers: An introduction.* White Plains, NY: Longman.

Visit study.sagepub.com/30skills for quizzes, eFlashcards, and more!

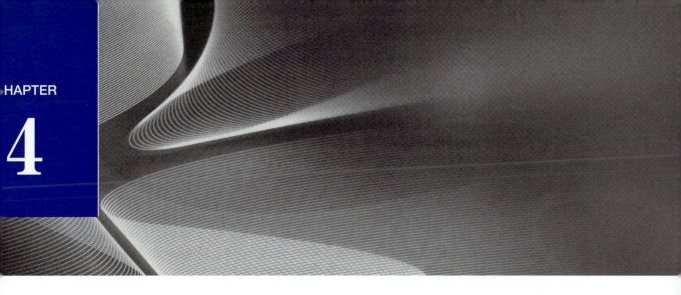

Managing Difficult Emotions That Come Up During Research

Skill

Develop the skill of being able to ride through the emotional highs and lows of conducting qualitative research.

Why the Skill Is Important

Research is typically one step forward, two steps back, then two steps forward, and so on. There will be setbacks and advances. The key to good research is to work steadily, take small steps, and rejoice in advances from time to time. If you can anticipate some of the challenges, they become easier to surmount.

The Emotional Journey of Qualitative Research

Anyone who has engaged in qualitative research will tell you that it is an **emotional journey**. Of course, this could be said about doing any form of research, but qualitative research is especially emotional because of at least three factors: the subject matter being explored, the lack of definite structure for conducting this form of inquiry, and the labor-intensive aspects of conducting this form of inquiry. These factors add up to an emotional rollercoaster for the qualitative inquirer. Unfortunately, books on qualitative research do not often address this process in any detail, but it needs to be made explicit because understanding it is central to planning and conducting good qualitative research.

Possible Steps in the Emotional Journey

Gilbert (2001) edited an entire book on the emotional nature of qualitative research. She was interested in this subject because of her own frustrations with how little had been written on the positive aspects of bringing emotions into the research process. These emotions for her included "feelings, sensations, drives; the personal; that which is intimate; personally meaningful, possibly overwhelming; being touched at a deeper level; something that comes from somewhere within ourselves; and that which makes us truly human" (p. 9). Topics that evoke these emotions—such as studies of loss, death, rape, abuse, and illness, as well as endangerment of oneself or a loved one—illustrate the subject matter often explored in a qualitative project. Undoubtedly, self-coping strategies need to be put into place. Gilbert asked, How do we manage difficult emotions that come up during research? Should they be hidden or kept from others? And what does it mean for the researcher to go through these experiences?

In one of the chapters in Gilbert's book, Rosenblatt (2001) discussed his own spiritual journey as a qualitative researcher. He spent a year studying grief and family life on the basis of readings of published and unpublished 19th-century diaries. On his first visits to the archive, he traveled to the archive each day at opening time and stayed until closing time. He would then "return to my motel room exhausted but also profoundly affected by the ways I had spent the day in contact with death and life" (pp. 117–118). He talked about "sliding down a deep well of depression" (p. 118). He finally took along his two sons so that he could spend part of his time with humans.

Reading this passage leads me to think about the self-care necessary when undertaking difficult emotional topics in our qualitative research. Certainly having someone to process our material with is important. Also, some time away from the field and the content provides a much needed reality check. Spending time on hobbies outside of the research project may also be helpful.

Another part of the emotional rollercoaster stems from the ups and downs of the general research process. This is an area largely untreated in the qualitative literature. One exception is a commentary by Kvale and Brickmann (2009), who identified the "emotional" steps in the journey of conducting one part of the qualitative research process: the interview. The steps qualitative researchers often go through were (pp. 100–101):

- The antipositivist enthusiasm phase. It starts with enthusiasm, commitment, a strong emphasis on carrying out realistic natural life research, and antipositivism in not wanting to approach the topic from a quantitative basis, collecting quantitative data, and abstract theories.

- The interview-quoting phase. This is the interview data collection phase. Initial ideological enthusiasm gives way to personal involvement, solidarity, and identification with participants. In qualitative research we speak about **"going native,"** an idea drawn from ethnography in which the researcher identifies closely with the people being studied.

- The working phase of silence. Silence falls upon the interview project. This is the transcription phase, characterized by sobriety and patience. Transcribing is a long, tedious process.

- The aggressive phase of silence. Interviews have been completed and still no results presented. This midproject crisis is characterized by exceeded time limits, chaos, and stress. At this phase, the researcher reads and rereads through the transcriptions and notes and tries to make sense of them.

- The final phase of exhaustion. The project has now become so overwhelming that there is hardly time or energy left for reporting. The researcher feels resigned to save what can be saved from the interviews and to recognize that he or she may not be able to pass on to readers the original richness of the stories.

I do think that the rollercoaster winds through these phases as well as more positive experiences of the research process. I call these the ups and downs of doing qualitative research.

The Upside of Qualitative Research

People report to me that qualitative research is fun, especially the *data collection phase*, when you can talk with participants, learn interesting stories, and go out to places of work, home, and friends. Others say that the key moment in qualitative research comes with the "aha" moment of *data analysis*, when, after spending days poring over the data, they finally make sense, and the story can be written. I think that I engage in qualitative research because of the creative *writing* part, where I can tell a good story and have fun actually developing it. Finally, some people feel that in working with qualitative research they are using the *latest, interesting methodology* in the social sciences. This fact puts them on the "cutting edge" of research, something they take great pride in doing.

The Downside of Qualitative Research

There are several challenges in doing qualitative research, and I will mention a few of them that students have suggested to me.

Feelings of Isolation

Here is what one doctoral student wrote to me:

> I have been talking to colleagues recently about the isolative process of dissertating . . . you really do feel quite alone in the process even when talking to others and processing with others. We all agreed that you tend to vacillate between feeling confident about your knowledge and feeling absolute uncertainty that what you're doing is accurate.

Expect to have both ups and downs in designing and conducting qualitative research.

This isolation period often comes during data analysis, when the researcher is poring over the transcriptions, notes, documents, and images (e.g., photographs). It is a lonely time, when you are working by yourself. Someone else cannot come into your project and make an interpretation of the data, because what he or she interprets may be different from what you see. Also, you cannot turn to your advisor for help and bring a sample of your transcriptions for analysis. Your advisor, too, will see something different, and possibly make interpretations that differ from your perspective.

Labor-Intensive Transcription

Another difficult period during the qualitative process is transcribing interview data. For a half-hour interview, about 20 single-spaced pages will result. Because beginning researchers often overestimate the number of interviews they want to conduct, the transcription process will take extensive time. I recommend that researchers plan for their interviews to last no more than 30 minutes and limit the overall number of interviews. Also, I recommend that researchers consider hiring out the transcription to someone who has experience in this task, who knows how to set up transcription (margins on each side of the page, double spaced, typing all of the words, etc.), and who can develop a good database for you to use. However, transcribing one's own interviews brings a closeness to the data and may reveal nuances not apparent when the transcription is hired out. Of course, computer programs may be helpful in translating verbal material into text.

Frustrations With the IRB

You may encounter individuals on the institutional review board (IRB) on your campus who may not be familiar with qualitative research and want large samples, the specification of variables, the advancement of hypotheses, and commentary about the reliability and validity of your protocols (see Chapter 5 on working with advisors and committees). Fortunately, this situation is changing, and more people are placed on IRB review committees with some expertise in qualitative research. Still, you need to detail your procedures, and be aware of the potential benefits and harm your research may create for participants.

Insecurity with personal interpretation. You need to trust your instincts and realize that all research has its interpretive elements (e.g., quantitative researchers make an interpretation when they choose a type of statistic). In qualitative research, you will look through transcripts and make an interpretation of what individuals are saying. You will then assign code names that you may create (recognizing that the best code words are words actually used by your participants) and form theme labels that reflect your own interpretive ideas. When you write your project, you will identify which themes to highlight in the report and what evidence to marshal to support the themes. All of these steps involve a personal interpretation. Fortunately, you have at your disposal validity checks, where participants review your theme labels, and the written report to check for accuracy. So, in the end, qualitative research is not, as some would allege, entirely interpretive, but based on whether your interpretation resonates with how participants see the issue being studied.

Fear of Being an Inadequate Writer

All of us have moments when we feel that we can improve our writing and may be shy about sharing it with others, or even become "blocked" as writers so that we cannot move forward. If these scenarios fit you, my best advice would be to go ahead and write out your qualitative report, and before you cast it aside because of inadequacy, check it out with others, such as fellow researchers or a few participants in your study. Also, writing is based largely, I think, on personal experience, and the more you write, the more comfortable you will become with it. This does not mean that even the most seasoned writers do not worry about the quality of their work, but they move through it and test out their material as they proceed. In qualitative research, the task does call upon you to be a good writer, as I noted in Chapter 1.

Working With the Unfamiliar Language of Qualitative Research

Start to look closely at the glossaries that are included in most introductory qualitative research books (as in this book). Also, a qualitative dictionary is available (Schwandt, 2009). It is sometimes helpful to think about the quantitative comparative terms for qualitative research if your background is in quantitative research. It takes time to master the vocabulary of qualitative research, and using the terms in your own writing will help you become accustomed to writing in this new language.

Fear of the Up-Close Nature of Qualitative Research

Dealing with sensitive topics is often difficult. I think that the best qualitative researchers are not afraid to go into sensitive topics, especially topics that may not easily lend themselves to measurement and scales collected on instruments. You need to be bold and be willing to go into difficult topics if you are to become a qualitative researcher. Just as good writing involves conveying emotions and feelings, so too qualitative research requires handling sensitive topics not only in your writing but also when you collect data and are face to face with individuals talking about difficult topics. A highlight of doing good qualitative research is to explore hard-to-study topics that deal with personal issues and individual challenges that are not typically found in our research literature.

Fear of the Graduate Committee's Rejecting a Qualitative Study

This fear arises out of a need to work with advisors or committee members who do not know qualitative research. It also arises out of not having individuals on your committee who know qualitative research and can become active supporters of your methodology (see Chapter 5 next).

SUMMARY

The skill introduced in this chapter is to be able to anticipate the ups and downs of doing qualitative research. This will not make the rollercoaster go away, but it will enable you to set aside time for those difficult phases and realize that they are simply part of doing good qualitative research.

ACTIVITY

Talk with another student who is close to or at the end of the thesis or dissertation (or who has had experience writing a qualitative study) stage of writing a qualitative project. Ask the following questions: What was the most challenging part of doing your project? Did you find transcribing your data time-consuming (or did you hire it out)? Was the IRB receptive to your project? Did you feel comfortable coming up with themes or findings on the basis of your own personal interpretation? Was your graduate (or undergraduate) committee or advisor supportive of qualitative research?

FURTHER RESOURCES

Here is a good text on the emotional side of conducting qualitative research:

Gilbert, K. R. (Ed.). (2001). *The emotional nature of qualitative research*. Boca Raton, FL: CRC.

Visit study.sagepub.com/30skills for quizzes, eFlashcards, and more!

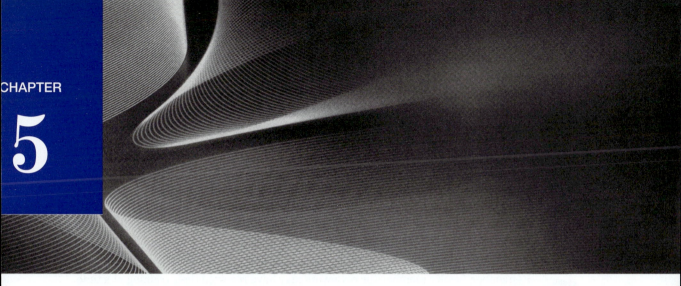

Working With Research Advisers and Committees

Skill

Develop the skill of being able to work effectively with research advisers and committees that review your qualitative project.

Why the Skill Is Important

With advisers, graduate committees, and external reviewers, you need to present a positive image and excitement about your project. How do you work with research advisers and committee members? You need to educate them about the importance and sophistication of your research project. You further need to always submit to them your best work—not incomplete drafts or partially worked out ideas. You also might consider how you are going to handle meetings with them.

Educating Your Committee

Patton (2002) urged individuals to find advisers and committee members who will support qualitative research before committing to a qualitative dissertation. There are other opportunities for qualitative research that do not involve a dissertation. If you decide to conduct a qualitative dissertation study, it may require educating your committee about qualitative research. How can this be done?

Qualitative research continues to bear some misunderstanding as being less rigorous in the eyes of professors (and even fellow students). Dealing with those perspectives can be frustrating and tiresome emotionally (see Chapter 4). In addition to seeking advice and support from your adviser, several other strategies can help. First, remember that your proposal is just that—a *proposal* to conduct a study through which you attempt to persuade others that it is worthwhile. The proposal is an opportunity to educate faculty advisers and demonstrate the legitimacy of the methodology. Second, students undertaking qualitative dissertations or theses often address concerns by including additional evidence about the legitimacy of their methodology (Meloy, 2002). The evidence may be presented by citing important works and by mentioning examples of published qualitative studies similar to yours. Remember, faculty members or reviewers may have received their training at a time or place where qualitative courses were not available. Skepticism is natural. It is your job to educate them about the rigor of your methodology and maybe even how to think like a qualitative researcher (see Chapter 1).

Putting Forward Your Best Material

How do you work with advisers and faculty research supervisors when you are preparing and presenting a qualitative project? Come prepared to your meetings. Consider each piece of writing you forward to reviewers as a significant component of your overall qualitative project. Do not consider your writing as "draft" material for their review. Instead consider it the "best" work you could put forward. Also, look at past dissertation proposals and completed dissertations, especially those supervised by your adviser or members of your graduate committee. Look at publications by members of your committee. In addition, put individuals with qualitative expertise on your committee. Consider the configuration of a good committee: a content specialist who knows your topics; a qualitative researcher who can help guide you toward a good, rigorous study; and a supporter who can always give you encouraging words about your project (and who brings the coffee and bagels). Certainly having an adviser who knows qualitative research would be most helpful. Otherwise, you will be educating your adviser about the methodology you plan on using. If this is the case, you might select a qualitative article published in your field in a leading journal and have your entire committee read the article. You might also consider starting your proposal meeting with a review of this article where you discuss each qualitative element in it, and then say something like, "And now I will apply these ideas of a good, rigorous study to my own project."

On Taking Feedback

When working with research advisers and committee members, consider their feedback mostly as "pearls of wisdom." When they react in writing, think about what useful ideas are included in their remarks. Furthermore, do not fasten closely to one remark that will cause you to "go back to square one." Most reviewers do not have this in mind. Instead, try to get as much feedback as possible from as many people as possible. Share your project with fellow students and ask for their candid reviews. The best researchers (and writers) I know are open to criticism, and are looking for good ideas that they may not have. This is good training for later receiving feedback on manuscripts submitted for publication or for proposals sent in for funding.

Research Committee Meetings

It is also helpful to think about the committee meeting at which you introduce your project to your committee. Here are some ideas about activities helpful before, during, and after the meeting.

Before the Committee Meeting

Putting together a good proposal that creates an immediate positive impression on the committee should be paramount in your mind. Look at proposals written by other students who have successfully passed through the proposal stage. Educate your committee members about qualitative research—attach a glossary of terms to your proposal, bring in a copy of a key qualitative study in your area, talk about the core characteristics of qualitative research (as discussed in Chapter 1). Above all, complete your proposal in time for committee members to review it, and then summarize the major features in your proposal meeting.

During the Committee Meeting

During the committee meeting this summary can be in the form of a PowerPoint presentation that is brief and to the point. Highlight the following in this presentation:

- The problem you are studying and its importance

- The purpose of your study and your key research questions

- The participants in your study, how you will collect data, and the types of data to be collected

- How you will analyze your results

- The significance of your study for audiences

- A timeline for completing the study and a budget

Recognize that your presentation is an argument for the need for the study, and you must convince your committee of the value of the project. Sometimes individuals not familiar with qualitative research will ask questions drawn from their quantitative training. I have summarized a few of these questions and the answers I would give:

> *Question:* Shouldn't you have a larger sample in your study?
>
> *Answer:* In qualitative research we study a few individuals and provide an in-depth understanding of their ideas. The intent of qualitative research is not to generalize from a sample to a population, as in quantitative research, but to learn from a few people and study them closely in their settings.
>
> *Question:* How do you know that your subjective interpretation of your results is accurate and valid?
>
> *Answer:* There are a number of ways to check for validity in qualitative research. I will use triangulation of data sources, member checking, and extensive time in the field. There are additional validity approaches so that my interpretation is not based solely on what I see [see Chapter 22].
>
> *Question:* How can you generalize your results if you study only a few people or sites?
>
> *Answer:* The intent of qualitative research is not to generalize findings but to provide an in-depth exploration of a few people or sites.
>
> *Question:* Why don't you have hypotheses that you intend to study in this project?
>
> *Answer:* In qualitative research we do not have hypotheses, only research questions. And these questions are open ended so that we can learn from participants. Furthermore, we do not have variables, because that would unduly limit what we hope to learn from participants, and participant perspectives are most important in qualitative research.

On the basis of feedback from advisers or committee members, anticipate changes in your project, although a supportive adviser should look out for comments that overhaul your entire study and change its emphasis. Summarize the major concerns committee members may have raised prior to the meeting so that they know that their ideas have been carefully considered.

After the Committee Meeting

There will always be suggestions for improvement from your committee. That is their role in working with you. Noting carefully their suggestions is most important, and keeping them informed about your progress is something within your control.

Beginning to write your dissertation or thesis chapters immediately after your proposal committee meeting helps you move forward. Start with easy-to-write chapters such as the literature review or the methods section. Work on your study each day, and you will be amazed at the progress you make.

SUMMARY

Working with research advisers and committee members can be challenging. Selecting a published qualitative article and having them read it prior to your meeting helps educate them.

Submitting drafts that are clean and reasonably complete helps create a positive reaction to your work. Careful attention to what will be required of you prior to the meeting, during the meeting, and after the meeting promotes a smooth process for receiving feedback.

ACTIVITY

Ask your adviser or a research supervisor for a copy of a qualitative thesis or dissertation he or she felt was a good model of research. Study this copy to see how it was written,

paying particular attention to the rationale given for using qualitative research. If a thesis or dissertation is not available, go to one of the leading journals in your field and look at a published article to use as a model for research.

FURTHER RESOURCES

Look at Marshall and Rossman (2011), chapter 9, on planning resources and the dissertation with graduate committees:

Marshall, C., & Rossman, G. B. (2011). *Designing qualitative research* (5th ed.). Thousand Oaks, CA: Sage.

Also, look at the type of evidence to justify a qualitative research project, as found in:

Meloy, J. M. (2002). *Writing the qualitative dissertation: Understanding by doing* (2nd ed.). Mahwah, NJ: Lawrence Erlbaum.

Visit study.sagepub.com/30skills for quizzes, eFlashcards, and more!

Considering Preliminary Elements

PART

II

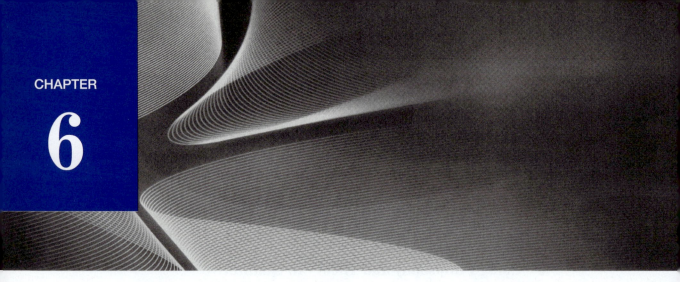

Using Philosophy and Theory in Qualitative Research

Skills

- Develop the skill of adding a philosophical perspective to your qualitative project.

- Develop the skill of using a social science or an advocacy theory to frame your qualitative study.

Why the Skills Are Important

We all bring a philosophical orientation to our research that informs, either consciously or unconsciously, our approach to inquiry. These beliefs are personal views that inform many aspects of our research, from the types of questions we ask, through our designs, and on to our conduct of studies and the write-up of projects. Qualitative researchers have long felt that these personal views need to be made explicit in good qualitative research, or at least the inquirer needs to be conscious of them, and perhaps write them into a study. Theory also informs a study, but at a less abstract level. Many qualitative studies incorporate theories, but not all, and the use of theory varies in priority from those studies that begin with theories, to those that build theories, and to those that disregard the use of theory. If you plan on using theory, it is helpful to know how it will inform your qualitative study and how to write it into your project.

The Philosophy Behind Qualitative Research

To understand the philosophy behind qualitative research, we need to follow the ideas of current writers, to learn the terms used to describe philosophy, to realize the origin of philosophy, to know about the four major types of philosophical schools, and to identify how they differ in basic beliefs and stances on practical issues.

How Philosophy Has Been Shaped by Qualitative Writers

Qualitative writers felt that it was necessary to distance themselves from quantitative research, and to do this they advanced different philosophical assumptions to guide their inquiry. The vanguard of this movement were Yvonna Lincoln and Egon Guba, who authored an important chapter on the use of philosophy in qualitative research beginning with the first *Handbook of Qualitative Research* (Denzin & Lincoln, 1994) and continuing on in each new edition of this book. Although others certainly articulated the philosophy behind qualitative research, my views and those of many others in the field have largely been shaped by Lincoln and Guba's perspectives. Through each of the four editions of the *Handbook* their ideas have shifted and developed. Most recently, in the fourth edition of the *SAGE Handbook on Qualitative Research* (Denzin & Lincoln, 2011), they have once again informed our understanding of the philosophy behind conducting qualitative research (see Lincoln, Lynham, & Guba, 2011).

What Are These Philosophical Beliefs, What Are They Called, and How Do They Originate?

These writers call the philosophical assumptions behind qualitative research "paradigms." This term comes from an important book on philosophical assumptions by Kuhn (1962), who discussed how fields move forward on the basis of individuals' challenging existing paradigms of thinking and advancing a new paradigm. A paradigm can be defined to be personal beliefs or ideas that shape a field. Kuhn advanced many different perspectives on paradigms, but he favored the idea that we are socialized by the scholarly communities to which we belong. These communities provide us with the important problems to study, and how to go about studying them. Individuals in education have a paradigm or set of beliefs that inform the types of problems they study as well as their methods. So too do nursing researchers, marketing researchers, psychologists, and others have their own paradigms.

A term often used synonymously with *paradigm* is *worldview* (Creswell, 2013). I tend to use worldview (or different schools of worldviews) to describe these beliefs, and I will use the terms interchangeably in my discussion.

How Do These Paradigms or Worldviews Shape Our Research?

As you see in Figure 6.1, I find it helpful to conceptualize how paradigms or worldviews fit into the larger process of research. Adapting the helpful diagram of Crotty

FIGURE 6.1   **How Philosophy Shapes Our Research**

There are multiple philosophical paradigms or worldviews consisting of basic beliefs, specific approaches to research, and applications

That inform our use of an interpretive or theoretical lens (social science or advocacy/participatory)

That shape our methodologies or the designs we use (e.g., narrative studies, ethnographies, grounded theory)

That lead to the methods we use and the data we collect (e.g., interviews, observations)

Source: Adapted from Creswell (2013) and Crotty (1998).

(1998), I see a hierarchical relationship among several parts of research. At the broadest level are the philosophical assumptions (or paradigms or worldviews) that inform research. According to Lincoln et al. (2011), there are different paradigms from which to choose, and within each paradigm are its basic beliefs and specific practical issues related to the process of research (e.g., inquiry aim, the nature of knowledge, knowledge accumulation, goodness or quality criteria, values, ethics, voice, training, inquirer posture, accommodation, hegemony). These paradigms (or worldviews) are personal beliefs that, in turn, inform our use of theory in qualitative research. Theory, in turn, informs our methodologies or research designs in qualitative research (e.g., grounded theory, case study). Within these methodologies, we then apply specific methods for gathering data to answer research questions.

What Philosophical Schools Exist?

According to Lincoln et al. (2011), there are four types (or schools) of philosophy from which qualitative researchers might choose: postpositivism (or positivism and postpositivism), which includes "hard science" researchers and those who take a cause-and-effect perspective; critical theory (e.g., feminism, race), whose adherents create change to the benefit of those oppressed by power; constructivism (or interpretivist), whose practitioners gain understanding by interpreting participant perceptions; and participatory (and postmodern), which attracts those who believe in transformation on the basis of democratic participation between the researcher and the participants.

What Are the Basic Beliefs of Paradigms (or Worldviews)?

These schools (or paradigms or worldviews) differ in terms of their central beliefs. What are their central beliefs? There are five basic beliefs I write about (Creswell, 2013). Ontology is the first basic belief, and this means that qualitative researchers differ in terms of how they see what is real or what exists. Epistemology speaks to the belief in the relationship between what we know and what we see (or between the researcher and that being researched). Axiology is the belief in the use of values and bias in a study and how these differ from paradigm to paradigm, while methodology relates to the research process, and how this process varies from a more set process to one that is emerging throughout the project. Rhetoric is the belief in the use of language that varies from more formal to informal (e.g., use of first-person pronouns).

How Do These Basic Beliefs Differ Among the Four Paradigms?

As shown in Table 6.1, we see the differences among the four paradigms in terms of reality, epistemology, values, methods, and rhetoric.

For those writers using postpositivism (or *positivism*), they believe that a singular reality exists, but we cannot know it exactly. This is why we do not ascribe

TABLE 6.1   Major Elements of the Four Paradigm Worldviews

Postpositivist Paradigm	Critical Theory Paradigm	Constructivist Paradigm	Participatory Paradigm
Single reality exists (ontology)	Social, political, and cultural reality	Individuals form their own realities	Reality is shaped by race, class, gender, or some combination
Independence between researcher and that being researched (epistemology)	Subjective opinions matter but within the social, political, and cultural context	Subjective participant views matter	Research is collaborative between researcher and groups
Objective/unbiased values (axiology)	Values of the researcher are present	Values of researcher are made explicit	Importance of both participants and researcher values
Deductive, "top-down" research (methodology)	Methods are negotiated with participants	Inductive research starting with participant views	Methods are collaborative to give power and agency to participants
Scientific language (rhetoric)	Rhetoric includes issues such as power, domination	Personal type of language	Language based on participants, stakeholders

The inclusion of philosophy in a qualitative project depends on the audience for the project.

"causality" to the relationships among variables, but we use "probable causality." Those who believe in this school also feel that we know something when the researcher is independent of the researched. In other words, we send out a questionnaire (at some distance) to gather data. In terms of values, we try to be objective and unbiased in our research, even to the point of commenting on the objectivity we have built into our study so that our personal views do not interfere with our conclusions. The methodology in this belief system is deductive and "top down," and we engage in the process of verifying a theory and use a set approach of specific measures and observations. Our overall rhetorical posture is to use scientific language and terms that are defined and precise.

Those who believe in **critical theory** feel that reality is shaped by social, political, and cultural events. How we know something, then, is shaped by subjective perceptions that are mediated by these events. Values are stated and present in our studies, and the methods of research are negotiated with participants through dialogues. The rhetoric of research is shaped by social, political, and cultural norms in which the researcher seeks to address some of the power issues that affect oppressed individuals. Alternatively, those who hold **constructivist** (or interpretive) beliefs feel that each individual holds different views, and the role of research is to uncover these multiple views. To do this, constructivists want to get as close as possible to participants, and will go out to sites or settings to collect data. Constructivists also place emphasis on conveying in their studies their values and biases. Furthermore, they view the participants as the experts in any study, and will rely on participants' views to construct the major themes in a study. Thus, the research methodology consists of building inductively from the "ground up" the various codes, themes, and perspectives that characterize a qualitative study. Constructivist rhetoric uses a personal type of language when discussing the research. Finally, those who embrace **participatory** beliefs hold that reality is political and constructed among the lines of race, class, and gender, or some combination. They believe in conducting research that is collaborative and political, with groups representing their interests. They advance values of the researcher as well as those being researched, and the methodology consists of involving participants, with the idea that such involvement will help empower them and bring about change. The rhetorical aspects of the participatory worldview then use the language of the participants to reflect the way they talk about the topic.

Writing About Philosophy in Your Qualitative Study

The decision to write philosophy into a qualitative study must be made on the basis of the type of study being developed for specific audiences. For a journal article, there is typically not enough space for a philosophy section, and one seldom sees it, except for a sentence or a passing remark in the methods section. For dissertations and theses, the philosophy is made explicit and is typically presented in a separate section in the literature review or the methods. In proposals for funding, the philosophy is often mentioned as "qualitative assumptions" and is found in a methods section. When you present at a conference, you should mention the philosophy behind your project. Qualitative researchers typically want to know where you stand and what philosophical beliefs have informed your study. When you are presenting a qualitative project in class, I usually recommend that the methods section include a passage on your philosophy.

In a passage on philosophy, what do you write about? I suggest that you mention which paradigm informs your study and why you adopted this particular stance. Because the reader or listener may not be familiar with philosophy in qualitative research, you should also briefly describe the major elements of the paradigm you are using and briefly discuss how it informs your practice of research. For example, write about how you value multiple perspectives (i.e., ontology) and move through each element. Here, I would refer you to the practical issues mentioned by Lincoln et al. (2011) as a guide to creating a discussion about the practice of incorporating philosophy into your qualitative project.

Use of Theory in Qualitative Research

Using theory in qualitative research has been a contentious area. Because qualitative researchers do not want to test theories, the exact nature of the use of theories has long been subject to debate. Still, within some types of qualitative studies, such as ethnography, the use of theories is quite evident. Also, in grounded theory, the idea is to develop or generate a theory, so theory occupies a position at the end of a qualitative study. My approach has been to consider theory as an interpretive lens (Creswell, 2013) that informs a qualitative study. It might be a theory introduced at the beginning of a study, one that emerges during the process of a study, or one generated toward the end of a study. It is helpful to think about the theory that goes into a qualitative study as one of two types: a social science theory or an advocacy theory. A social science theory would be a theory from one of the social science fields (e.g., psychology, sociology, management) that is used deductively in a qualitative study. In short, it begins the study and helps shape the questions asked and the results obtained. An advocacy theory, on the other hand, is one used to help oppressed individuals or groups. It might be a feminist theory, and ethnic or racial theory, a social class theory, a gay or lesbian theory, a disability theory, or some combination. In each case, the group or individuals who have been marginalized, oppressed, or not considered mainstream have been helped through the research of a qualitative study.

A Social Science Theory

One sees this type of theory at the beginning of a study. It often shapes the research questions asked, and the researcher returns to the theory at the end of the project. You might view this **social science theory** as a broad explanation as to what you hope to find in your qualitative project. This theory may be a leadership theory, a political theory, a psychological theory, or a marketing theory, to give just a few examples. You find these theories in the literature, and researchers often label them as theories, such as Bandura's social learning theory. They are prevalent in quantitative research. In the opening passage (or the literature review), you mention the name of the theory, who developed it, in what year, and how it has been used to explain social science phenomena. It becomes a deductive approach that is actually tested using qualitative data and results.

An Advocacy Theory

An interpretive **advocacy theory** in a qualitative study is used to inform the entire research process and ends with advocating for change or improvements for individuals or groups that have been oppressed. Previously, I mentioned "critical theory," which is a theoretical orientation to address the wrongs of marginalized groups. It could serve as a broad philosophy or, in this case, as a theoretical lens used in a project. As distinct from a social science theory, an advocacy theory in qualitative research is typically found threaded throughout a project. In the introduction to a study, the researcher raises a theoretical issue about a marginalized group (e.g., women are not treated equally in pay). The researcher then brings in some of the issues related to the marginalized group (e.g., lack of power, lack of authority to make changes). The study aims or purpose statement then conveys what we might call an advocacy or a directional research question, pointing out the marginalization (e.g., "This project will uncover the inequities women face because of their lower pay"). The purpose statement or questions may call for actual change in the situation for the oppressed. The purpose statement and research questions do not stay neutral; instead, they are framed to highlight the marginalization or the oppression that exists. This framing is in distinct contrast to most qualitative purpose statements and research questions that are neutral and address broad, nondirectional emphases. Some common errors beginning researchers often experience in using an advocacy theory are to assume that readers are familiar with the theory, and therefore they do not explain it well enough. Researchers, too, need to read extensively about the theory in order to explain it well. Furthermore, researchers can assume that an action-oriented step of using an advocacy theory will be embraced by the reader, when in fact the reader may be more objective, or quantitatively oriented and wish to keep advocacy to a minimum.

Here are some examples of advocacy research questions:

Example #1

Changing a standard central question to an advocacy question:

> Original standard qualitative central question: "How do adolescents describe dating violence?"

> Improved: "How are female adolescents abused in violent dating relationships?"

To change this to a feminist perspective, I added "female adolescents," the participants you will be studying, so that an often marginalized group could be studied. And I added the "issue" or "problem" of "abuse." The word *abused* infuses this with an advocacy angle.

Example #2

Use of an advocacy framework in a central question and in sub-questions:

> The purpose of this portraiture (Lawrence-Lightfoot & Davis, 1997) was to understand the empowerment of eight activists (six women and two men) of the One Million Signatures Campaign. (Badiee, 2011)

The research questions were:

1. What do the stories of One Million Signatures Campaign activists tell us about empowerment? Sub-questions: What was their path to the Campaign? What strategies have they used along the way to gain control of the environment? How have they been personally changed in the process of their activism?

2. How do individuals feel connected to the wider movement of the One Million Signatures Campaign? Sub-questions: How did they attempt to understand their environment? How did participants use resources in this movement? How were these resources mobilized?

Example #3

A purpose statement written in a directional, advocacy way about gender hierarchies in the leisure game of lawn bowls in Australia:

> In summary, there are marked differences in both the quality and quantity of leisure between older men and women. We suggest that these differences both are produced by and help to reproduce other gender hierarchies in society. (Boyle & McKay, 1995, p. 557)

The phrase "gender hierarchies" orients this study toward an advocacy or participatory study.

The review of the literature that follows the research questions may speak to a review of the issues of marginalization for the participants under study, and provide evidence that these issues exist and are well documented (e.g., a section might cover inequality in salary). The methods of data collection should not further marginalize the individuals under study. Instead, the process should emphasize collaboration, involve efforts to create "safe" environments for data collection, and promote helpful strategies for the individuals under study (e.g., the researcher may enlist the participants to help collect data). The data collection questions asked during interviews, for example, would have participants comment on their issue (e.g., questions about how the inequality of pay played out in the workplace). The findings would highlight themes that suggest inequality and how it manifested for the individuals under study (e.g., lack of respect in the workplace). We would hear the voices of individuals marginalized through ample quotations provided by the researcher. The conclusion of the study would emphasize what needed to be changed to promote greater equality and fairness for the participants. These "calls for action" might vary from recommendations from the research (i.e., that inequity in pay exists) to distinct action steps that might be taken (e.g., a new review process for salaries by the leaders is required). In either case, a call for change is issued as a result of the study.

SUMMARY

Philosophical ideas inform our qualitative projects, whether we make them explicit or implicit. Several beliefs (or paradigms or worldviews) have been extensively discussed in the qualitative literature. They inform our use of theories, our methodologies or designs, and our methods of data collection. Four schools of beliefs or worldviews are postpositivism, critical theory, constructivism, and participatory approaches. They shape how we view what is real, what warrants knowledge, our use of values, our methods of research, and our language when we talk about research. How we write these beliefs differs on the basis of our audiences; what we write needs to clearly convey the key philosophical ideas of the belief system we are using. Theory can also be written into a qualitative project, although the use of theory varies considerably in qualitative research. The use of theory falls into two types: social science theory that provides guidance as to what we hope to find in our qualitative project and advocacy theory that informs various components of the research process (e.g., how we phrase the research question) and that calls for change or improvements for individuals or groups we study.

ACTIVITIES

1. Look at a feminist qualitative journal article for an advocacy theory perspective: Pohl, S. L., Borrie, W. T., & Patterson, M. E. (2000). Women, wilderness and everyday life: A documentation of the connection between wilderness recreation and women's everyday lives. *Journal of Leisure Research, 12*, 415–434. This is an article about how women make sense of their lives through wilderness recreational activities.

Respond to the following questions about the article: What theoretical issue is introduced at the beginning? How is advocacy written into the research question? How is literature reported about the theoretical issue? Are data collected to reflect sensitivity to the sample being studied? How do the authors position themselves in the study? What types of change do the authors call for at the end of the study?

2. Look at the use of social science theory in this article: James, D. C. S., Pobee, J. W., Oxidine, D., Brown, L., & Joshi, G. (2012). Using the health belief model to develop culturally appropriate weight-management materials for African-American women.

Journal of the Academy of Nutrition and Dietetics, 112(5), 664–670. This article explores the use of the Health Belief Model in developing culturally appropriate weight management programs for African American women.

Respond to the following questions about the article: What was the social science theory used in the study? How did the authors use the theory in the study? How did they limit the application of the theory at the end of their study?

FURTHER RESOURCES

For the use of philosophy in qualitative research, see:

Lincoln, Y. S., Lynham, S. A., & Guba, E. G. (2011). Paradigmatic controversies, contradictions, and emerging confluences, revisited. In N. K. Denzin & Y. S. Lincoln (Eds.), *The SAGE handbook of qualitative research* (pp. 97–128). Thousand Oaks, CA: Sage.

For the use of theory in qualitative research, see:

Creswell, J. W. (2013). *Qualitative inquiry and research design: Choosing among five approaches*. Thousand Oaks, CA: Sage.

For a good article that uses advocacy theory, see:

Yakaboski, T. (2010). Going at it alone: Single-mother undergraduates' experiences. *Journal of Student Affairs Research and Practice, 47*, 463–481.

Visit study.sagepub.com/30skills for quizzes, eFlashcards, and more!

Anticipating Ethical Issues

Skill

Develop the skill of anticipating ethical issues that might arise in your qualitative study.

Why the Skill Is Important

The qualitative research community is quite vocal about the importance of identifying and addressing ethical issues that arise in qualitative research. It is a topic that is underscored in the *Publication Manual of the American Psychological Association* (American Psychological Association [APA], 2010) and it is given emphasis in qualitative research classes. Furthermore, the ethics of protecting human subjects in your research are important because institutions require **institutional review board (IRB)** approval to protect human subjects before you can begin your research. Also, because qualitative research often involves collecting data personally from individuals on emotional topics (see Chapter 4) and collecting up-close data, a need exists to be sensitive to the rights of individuals and to make sure that your study does not cause participants harm. It also means being respectful to other authors who may work with you on your project and whose materials you may borrow to use in your qualitative study. Patton (2002) underscored the importance of ethics:

> Because qualitative methods are highly personal and interpersonal, because naturalistic inquiry takes the researcher into the

real world where people live and work, and because in-depth interviewing opens up what is inside people – qualitative inquiry may be more intrusive and involve greater reactivity than surveys, tests, and other quantitative approaches. (p. 407)

Thus, you need to anticipate ethical issues and actively address them in your qualitative projects. This means knowing the safeguard you need to put in place from the IRB, what ethical issues may arise in a project, and what permissions you will need for borrowed material in a qualitative study.

Human Research Protections in Your Qualitative Research

Before collecting qualitative data, you need to receive approval from your IRB that you have protected the rights of human subjects. Most researchers are familiar with IRBs on their campuses. These boards review your qualitative project and provide permission for you to proceed. You need to know that these boards exist, because they are required by federal mandate to review projects. Some campuses do not have access to boards, and they outsource IRB responsibilities.

On many campuses, IRBs have been created, and they need to approve your qualitative project so that you have protected the rights of human subjects. More frequently these days, qualitative researchers are found on review boards, and the boards are open to and knowledgeable about qualitative inquiry.

These boards have established procedures for reviewing projects and have classified projects in terms of risks. An exempt project means that your project poses less than minimal risk, an expedited project is one that includes minimal risk, and a full-board project is one where your project would present more than minimal risk to individuals. Typically, a more than minimal risk case would be one that involves minors (18 years of age or younger) or sensitive populations (e.g., individuals with HIV infection). Most qualitative projects involve minimal risk in that you may be interviewing, observing, or videotaping individuals and potentially placing participants at risk.

As a qualitative researcher, you need to do two things: (a) submit an application describing your project and (b) have participants in your qualitative study complete a consent form (also, when studying minors, have them complete a form). The application process is often conducted online and involves detailing your data collection procedures and providing an overview of your study. In this application, you typically need to convey the purpose of the study; describe the data collection procedures (what participants will do, how long they will participate); provide names and contact information for participants to reach you; describe how participants will be approached; state the benefits that will likely accrue to participants and whether compensation will be provided to them; describe how informed consent (or assent) will be obtained, how confidentiality will be protected, and the potential identification of participants; and describe the procedures for record storage and access. You also need to attach protocols (e.g., interview, observation, instruments, recruitment flyers, and confidentiality agreements) that will be used in the qualitative study. The consent form also needs to be drafted (see Chapter 13 for a sample consent form, the elements that go into the form, and alternative forms that exist).

You can anticipate finding ethical issues in many phases of the process of research.

So, the practice of qualitative research requires becoming familiar with the institutional review board, the types of classifications of risks of projects, the process of advancing a proposal for a project for approval, and the inclusion of a consent letter when you are collecting data.

Ethical Issues at Different Phases in the Research

Besides adequately responding to the institutional review board, you, as a qualitative researcher, need to anticipate the types of ethical issues that will likely arise in your project and actively write about how you intend to address (or have addressed) these issues. I think about ethical issues as arising during different phases of the research process. These issues arise prior to conducting the study, when the study begins, during data collection, during data analysis, during the interpretation of the data, and when publishing or disseminating your study. I think that the assumption exists that ethical issues arise only during data collection. Although many issues arise at this time, they also appear in other phases of the process, from negotiating a topic to data analysis and the report of the research. My best advice would be for you to consider how ethical problems arise throughout the research process and how they might be addressed in your project, as shown in Table 7.1.

In research plans, you need to discuss what ethical issues will likely arise and how you hope to address them. This discussion can be found in a methods section under "data collection" if the issues arise during the data collection phase of your study. In a proposal for funding, the anticipated ethical issues and your solutions will likely be found in a separate section. In published journal articles, the ethical issues that arose and how they were addressed are found in a methods section.

I have had my share of ethical dilemmas in my own research, and I will share a few of these and indicate how I addressed these issues.

Ethical Issues I Have Faced as a Qualitative Researcher

- *Having high school students disclose their use of illegal drugs during an interview about adolescent smoking.* This project addressed the relationship between depression and smoking among high school students. During my interviews with the

TABLE 7.1   Ethical Issues in Qualitative Research

Where in the Process of Research the Ethical Issue Occurs	Type of Ethical Issue	How to Address the Issue
Prior to conducting the study	• Adherence to professional association standards • Obtain college/university approval on campus through IRB • Gain local permission from site and participants • Select a site without a vested interest in outcome of study • Negotiate authorship for publication	• Become familiar with code of ethics for professional association in your area • Submit proposal for IRB approval • Identify and go through local approvals; find gatekeepers or key personnel to help • Select site that will not raise power issues with you • Give credit for work done on project; decide on author order in the future publication
Beginning the study	• Identify a research problem that will benefit participants • Disclose purpose of the study • Refrain from pressure for participants into signing consent forms • Respect norms and charters of indigenous societies • Sensitivity to the needs of vulnerable populations (e.g., children)	• Conduct a needs assessment or informal conversation with participants about their needs • Contact participants and inform them of general purpose of study • Tell participants that they do not have to sign the consent form • Find out about cultural, religious, gender, and other differences that need to be respected • Obtain appropriate consent (e.g., parents, as well as children's assent)
Collecting data	• Respect the site and disrupt as little as possible • Avoid deceiving participants • Respect potential power imbalances and exploitation of participants (e.g., interviewing, observing) • Avoid "using" participants by gathering data and leaving site • Avoid collecting harmful information	• Build trust, convey extent of anticipated disruption in gaining access • Discuss purpose of the study and how the data will be used • Avoid leading questions; withhold sharing personal impressions; avoid disclosing sensitive information; involve participants as collaborators • Provide rewards for participating • Stay to questions in the protocol

(Continued)

TABLE 7.1	(Continued)

Where in the Process of Research the Ethical Issue Occurs	Type of Ethical Issue	How to Address the Issue
Analyzing data	• Avoid siding with participants (going native) • Avoid disclosing only positive results • Respect the privacy and anonymity of participants	• Report multiple perspectives • Report contrary findings • Assign fictitious names or aliases; develop composite profiles of participants
Reporting and storing data	• Falsifying authorship, evidence, data, findings, conclusions • Refrain from plagiarizing • Avoid disclosing information that would harm participants • Communicate in clear straightforward, appropriate language • Keep raw data and other materials (e.g., details of procedures, instruments) • State who owns the data from a study	• Report honestly • See APA (2010) guidelines for permissions needed to reprint or adapt work of others • Use composite stories so that individuals cannot be identified • Use unbiased language appropriate for audiences of the research • Store data and materials for 5 years (APA, 2010) • Give credit for ownership to researcher, participants, advisers
Publishing the study	• Share data with others • Refrain from duplicative or piecemeal publications • Complete proof of compliance with ethical issues and lack of conflict of interest, if requested	• Provide copies of report to participants and stakeholders; share results with other researchers; consider Web site distribution; consider publishing in different languages • Refrain from using the same material for more than one publication • Disclose funders for research; disclose who will profit from the research

Source: Adapted from APA (2010), Creswell (2013), and Mertens and Ginsberg (2009).

Note: APA = American Psychological Association; IRB = institutional review board.

students, one chose to disclose drug use. I chose not to report this information because as a university researcher, I was not legally required to report such information (as distinct from teachers, who are required to report this behavior). In my interviews, I did ask students if they smoked, but I did not ask about drug use.

- *Taking research team members into a homeless shelter and soup kitchen where an individual trailed one woman on my research team (this individual carried a knife).* The homeless man who was trailing this woman had brandished a knife in the kitchen, and I had heard that he had threatened other people at the homeless shelter. As soon as I found out about this situation, I talked with a female research colleague on my team and advised her to have a companion from our team accompany her on her walk home.

- *Having a colleague write up a complete research study and publish it without my knowledge (I later learned about its publication).* I found out about this issue when I saw the publication in the journal. This individual had not contacted me, and he simply substituted his name for mine on my work and submitted it to a journal. It is difficult to address this issue after the fact, and I ended up not publishing with this individual again. If I had discovered this before publication, I would have asked that the manuscript be withdrawn.

- *Handing over a tape of an interview to a participant and having the participant pocket the tape so that I lost the interview data.* This participant had requested to see the tape, and then she left with it. Undoubtedly, I had touched on a sensitive nerve when I interviewed her. In retrospect, I would probably not have handed over the raw data on the tape unless she had specifically asked to withdraw her interview. I learned how to handle this situation the hard way.

- *Having an interviewee dominate the interview conversation with a "pet" topic of the day, so that I did not receive the type of information I needed.* I think that this situation frequently happens. If a person goes off track during an interview, I simply say, "We can talk about that important issue after the interview concludes." Partly this situation involves knowing how to conduct a good interview, but it also raises the question as to whether an interviewee is intentionally trying to subvert the interview process, and researchers need to be able to anticipate this potential problem.

- *Having a colleague ask me whether a student could publish the student's own data without the colleague's name on the article. This colleague was an adviser for the student.* If a person has gathered and analyzed the data, his or her name should appear on the publication. Although the resolution of this issue differs among fields, my own perspective is that an individual should be an author if he or she provides a substantial contribution to an article. The student needs to weigh whether the adviser played a substantive role in the creation and writing of the study. The APA's (2010) publication manual discusses this situation and provides useful advice.

- *Having a Native American tribal council challenge whether the researcher has the right to publish information gathered from the tribe because the individual is not a member of the tribe (although permission had been granted by the council earlier, before the results were compiled).* Participants can actually withdraw information at any time during the research process, even though they initially gave permission for the study. Studies change, as do the needs of both the researcher and the participants, and flexibility needs to be built into the process to allow individuals to withdraw from the research. The researcher in this case could not publish his report about the tribe.

- *Having an inmate at a prison tell the interviewer that a "breakout" was occurring that night.* How do you think the interviewer responded to this "private" information? An anthropologist friend of mine encountered this situation. Even though the inmate mentioned the possible breakout, the anthropologist did not report the information to the warden or the prison authorities. Fortunately for all, no breakout occurred that night. I like the idea that the anthropologist honored the privacy of the inmate.

- *Having a researcher submit a journal article to my journal (I was the editor) when it had been published earlier in another journal.* In this case, we wrote to the author saying that we had found a duplicate of the article published in another journal. As the editor of a scholarly journal, I always did a background check on articles to see if the same words were used in other publications. The author in this case withdrew the article from our journal.

Permissions for Borrowed Material Used in Qualitative Research

A related idea to ethical issues is the need for permissions for borrowed works. As you compose your qualitative study, it is helpful to keep in mind the permissions you need to seek when you use material borrowed from another source. The APA's (2010) publication manual outlines the types of materials you may borrow for your study that require letters of permissions from authors or from publishers (depending on who owns the copyright to the material):

- *Figures and tables* that are direct reprints from other authors require letters of permission. When you use three or fewer figures or tables from a journal article or book chapter, or five or fewer figures or tables from a whole book, you do not need written permission. But if your material does require written permission from authors or publishers, you need to put below the figure or table a comment such as "Source: Jones and Smith (2014). Copyright 2014 by [the publisher's name]. Reprinted with permission." Publishers may require a variation on this template, but it is a good model to use for drafts before you seek the exact language the publisher would like you to use.

- *Numeric data* that are reproduced in their exact form from another source. However, when you reconfigure or reanalyze data to produce new numbers, you do not need to obtain permission.

- *Text data* borrowed from another source as a long quotation. The APA requires permission when the text exceeds 400 words or a series of text extracts totals more than 800 words. You need to check with the particular copyright holder for their requirements.

- *Test and scale items, questionnaires, and vignettes* require permission from authors and publishers. You need permission especially when the materials are copyrighted and commercially produced.

A Checklist for Ethics

I have personally found useful the "Ethical Compliance Checklist" from the APA (2010, p. 20). It provides a good summary of IRB provisions, ethical issues, and permission concerns that I have discussed in this chapter. The checklist is reproduced here with some adaptation:

_____ Have you obtained permission for use of unpublished instruments, procedures, or data that other researchers might consider theirs (proprietary)?

_____ Have you properly cited other published work presented in portions of your manuscript?

_____ Are you prepared to answer questions about institutional review of your study or studies?

_____ Are you prepared to answer editorial questions about the informed consent and debriefing procedures you used?

_____ Have all authors reviewed the manuscript and agreed on responsibility for its content?

_____ Have you adequately protected the confidentiality of research participants, clients-patients, organizations, third parties, or others who were the source of information presented in this manuscript?

_____ Have all authors agreed to the order of authorship?

_____ Have you obtained permission for use of any copyrighted material you have included?

SUMMARY

As a qualitative researcher, you need to be aware of potential ethical issues that may arise in your project and develop strategies or approaches for addressing these issues. The first element in this area is to be aware of the institutional review board procedures for your institution or company. These provisions protect the human rights of individuals participating in your study. You will need to apply for permission to proceed with your participants, and have them complete an informed consent form giving you permission. Certain provisions need to be addressed in these consent letters. Also, you need to anticipate the ethical issues your project might raise and actively put in place approaches for addressing them. Ethical issues arise before the study begins, during data collection, during data analysis, during the interpretation of data, and when publishing or disseminating your study. Also, remember that permissions will be required for using borrowed material from other authors, and guidelines exist for how to handle these issues.

ACTIVITY

It is helpful to respond to some ethical problems and share with others how you would address each issue. Examine the following ethical dilemmas posed by Sharona Levy of Israel (personal communication, 2013). How would you respond to each issue?

- In designing a research project that focuses on racism inside a school, a researcher believes that only by not revealing the real objective of the study will he get access to the school. Is his approach correct?

- During research aimed at improving education in jails, the research head decides to randomly assign the prisoners to one of two teachers, whom he had trained with contrasting pedagogical styles. Is this legitimate?

- In research that addresses educational development for students with disabilities, the researcher is presented with a young person who has significant learning disabilities and demands to be part of the research, even though his parents did not agree that he will participate. What should the researcher's response be?

- What is informed consent? What does one need to be informed about—the study's goals? Its form of execution? How its results will be published? Do participants need only to know or also to understand?

- A graduate student conducts research in which two advisers are involved. In the process, the student designs the research, collects the data, and analyzes it with the help of a statistical assistant. While writing up the research, the student puts her own name first, and then the names of her two advisers. When getting back the draft, the graduate student discovers that the second adviser has moved his name to the last position and added two of his postdoctoral researchers to the list of authors.

- A graduate student has put in a great deal of work to design a computer-based learning unit. During its design, several questions came up regarding the design that required going to the literature and to experts to learn and ask for advice. A year later, a new student joins the research group. He designs a learning unit that is based on the same design principles as those of the first student. When this new student writes up the report, the first student is not mentioned.

- A student conducts research as part of a school-based project. After receiving consent from the participants to be part of the research, the student collects data and analyzes it. A year later, a new student comes to the lab, and the adviser suggests that the same set of collected data may be suitable for a different study as well.

FURTHER RESOURCES

Examine:

Mertens, D. M., & Ginsberg, P. E. (2009). *The handbook of social research ethics*. Thousand Oaks, CA: Sage.

Also, consider reviewing the guidelines for ethics and permissions in the APA's style manual:

American Psychological Association. (2010). *Publication manual of the American Psychological Association* (6th ed.). Washington, DC: Author.

Visit study.sagepub.com/30skills for quizzes, eFlashcards, and more!

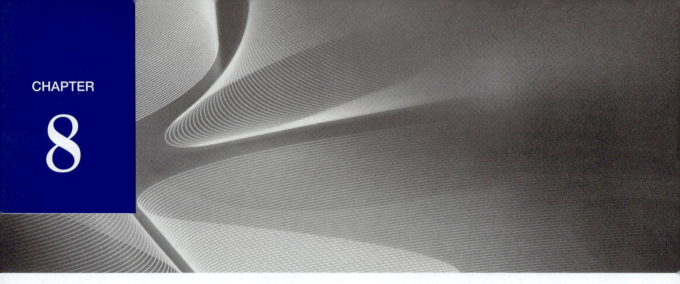

Developing a Literature Map

Skill

Develop the skill of creating a literature map that positions your study within the larger scholarly literature.

Why the Skill Is Important

The literature review plays an important role in research. One of the main ways the literature review can be used is to *share the results of other studies*. This provides a frame of reference for your study and *relates your study to the larger dialogue in the literature*. This is an important aspect, as it creates a link between your study and research that has already been conducted, which helps *provide a framework for establishing the importance of the study*. By providing this framework, you have demonstrated as a researcher that your study is valid and significant for your field. The literature review also *provides a benchmark for comparing the results to other findings*. Through a literature review you can create a dialogue in which your findings are compared with the existing body of literature and point toward future directions for your topic. A literature review is not easy. It calls for higher level reading skills in being able to interrelate different topics from diverse literature. This is a skill in and of itself. In this chapter we will consider options for placing the literature review in a qualitative study, conducting a literature review, setting a priority for the literature to be reviewed, developing a map of the literature, and creating a narrative for discussing and presenting your literature review.

Challenges in Reviewing the Literature

Pulling together many studies from the literature is not an easy task. It requires one of the most advanced reading techniques—interrelating ideas from diverse literature (Lacroix, 1999). Moreover, finding the articles in the library may be a problem, especially as libraries cut back on holdings. You also need to learn to search the digital databases and try out multiple terms before you find articles that relate to your topic. Also, becoming familiar with the various digital databases and what they have to offer takes experience and time. Another issue is knowing when to stop reviewing the literature—when do you have enough? There is no easy answer to this question, except that I often use the approximate length of a literature review chapter as a guide, whether this length is 30 pages or 60 pages. Also, I use the idea of repetition. I stop reviewing the literature when I am no longer coming across useful sources and I am finding repetitions of sources cited by different authors. Also, other challenges are writing the reviews of studies in chronological order when that order may not best convey the literature, or simply writing a collection of single paragraph summaries without tying them together as a meaningful unit. Finally, it is a challenge to review the literature and write it into a qualitative study. Here is where thinking about where I will use the literature in a qualitative study as well as the literature map comes in.

Options for Placing the Literature in a Qualitative Study

How is literature used in qualitative research? There are several possibilities, as shown in Table 8.1. For many years there was the thought that you did not have to do a literature review in qualitative research, because it is an inductive process and as a qualitative researcher you wanted to learn from the participants. During this time, scholars did not go out and read the literature about their topics or research questions. Over time, as the field of qualitative research progressed, our thinking on literature reviews changed.

References to the literature will end up in four different places. One place you will find literature is in the *introduction section*, which serves to frame and provide evidence for the problem. Second, you could have a separate *literature review section* where you summarize the broad subtopics of the topic you are exploring. A popular approach is to present the literature *at the end of the study* as a basis for comparison. Alternately, the literature could even be *threaded throughout the study*. In this case you would find literature in the problem section, the methods, the findings, and the conclusions.

A separate literature review is not a universal practice in qualitative research. In fact, for many of the qualitative dissertations I have directed, students do not have separate literature review chapters. My personal approach is to put literature up at the beginning of the study, to frame the problem, and to put literature toward the end as a means of comparison within findings. In this approach, the literature does not dictate the questions and the theory we are going to use, because in qualitative research we need to keep the research questions open ended. Yet, as you can see in Table 8.1, there are many different ways literature plays a role in qualitative research, and there is no one right way to include it in a study.

Steps in Conducting a Literature Review

The first step in conducting a literature review is to *identify key words* that will help you learn about your study. These key words can be made up of different combinations of words related to your study. For example, if you want to research strong GLBT (gay, lesbian, bisexual, and transgendered) families, you might pick the words *gay*, *lesbian*, *GLBT families*, *strong families*, and *family strengths*, or any combination of those words.

Next, you will use those key words to *search digital databases*. Most libraries have extensive online databases and search engines you can use to refine your search. These engines should tell you whether your library has the journal or book you are looking for and sometimes provide access to an online digital copy of the work. Some common databases used in the social and health sciences are ERIC (Education Resources Information Center), Academic Search Premier, PsycINFO, PubMed, and Sociological Abstracts. Also, look through the library holdings. If your library does not subscribe to the journal or book you are looking for, you can request it via interlibrary loan. Other partner institutions that do have the book can loan it to your library or scan a journal article and e-mail it to you. Remember that you can look through the reference sections of a few books or journal articles to get more sources that may fit your topic and expand your literature base.

To have a solid review of the literature you will need to *identify about 50 research reports in articles or books* to get started. That is not to say that you will use all of these books or research reports, but it will give you a substantial base from which to begin your review.

After you have identified your articles and books you will need to *photocopy, scan, or save on your computer those that are central to your topic*. Many journals have online resources that you can save and print, or refer to later. Those journals that are not online can be scanned and saved or photocopied. This will allow you to not only read and absorb all of the information but also to refer back to it throughout your research project.

An important way to stay organized and avoid getting overwhelmed with all of the literature you have uncovered is to *draft summaries of the relevant articles*. This can take the form of an annotated bibliography or a simple view of the major content of the article. These summaries are important, as they will allow you to

TABLE 8.1   Options for Using the Literature in a Qualitative Study

Use of the Literature in Qualitative Research	Criteria	Examples of Suitable Strategy Types
The literature is used to "frame" the problem in the introduction to the study.	There must be some literature available.	This approach is typically used in all qualitative studies, regardless of type.
The literature is presented in a separate section as a "review of the literature."	This approach is often acceptable to an audience most familiar with the traditional, quantitative approach to literature reviews.	This approach is used with studies using a strong theory and literature background at their beginning, such as ethnographies and critical theory studies (see Chapter 30).
The literature is presented at the end of the study; it becomes a basis for comparing and contrasting findings of the qualitative study.	This approach is most suitable for the "inductive" process of qualitative research; the literature does not guide and direct the study but becomes an aide once patterns or categories have been identified.	This approach is used in all types of qualitative designs, but it is most popular with grounded theory, where one contrasts and compares a theory with other theories found in the literature (see Chapter 30).
The literature is threaded throughout the study: problem section, methods section, findings, and conclusions.	The literature is seen as not something to be "added in" but to be an integral part of the entire story.	This approach is best used within narrative studies in which the entire article essentially details a story of an individual's experiences (see Chapter 30).

Source: Adapted from Creswell, J. W. (2014). *Research design: Qualitative, quantitative, and mixed methods approaches* (4th ed.). Thousand Oaks, CA: Sage.

understand results and findings from the studies, and to keep an organized list of references as your research project progresses.

Once you have read, understood, and summarized the articles you have found in your literature search, you need next to *write a literature review, organizing it by important concepts*. As was covered earlier in this chapter, where this literature comes into a qualitative study is in many ways up to the author of the study. The last step in the literature review process is to *design a literature map*. This is a great way for you and your readers to get a visual picture of how and where your study will contribute to the literature on your topic.

Priority for Reviewing the Literature

Before going into the design of a literature map, it might be helpful to briefly discuss what types of literature to review and which ones would net the highest content yield in the shortest amount of time. This is roughly the order in which I look at material for compiling my literature review. When I am faced with a new topic to review, I run computer searches on the topic, but then I focus my attention on articles, chapters, or books that provide a broad synthesis of the literature. Encyclopedias often help. Also, look for journal articles that provide reviews of the literature on the topic. After this, I turn to leading journals on the topic. These are journals that are national or international in scope and that are refereed by a panel of experts in the field. Next, I would turn to books on the subject, followed by conference papers. So now I am beginning to turn to the more fugitive literature, which may be of lesser quality and not screened or reviewed for quality. Finally, I might look at student dissertations and reports posted on the Web. Unquestionably, the material posted to the Web is being reviewed more and more, and some of it meets high standards for inclusion.

How to Design a Literature Map

Nature of a Literature Map

A literature map is a visual summary that allows the reader (and author) to understand how the proposed qualitative study adds to, extends, or replicates the existing research. The literature summarized in this map may be conceptual discussions or empirical databased research studies. It may consist of quantitative or qualitative articles. Furthermore, this literature map is typically presented in a figure. The layout of this figure can take many forms. It can be a flowchart in which the reader sees the literature unfolding from left to right with the farthest right-hand section discussing the proposed study. It could also look like a cycle or a series of circles, with each circle representing a body of literature and the intersection of the circles denoting the areas where future research is needed. This map could also be organized as a hierarchy with a top-down presentation of the literature and the proposed study at the bottom, or any other visual representation that makes sense to you and actually displays the current literature of the field. Our examples will focus on the hierarchical arrangement, which is one that I prefer because a reader can work down from the broad topic to the narrow idea at the center of your qualitative study.

> A literature map can be a good way to argue for the need for your study and to present a visual to audiences in which you convey that you know the existing literature on your topic and can position your study within it.

Procedure for Designing a Literature Map

Figure 8.1 is an example of a literature map used by a student in my class to organize the literature on her topic related to justice in organizations. I will use this map as a basis for explaining how to create a literature map on the topic of your qualitative study.

FIGURE 8.1 **Example of a Literature Map**

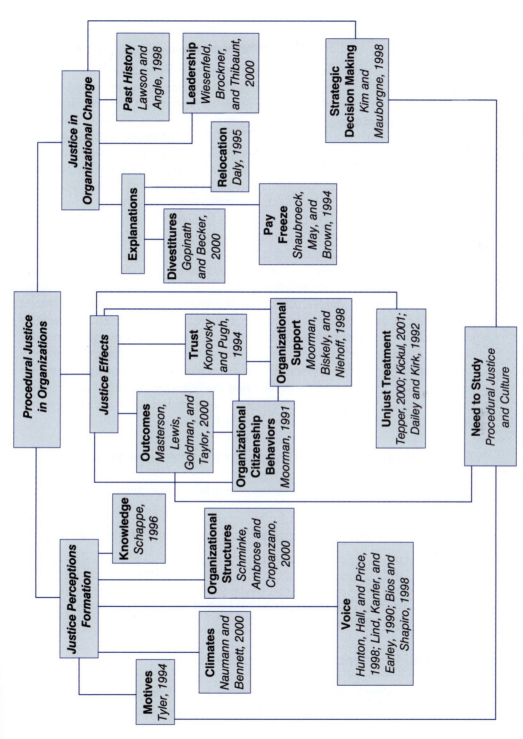

Source: Janovec, T. *Employees' Concerns about the fairness of and the making of managerial decisions.* Reprinted by permission of T. Janovec.

Start With Your Topic (Central Phenomenon)

In a hierarchy, this will be the top box of the page, but it will be located in other areas depending on the style you have chosen. Think about grouping studies together (*what broad subtopics have researchers studied about your topic?*). It can be helpful at this stage to look back at what you have found in your literature search and group the studies into categories.

> To create the top box in your literature map, ask yourself, to what literature does my study add? If I broaden my central phenomenon to a literature topic, what would I start searching for in the library computer bases? Narrow your topic to one or two words.

After you have thought about the broad subtopic in your area, *begin to sketch out your map once you have a sufficient number of studies*. Some find this easiest to do with paper and pencil, others like to use sticky notes and move them around on a whiteboard, or on a piece of paper. Some may find it easiest to begin with a computer program, such as Microsoft Word or PowerPoint, to begin this process. Whichever method you choose, *map out in terms of the broad subtopics to the narrow ones*. Again, this will be a top-down approach in the hierarchical methods, or side to side in the flowchart style. As you go through this process, *give a label to each box and cite general references*. There could be only one study on a subtopic or, more likely, several. Try to keep your literature as current as possible (within the past 10 years, except when older papers are "classics" or important for describing the literature). Last, *draw arrows or connectors from the boxes you will build on for your study*. You will mention your proposed study in a box, as well as how your study will add to the literature. This box will be at the very bottom on the page in a hierarchical layout. The final step is to write a paragraph summarizing the literature map.

Additional Ideas About Designing a Literature Map

- Start with the broad subtopic first before narrowing to your particular study.

- It takes time and many drafts to put together a complete map.

- Develop the map over time by continuing to add to it as you collect new articles and studies.

- To design the starting box at the top of the map, narrow your topic to one or two words.

A Sample Description of a Literature Map

After you have drawn your literature map, it is helpful then to develop a narrative that explains the literature map. This narrative could be used in a presentation of your qualitative proposal or at the beginning of a conference presentation. It has the impact of establishing your scholarly credibility with an audience and conveying to them the unique contribution of your study. Here is a script that may be helpful in creating this discussion:

> My topic adds to the overall literature on . . . . This literature divides into three types of studies . . . 1, 2, 3. You can see how under each topic the literature further subdivides into subtopics. Now my study will extend branch 2 [or multiple branches in the literature]. More specifically, it will add to the subtopic [or subtopics of several branches in this map] of . . . in the following way. . . . You can see that subtopics a, b, and c have been discussed in the literature. One area not addressed in this literature is . . . . Hence, the need for my study is to develop a project that adds to the literature by . . . .

Now I will apply this script to an actual project. The following is a description of a literature map by one of my former students using the above script:

> My topic, GLBT Family Strengths adds to the overall literature on both family strengths research and GLBT family life. This literature divides into several types of studies: Measures, International Applications, and Special Populations. You can see how under the topic, "Special populations" the literature further subdivides into subtopics: gay and lesbian families, cohabiting families, traditional families and single parent families. My study will extend the branch labeled gay and lesbian families as well as the family strengths literature overall. More specifically, my study will add to the literature on gay and lesbian families in the following ways. You can see that there has been a great deal of research on children in Gay and Lesbian families, as well as Coming out Processes and some research on relational quality of Gay and Lesbian couples. One area that is not addressed in this literature is the strength that gay, lesbian, bisexual and transgendered (GLBT) families have, and what these qualities of strength are in these family types. Hence, the need for my study is to develop a project that adds to the literature by generating a theory of GLBT family strengths. (Maureen Todd, personal communication, December 12, 2010)

SUMMARY

A literature review helps you share the results of other studies, relates your study to the larger dialogue in the literature, establishes the importance of your project, and provides a benchmark for comparing the results with other findings. It is challenging to write a good review of the literature. One issue is where to place the literature in a qualitative study, such as at the beginning, in a separate section, at the end, or threaded throughout a study. Begin your literature review by searching digital databases for good articles, locating the articles, and then summarizing them. I generally look for published journal articles in national, refereed journals. I then design a literature map of the articles and books on my topic. This map is a hierarchical presentation of existing literature on my topic, and I create links between this literature and my proposed topic. In this way I can justify and situate my study within the larger literature. I present a script of a discussion of a literature map in this chapter that you might find useful as you present your map to other researchers.

ACTIVITY

Draw your own literature map on the topic of your qualitative study. Draw it on one page as a rough sketch and then keep adding to it as you proceed by collecting more studies and reviewing more articles. So this is a map that expands over time.

FURTHER RESOURCES

See:

Creswell, J. W. (2014). *Research design: Qualitative, quantitative, and mixed methods approaches* (4th ed.). Thousand Oaks, CA: Sage.

This book has a chapter on reviewing the literature and introduces the concept of a literature map.

Visit study.sagepub.com/30skills for quizzes, eFlashcards, and more!

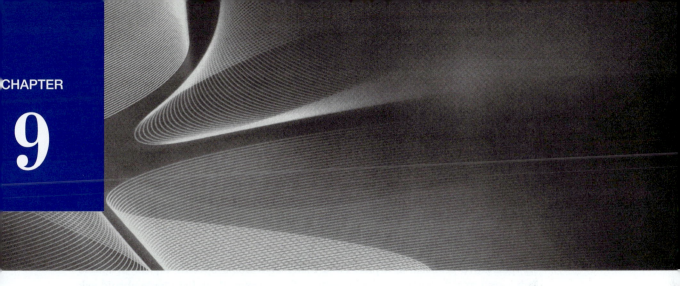

Viewing the Structure of a Thesis or Dissertation for a Qualitative Study

Skill

Develop the skill of diagramming the macrostructure of your qualitative project.

Why the Skill Is Important

When we come to a research study we are often focused on the content of the article and the conclusions about the topic presented by the author. We do not stop and think about the underlying research structure on which the study is based. I am reminded of how Natalie Goldberg, who has written about how to write in *Long Quiet Highway* and is a noted poet and painter, said that she finally figured out how to write poems after she began to look closely at their structure (Goldberg, 1993). Looking at the macrostructure—how a study is composed and the topics and flow of the topics—helps you build a model of the structure for designing your own study. People often ask me what format they should use for preparing their qualitative dissertation or master's thesis proposal. Later, after they have completed their studies, they then return and ask how they should organize their topics in their qualitative articles for journal publication. Unquestionably, qualitative proposals and journal articles differ in their organization and structure from more traditional quantitative proposals and articles. In this chapter we will stop and consider the structure—the macrostructure—of qualitative research through the lens of a dissertation or thesis proposal and then through the lens of a published qualitative journal article. In the end you should be able to better organize and stage your ideas for your qualitative project.

Topics Typically Included in a Qualitative Proposal or Plan

A qualitative proposal is a plan for a study addressing specific topics. Graduate advisers typically have favorite structures for a proposal, and students should ask their advisers for copies of proposals they have supported in the past. Knowing how to organize topics is essential to the successful acceptance and defense of a plan for your qualitative study.

A plan for a research study typically follows a general outline of topics, as shown in Figure 9.1. This framework works from the topic of a problem, through questions, on to data collection and analysis, through carrying out the plan, and then to reporting the findings. This might be called the "scientific process of research." It applies equally to all forms of social, behavioral, and health science research, whether a study is qualitative or quantitative.

Structure of a Dissertation or Thesis Qualitative Proposal

In planning a qualitative project, there are certain topics that are usually advanced. One model I have used over the years is the nine topics Maxwell (2013) identified that should go into an argument for a dissertation project. Adapted from his writings, these topics are:

1. We need to better understand . . . (the topic)

2. We know little about . . . (the topic)

3. For these reasons, I propose to study . . . (purpose)

4. The setting and participants are appropriate because . . . (participants)

5. The methods I plan on using are . . . (methods)

6. Analysis will generate answers to these questions . . . (data analysis)

7. The findings will be validated by . . . (validation)

FIGURE 9.1   **The Process of Research**

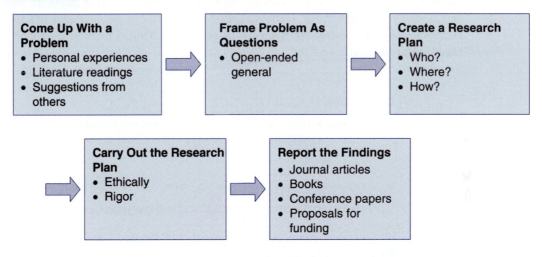

8. The study poses no serious ethical problems . . . (ethics)

9. Preliminary results support the practicability and the value of the study . . . (value)

    I have often felt that if students write out answers to these nine topics, they will have a compete proposal. The proposal could be short, no more than about 20 pages in length, with appropriate references and protocols for data collection included.

    The overall final structure of a qualitative proposal or a dissertation or thesis may vary in form. Some individuals may present the structure as a scientific layout of topics, such as the problem, literature, methods, findings, and discussion. Others may rely on narrative structures where they tell a story from beginning to end and interweave into this story the major elements of the research process (e.g., questions, data collection). A personal story told in an autoethnographic format is an example of the structure of this approach. Some individuals may create performance structure, such as developing their studies into experimental poems, plays, musicals, or other art forms. Because of these varieties, as qualitative researchers we need to be open to various structures for our proposals and for our final studies.

    Having said this, however, beginning qualitative researchers, I believe, profit from a general structure for how to organize their dissertations or thesis proposals. Over the years, I have advanced a format for topics included in a qualitative study. This format is my approach, one that I am comfortable with, and one that I assign to my advisees as they think about dissertations or thesis plans. At times I have distinguished between a qualitative constructivist approach and a qualitative advocacy or participatory approach to the structure (see Creswell, 2014). In the end, I really feel that there is one structure that is comprehensive and fits the numerous ways qualitative research can be presented. Thus, I present the following structure as one model for you to consider in outlining your proposal or plan for a qualitative study:

- Introduction
  - Statement of the problem (including existing literature about the problem, significance of the study)
  - Theory (if used)
  - Purpose of the study and how the study will be delimited
  - The research questions (central and sub-questions)
- Philosophical assumptions of qualitative research and how they apply in present study
- Literature review (optional)
- Procedures
  - Qualitative research design (e.g., ethnography, case study) or basic characteristics if qualitative research
  - Role of the researcher (i.e., reflexivity)
  - Data collection procedures
  - Data analysis procedures
  - Strategies for validating findings
  - Proposed narrative structure of the study
- Anticipated ethical issues
- Preliminary pilot findings (if available)
- Expected outcomes and significance of the proposed study
- Appendices: interview questions, observational forms, timeline, and proposed budget

As you will note, this structure provides for a discussion about philosophical assumptions, the advancement of a theoretical model, a sensitivity to reflexivity, a discussion about ethical issues, the inclusion of pilot data that will hopefully demonstrate the feasibility of a study, and the expected outcomes of a study. In the appendices you will see a proposed timeline and a budget for the project. This structure will work well, but, of course, it may need to be adapted to fit the particular topical requirements of advisers or fields of study.

A Concept Map of the Structure of a Qualitative Journal Article

It is helpful in designing qualitative research to look closely at the topics included in a qualitative journal article and map out the flow of these topics. This flow can then inform your present project and provide a sample roadmap for the structure of your research study. I would recommend that you draw out a concept map of your favorite qualitative article. You might follow these steps:

- Create circles that indicate the major flow of ideas

- Link the circles to show how the study unfolds

- Refrain from being overly detailed in your drawing

- Disregard headings used by the author unless they indicate major ideas

- Keep the diagram to one page in length

One of my favorite journal articles is the study of an individual with a mental disability, Vonnie Lee, by Angrosino (1994). I like having my students draw out this study because it follows more of a storytelling format than a scientific format. It helps students see how ideas can be staged to build interest in the key participant. I like how the author integrates good qualitative research components into this unfolding story. Figure 9.2 depicts the concept map I drew of the flow of topics in the article.

This journal article was about an individual with mental disability (Vonnie Lee) who found meaning for his life in his travels on a bus from his house, an agency for the rehabilitation of adults with the dual diagnosis of mental disability and psychiatric disorder and criminal records, to his job at a plumbing supply warehouse. This bus ride became empowerment, escape, and status for Vonnie Lee.

This map in Figure 9.2 shows the flow of topics in this narrative, literary-style qualitative journal article. The map begins with a description of Vonnie Lee to set the stage for discussing him. Then, the author comes into the picture as an individual to help Vonnie Lee. At this point, data collection is introduced, and then the article focuses on the major feature in the study—the bus trip Vonnie Lee goes on that gives meaning to his life. Angrosino (1994) next highlights the meaning of this bus ride, in its images and symbols. At the end of the article, the author broadens the perspective beyond the one individual and interprets the larger meaning of it, anchors the

> Once you see the macro-structure of a published journal article, you can use this structure to organize your own qualitative project.

FIGURE 9.2   Flow of Ideas in Angrosino's (1994) Journal Article on Vonnie Lee

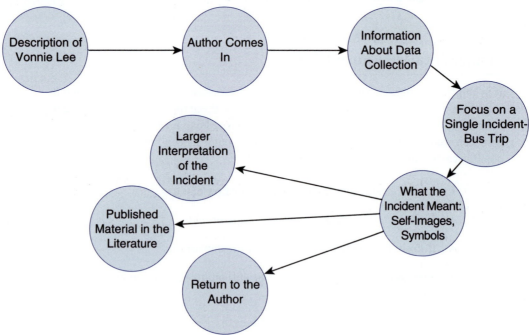

meaning in current literature, and brings himself back into the picture. In all, this is a literary approach to writing a qualitative research article because it does not flow from problem to literature, methods, results, and discussion. Still, within the flow of the story, one can find all of these elements.

SUMMARY

Examining closely the structure of qualitative dissertations and theses or published journal articles helps create a model for your own qualitative project. In this chapter I have offered a typical structure for a qualitative proposal or plan and the sequence of topics that might be included in such a plan. I presented several models, including one model in which you answer nine questions about your project. Then I examined how to analyze the structure of a qualitative journal article and focused on one that presents a literary story of an individual's experiences. Drawing a concept map of a journal article provides a template for organizing the structure of your own project.

ACTIVITY

In this chapter I discussed the nine steps Maxwell (2013) identified for writing a good qualitative proposal. Take these nine steps and construct a brief qualitative proposal on a topic of your choice. Be prepared to present and defend your proposal to others.

FURTHER RESOURCES

To learn more about writing a qualitative dissertation proposal and to examine a sample proposal, I recommend Maxwell's book:

Maxwell, J. A. (2013). *Qualitative research design: An interactive approach* (3rd ed.). Thousand Oaks, CA: Sage.

Although I have not seen much on concept mapping of the flow of ideas in research, there is one book that looks at research methods from a visual display perspective:

Wheeldon, J., & Ahlberg, M. K. (2012). *Visualizing social science research: Maps, methods, & meaning*. Thousand Oaks, CA: Sage.

Visit study.sagepub.com/30skills for quizzes, eFlashcards, and more!

Introducing a Qualitative Study

PART

III

Writing a Good
Qualitative Title and Abstract

Skill

Develop the skill of writing a good title and a complete abstract for your qualitative study.

Why the Skill Is Important

When Glesne and Peshkin (1992) decided to suggest that researchers begin their studies by stating a draft or tentative title, I felt that they were on to something good. I have since followed the practice of beginning my studies (or asking students to begin their studies) by advancing a draft title. I think that this is good practice in qualitative research, and I routinely have drafted titles for my research team members as they have pondered how to title journal articles, their dissertations, and their books. A title written early in a qualitative project provides a general roadmap for the study, offers a direction and focus that is helpful in sharing the project with others, keeps one on track (as well as any team members working with the author), and delineates the search of the literature. Furthermore, titles can be revised as the project proceeds, so I consider my early titles as "drafts."

Another important part of describing research at the beginning of a study is the abstract. Often qualitative researchers save the abstract for the last component they write in their qualitative projects. I turn this idea around and typically have qualitative researchers draft the abstract as one of the first elements, just like writing the title early in the project. Writing the abstract gives an overall sense to the project, and it covers the major elements that go into a good qualitative study. Granted, students may not have all of the information for their abstracts (e.g., the findings or results), but I ask them to conjecture and put something down on paper as to what they hope to find. Hence, writing an abstract at the beginning of the study is an orienting device that helps set the direction for the study. I have developed a structure for how this abstract might be written. If you use this structure, your abstract will contain all of the necessary parts of a good model and will not leave the reader wondering about the essential nature of the study. Furthermore, writing the abstract clarifies at the outset of a study major components that are helpful in planning a study.

Good Qualitative Titles

Here are some ideas about writing a good qualitative title.

I look for *short* titles consisting of no more than about 10 words at the most. The best titles are extremely short. Of course, I like even 1-word titles for books, such as *White*, or 1-word titles for movies, such as *Red*, or even 1-word titles for musical theater productions, such as *Rent*. More would be required for qualitative titles, but brevity is the key idea I want to emphasize.

I further keep the language as *open ended* as possible to allow multiple perspectives to emerge. Examine your drafts of titles to see if they narrow your project unnecessarily by the words that are used. Look at this draft title and then its revision to see how the directional words *boredom* and *exhaustion* were eliminated:

- Original title: "Fighting Boredom and Exhaustion: What Do Chinese Ph.D. Students in Computer Science Do in Leisure Time?" (R. Zhao, personal communication, December 10, 2011)

- Improved title: "How Do Chinese Ph.D. Students in Computer Science Spend Their Leisure Time?"

Then I also consider an array of *literary forms* for writing titles. A title can be a statement, but typically not what a researcher would expect, such as found in good quantitative titles. You can write the title as a question. There might be some redundancy with the central question, but that would be acceptable, especially in dissertations or theses. Because purpose statements populate qualitative journal articles, the use of a question in the title would not be redundant with the statement found in a good purpose statement. Then the title could also be a two-part title, with the parts separated by a colon. In this case the researcher needs to be certain that that two parts actually connect, and that connection is typically found tying together the central phenomenon in one part of the title and the other part of the title. I would refrain from using two colons (creating a three-part title), as this simply becomes too confusing.

An important element of writing a good title is to consider what the essential parts might be. Here are the elements I often consider in the order in which they appear in the title:

- Begin with a *gerund* verb. By using an "-ing" word, you convey action in the study. Action implies something unfolding, something in progress—all ideas central to good qualitative research. This gives the project an action and forward momentum. A good example is "Waiting for a Liver Transplant" (Brown et al., 2006), which begins with a gerund doubling as a central phenomenon, with patients as the participants, and the site implied (patients would be waiting at home, at the hospital, etc.). Good qualitative gerund words might be *developing*, *understanding*, and *exploring*.

- Next state the *central phenomenon*. The central phenomenon is the one concept or idea being explored in the study. It is probably best not to phrase it from a social science perspective but to phrase it using common language. In this way, it mirrors the phenomenon being asked of interviewees or being observed in the study.

- Identify the *participants*. The individuals being studied need to be included in the title of a project. In some cases, the focus could be on an entire case, and it would be more appropriate to mention the case rather than specific individuals. When participants are mentioned, it is somewhat of a judgment call as to whether the number of individuals might be stated. If multiple cases are studied, then the number of cases would probably be germane. The details about the number of participants can be conveyed later in the study in the methods section. What is important is to mention who exactly the participants might be. Rather than underrepresented students, for example, I would mention "Latino students." Rather than undergraduates in a class, I would mention that they are "undergraduates in a class on leadership skills."

- The final part of a good title is to mention the *research site* or place where the research took place. This may be implied in some studies, such as "individuals undergoing treatment for chronic pain," with the hospital or clinic as the implied setting.

In many cases mentioning the research site needs to be specific, such as "in a midwestern metropolitan city" or "in two middle schools in a state on the East Coast." In some cases, the site would be all around the United States or some other country. It may not be necessary to specify the geographic region if it is implied by the information about your participants. Also, the site may be a virtual site, and again this may be implied when you talk about your participants.

The order or position of these four elements is also important to consider. My title script would be as follows: "_____ (gerund) _____ (central phenomenon) for _____ (participants) at _____ (site)." This orders the elements from gerund verb, through central phenomenon (the most important component in the title) and participants, and on to where they are located (or where the study took place).

Finally, remember that in Chapter 3 I talked about how to make your project interesting through the study of an unusual group, angle, location, data collection, or data analysis, or through the study of a timely topic. One or more of these elements need to go into your qualitative title in addition to the above considerations. In this way, your title will engage readers, encourage them to read on, and require a thorough reading of your qualitative study to understand how the title was resolved or completed.

> The main components of a title are an opening gerund, the central phenomenon, the participants, and the research site. Does your title contain these components?

Improved Titles

The draft of a student's title stated in its original and revised forms can illustrate how titles can improve.

Example

Eliminating extra words and repositioning elements:

> Original: "The Emergence of the Competitive Cusp Within Entrepreneurial Firms in an Artistic Context" (E. Bass, personal communication, December 10, 2011)

> Revised: "The Competitive Cusp of Company Founders in Competitive Dance Studios." This change again positions the central phenomenon first, followed by the participants, and then the research site. Also, extra words are eliminated, and the "artistic context" is narrowed to the actual site of competitive dance studios.

Definition of an Abstract

An abstract is a brief summary of the contents of the qualitative study, and it allows readers to quickly survey the contents of an article. It is placed at the beginning of a study, and you will find it as the first discussion following the title in a journal article. The *Publication Manual of the American Psychological Association* (American Psychological Association [APA], 2010) indicates that it can be the most important single paragraph in an article. It also goes on to say that it must be accurate, non-evaluative (i.e., do not add comments beyond the scope of the research), coherent, readable, and concise.

A Word About Word Count

Abstracts written for journal publication vary in length, and editors often specify this length. Likewise, the length of an abstract for a dissertation or thesis is often dictated by college or university guidelines. At my institution, the abstract cannot be longer than 250 words. For one of the journals I published in, the abstract could be no longer than 50 words. The APA (2010) guidelines say that most abstracts range from 150 to 250 words. For some journals, the editorial guidelines require that the author write an abstract in an outline form (a "structured abstract"), with headings such as "Problem," "Objectives," "Data Collection," and so forth. This is the case for many health science journals. For purposes of our discussion, I will specify that the abstract can be no longer than 150 words.

Topics of a Good Abstract

There are major topics I would include in an abstract. The APA's (2010) publication manual indicates that the content varies for abstracts for a report, a literature review, a theory-oriented paper, and a methodological paper. I will focus here on the abstract for an empirical article. I see several major topics as part of the qualitative abstract, and I would order these components in the order in which I present them:

1. Start with the *issue* or *problem* leading to a need for the research. This issue might be related to a need for more literature, but I like to think about a "real-life" problem that needs to be addressed, such as the spread of AIDS, teenage pregnancies, college students dropping out of school, or the lack of women in certain professions. These are all real-life problems that need to be addressed. You could cite a reference or two about this problem, but generally the abstract is too short to include many citations.

2. Indicate the *purpose of the study*. Use the word *purpose*, and talk about the central phenomenon being explored, the participants who will be studied, and the site where the research will take place.

3. Next indicate what *data will be collected* to address this purpose. You might indicate the type of data, the participants, and where the data will be collected.

4. After this, report *themes* that will likely arise in your study. At the early stages of planning a project, you will not know what themes arise, so you might have to guess as to what they might be. Indicate four or five themes as possibilities.

5. Finish the abstract by mentioning the *practical implications* of the study. State the specific audience that will benefit from the project and why they will profit.

Examples of Abstracts

I want to provide three examples of abstracts. Examine these abstracts for the flow of topics from the problem, through the purpose and the methods, and on to the themes and the practical significance. Most of these abstracts are reasonably complete.

Example 1: Needing Additional Components

The purpose this narrative study is to deconstruct lived experiences of wartime rape through the perceptions of rape victims from the former Yugoslavian conflict between Bosnia, Croatia, Kosovo, and Serbia. The present study takes a unique methodological stance by exploring the narratives from courtroom testimonies of two Bosnian rape victims. The limited research has been conducted on how wartime rape victims perceive their victimization. The violation of the female body leaves women with long-lasting impact of psychological and physical trauma, which needs to be understood before providing victims with assistance and treatment (Sharlack, 2000). Therefore, this study explores the repercussions of wartime through the perceptions and narratives of rape victims. (T. Zohra, personal communication, December 12, 2010)

This is an example of a good abstract, but the ideas do not follow the five steps in the order in which I have provided them. It starts with the purpose, and then moves on to the problem. Reversing these two topics would create, I believe, stronger reader interest in the study. This abstract could be enhanced by the inclusion of the specific procedures, the themes, and the significance of the study for audiences.

Example 2: Adding One More Component

The national Boy Scouts of America announced in 2009 a new set of training requirements that annually affect over one million volunteer leaders across the United States. These heightened training requirements include new courses such as Hazardous Weather and revised courses such as Youth Protection, without which, a returning leader may not be re-registered. Previous studies indicate that increased training requirements of organizational volunteers may lead to an overall decrease in membership and attrition of qualified leaders. This qualitative study provides unique perspectives of volunteer leaders as they attempt to fulfill and comply with the new training expectations. Twelve leaders from three Midwest Councils were asked open-ended, one-on-one interview questions about how these training requirements affect their personal and professional lives and their ability to navigate a national online training site. The study provides a rich introspective into the lives of these volunteers and programmatic implications for non-profit organizations that seek to balance the need for increased training and education with the limits of volunteers' commitment. (T. Rolfes, personal communication, December 12, 2010)

This abstract is better than the first, but it is missing the part about advancing the themes in the study. All other parts seem to be in place and in the order in which I would like to see them.

Example 3: Adding a Clear Problem Statement

The issue that this study addresses is the lack of women in martial arts competitions. To address this problem, the purpose of this study will be exploring motivation of female athletes in Tae Kwon Do competitions. To gather data, interviews with 4 female Tae Kwon Do tournament competitors were conducted. The interviews were transcribed and analyzed. This data led to the following 3 themes: social support, self-efficacy, and goal orientation. These themes will be useful for understanding the optimal way to increase motivation in female martial artists. (Amanda Witte, personal communication, December 12, 2010)

This abstract is a good one, with all of the parts. My only concern would be that the problem is not clearly addressed at the outset. What is the issue when few women participate in martial arts competitions? Some possible "problems" might be: gender inequality, a lack of women to compete for the highest honors, and a missed opportunity of the empowerment for women. We simply do not know what problem results from the "lack of women in martial arts competitions." The first sentence does not clarify the problem clearly and could be improved. Otherwise, this abstract contains all of the topics necessary for a good qualitative abstract.

Writing an abstract when planning a study can give a general sense of the project and provide an overall direction for the study.

SUMMARY

Two important components that begin a qualitative study are the title and the abstract. These need careful attention. The title needs to be short, open ended, and creative. I recommend a structure as follows: begin with a gerund verb, next identify the central phenomenon, and then add the participants in the study and the research site. A script that I provide in this chapter can help with this design. Then write a good qualitative abstract for your study. I believe that there are essential components of this abstract, and they follow this order: the issue or problem, the purpose of the study, the data collection, the themes or findings, and the practical implications of the study. I provide several examples of abstracts for you to examine as you design your own abstract.

ACTIVITY

Write your draft title for a qualitative study. Use the guidelines I have provided in this chapter to write it, and be aware of what unusual features you have added to make it interesting to readers and audiences.

Critique an abstract. Find a published article in a qualitative journal and critique it. Ask yourself: Does it contain a problem, a purpose, the procedures, the themes, and the significance, reported largely in that order?

FURTHER RESOURCES

Consult the APA's (2010) publication manual for guidelines about writing a good title and abstract for an empirical study. It is difficult to find specific discussions about the creation of titles in qualitative studies. In one of my books, I discuss this topic:

Creswell, J. W. (2015). *Educational research: Planning, conducting and evaluating quantitative and qualitative research* (5th ed.). Boston: Pearson.

Visit study.sagepub.com/30skills for quizzes, eFlashcards, and more!

Writing a Good Introduction and Opening Sentence to a Study

Skill

Develop the skill of writing a good introduction to your qualitative study that includes a strong opening sentence.

Why the Skill Is Important

When we write papers or essays, we often develop the papers complete with the topics and then go back and write introductions that summarize the topics in our papers. Writing the introduction to a research study is a craft unto itself, and the introduction needs to be carefully developed, with attention toward engaging the reader in the study. If the introduction does not attract the reader, he or she is not likely to read the rest of the study. The introduction is not casually developed; it has a specific structure and organization, and once you have mastered this structure, it will be easy for you to write a good introduction in the future. I call this structure the "deficiencies model" of a good introduction, and I have been writing about it in my books during the past 20 years (see Creswell, 2014). Essentially, the introduction sets forth the problem or issue being studied in your qualitative project.

Also, part of a good introduction is the opening sentence. This is an important phase of your introduction. It needs to draw the reader in, present information that is at a level that she or he can understand, and be scholarly in its tone. We will spend time in this chapter learning both how to write a good introduction to your qualitative study and how to phrase your opening sentence so that both together engage your audience. How does a novice qualitative researcher write a good introduction?

Positioning an Introduction Within a Qualitative Study

Assuming that the purpose of an introduction is to present the problem or issue leading to the need for the study, let us position this introduction within the important first phases of a project. Already I have discussed the importance of finding a topic and then writing a good title and an abstract. The opening section in a qualitative study then introduces the problem or need for the study. After this, the opening section ends with a purpose statement that narrows the problem down to a manageable objective or focus. Then the research questions narrow it further to specific questions that will be answered in the study. Finally, the research design presents the data that will be collected to answer the research questions. Through the beginning of a study we are starting to narrow the focus of the project to research questions that can be answered with specific individuals. As shown in Figure 11.1, this information would represent a hierarchy of levels from the broad opening of a study to its narrowing.

Five Key Elements of a Good Introduction

I cannot emphasize enough how important it is to have a good introduction to a qualitative study. Care needs to be taken in presenting the opening material of a study.

FIGURE 11.1   **Hierarchy of Levels From the Topic to the Methods**

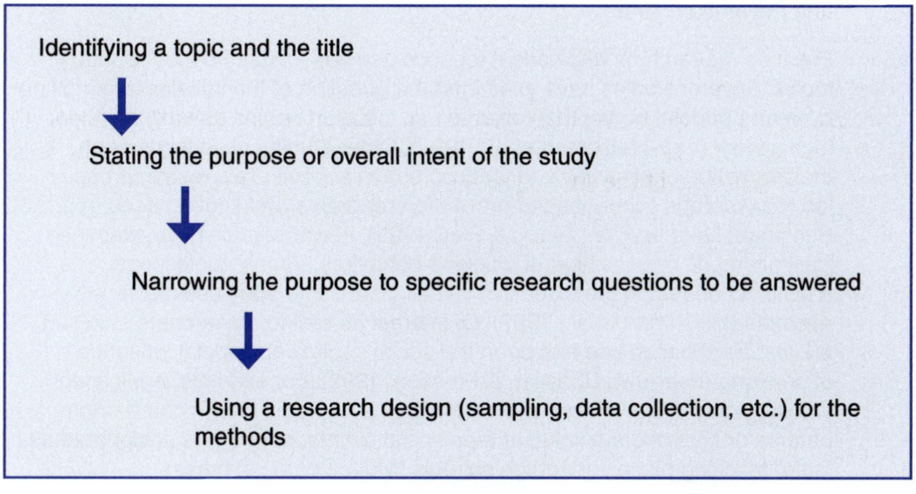

Identifying a topic and the title

Stating the purpose or overall intent of the study

Narrowing the purpose to specific research questions to be answered

Using a research design (sampling, data collection, etc.) for the methods

One way to learn about how to write the introduction is to study good introductions. This was the approach I took in the first edition of *Research Design: Qualitative and Quantitative Approaches* (Creswell, 1994). In that book, in Chapter 3, I reproduced the entire introduction to a journal article by Terenzini, Pascarella, and Lorang (1982) and then highlighted what I felt were the major elements of their introduction. I called the approach the "deficiencies" model of writing an introduction and have often described it as a standard form of writing a good introduction to a research study, regardless of whether the study is qualitative or quantitative (although there are elements that go into a qualitative introduction that set it apart from a quantitative introduction). I next used this same approach in my text *Educational Research* (Creswell, 2015). In that book I included as a figure the entire introduction to one of my studies addressing teen smoking and depression among high school students, and I placed marginal notes alongside the text to show what elements of an introduction were being used at certain points in the text. This figure is shown as Figure 11.2 here.

> An introduction is not casually written—it has a distinct structure and content.

FIGURE 11.2   Sample Introduction to a Qualitative Study

Exploring the Conceptions and Misconceptions of Teen Smoking in High Schools: A Multiple Case Analysis	
The Topic The Research Problem	Tobacco use is a leading cause of cancer in American society (McGinnis & Foefe, 1993). Although smoking among adults has declined in recent years, it has actually increased for adolescents. The Centers for Disease Control and Prevention reported that smoking among high school students had risen from 27.5 percent in 1991 to 34.8 percent in 1995 (USDHHS, 1996). Unless this trend is dramatically reversed, an estimated 5 million of our nations children will ultimately die a premature death (Centers for Disease Control and Prevention, 1996).
Evidence from Literature Justifying Problem	Previous research on adolescent tobacco use has focused on four primary topics. Several studies have examined the question of the initiation of smoking by young people, noting that tobacco use initiation begins as early as junior high school (e.g., Heishman et al., 1997). Other studies have focused on the prevention of smoking and tobacco use in schools. This research has led to numerous school-based prevention programs and interventions (e.g., Sussman, Dent, Burton, Stacy, & Flay, 1995). Fewer studies have examined "quit attempts" or cessation of smoking behaviors among adolescents, a distinct contrast to the extensive investigations into adult cessation attempts (Heishman et al., 1997). Of interest as well to researchers studying adolescent tobacco use has been the social context and social influence of smoking (Fearnow, Chassin, & Presson, 1998). For example, adolescent smoking may occur in work-related situations, at home where one or more parents or caretakers smoke, at teen social events, or at areas designated as "safe" smoking places near high schools (McVea et al., in press).

Deficiencies in Evidence	Minimal research attention has been directed toward the social context of high schools as a site for examining adolescent tobacco use. During high school students form peer groups which may contribute to adolescent smoking. Often peers become a strong social influence for behavior in general, and belonging to an athletic team, a music group, or the "grunge" crowd can impact thinking about smoking (McVea et al., in press). Schools are also places where adolescents spend most of their day (Fibkins, 1993) and are available research subjects. Schools provide a setting for teachers and administrators to be role models for abstaining from tobacco use and enforcing policies about tobacco use (OHara et al., 1999). Existing studies of adolescent tobacco use are primarily quantitative with a focus on outcomes and transtheoretical models (Pallonen, 1998). Qualitative investigations, however, provide detailed views of students in their own words, complex analyses of multiple perspectives, and specific school contexts of different high schools that shape student experiences with tobacco (Creswell, in press). Moreover, qualitative inquiry offers the opportunity to involve high school students as co-researchers, a data collection procedure that can enhance the validity of student views uncontaminated by adult perspectives.
Importance of Problem for Audiences	By examining these multiple school contexts, using qualitative approaches and involving students as co-researchers, we can better understand the conceptions and misconceptions adolescents hold about tobacco use in high schools. With this understanding, researchers can better isolate variables and develop models about smoking behavior. Administrators and teachers can plan interventions to prevent or change attitudes toward smoking, and school officials can assist with smoking cessation or intervention programs.

Source: Adapted from Creswell (2015).

The five major components that go into a good "deficiencies" introduction are:

1. The topic being examined in the study

2. The research problem or problems

3. The literature evidence justifying the problem

4. Deficiencies in this literature (hence the name of this type of introduction)

5. The audiences that will profit by the study's addressing these deficiencies

The Topic

It is important to state the topic in the opening sentence or two. This is not as easy as it might seem. The topic needs to be presented in a way that readers can immediately identify. It cannot be so narrow that the reader does not understand the general orientation of your qualitative study. Likewise, it cannot be stated so broadly that the reader cannot relate to the topic. The way I talk about this topic is that you need to lower the reader slowly down into a well rather than dropping the reader suddenly into the depths of your project. The well analogy is effective because you have a hand on the rope and can let the rope out slowly, placing one hand on top of the other over and over again. One way to determine if you have the topic framed at the right level of understanding is to ask people in your class or your friends to read the opening lines and see if they relate to your topic. It is best if these individuals are not people who work in your specific subject field. One more point: this topic can be referenced in the literature, it can include numbers or statistics, and my preference would be that it relate to a content area (even a timely topic) rather than simply saying "There is a lack of literature on X." Notice in Figure 11.2 that I talk about tobacco as a leading cause of cancer. I have pitched this qualitative study at a level that I believe most readers can understand—a topic with which they are familiar.

The Research Problem

The second idea to convey, then, in the introduction would be to state the problem or the issue leading to a need for the study. I have often felt that the **research problem** or issue is something that needs to be addressed and potentially solved. It is, indeed, a "problem." Think about how novels start (with a dilemma), how plays begin (with controversy), how music moves (from dissonant chords that need to be resolved to pleasing chords), or how sitcoms on television typically introduce several dilemmas that often run simultaneously. Research is no different—it begins with a problem or an issue. In short, the author presents the need for the study, and if this need is not clearly announced at the beginning of the qualitative study, then readers have no need to continue reading.

Also, it is helpful to think about this problem from two perspectives. First, there is the "real-life" problem, something occurring in our real world of work, home, friends, family, and so forth. Today, the Ebola virus is a problem, and it seems to be spreading. Also, teenage pregnancies are an issue. Gun control is certainly a controversial issue that needs to be addressed. I could cite other examples, but as you frame the "problem" in your qualitative introduction, think about commenting on some "real-life" problems that relate to your research topic. Second, there are problems with the literature. We often see people talk about the "need for more literature" or state that "the topic has been understudied" or that "there is little literature on the topic." These are problems that can lead to a study, but coming from the practical field of education, the social sciences, and health sciences, I find addressing the gaps in the literature as a somewhat weak rationale for a problem. To me it indicates a need, but I am still left thinking, "Why has it not been addressed in the literature?" Perhaps the best problem statement in your introduction would actually be a combination of a "real-life" problem as well as a "literature" problem. It is not difficult to state both types of problems to cover your bases. Also, remember to cite literature that supports your argument that a problem exists. Notice in Figure 11.2 that I talk about the problem of smoking leading to the premature death of children.

Colson Whitehead wrote an article titled "How to Write" in the *New York Times Sunday Book Review* of July 26, 2012. He advanced several rules for writing, and one of them was "What isn't said is as important as what is said." In good writing, he went on to say, the key idea is this thought: "Something is wrong—can you guess what it is?" Probably one difference between literary writing and good qualitative research writing is that the author specifies exactly what is wrong. It is not left to guesswork by the reader. But the larger point here is that in all writing, "something is wrong." This is good advice for your qualitative research: you need to make it clear early in your study that "something is wrong." This is the problem statement.

Evidence About the Problem

The next step in the introduction is to provide evidence on what has been studied about the problem. This evidence is typically based on the literature and the studies of the problem. Now here a clarification is needed. This reference to the literature is not a literature review citing specific studies or specific results of studies. It is instead a general review of the literature to set the stage for your study. Think about your literature map and the broad headings just below the top box in your map. These broad headings will help you map the general terrain of what authors have studied, not specific studies. But you may say, "No one has studied my topic." Of course, your particular topic may be quite focused (on a special population, a special site, or an unusual angle, as I suggested in Chapter 3, on making your project interesting). If you are to branch out beyond your topic (think about an inverted triangle with your project at the apex), you can find others who have studied topics closely related to your topic. In this section you need to summarize the research that has been done on your topic and then point toward deficiencies in that literature. You may draw on quantitative, qualitative, and mixed methods studies as you describe the extant literature. See that in Figure 11.2, I talk about four major topics related to smoking in schools.

Deficiencies in the Literature

The next passage refers to comments you would make about the shortcoming of the literature on the problem. You might mention several shortcomings, and draw on deficiencies such as topics not addressed, issues in research methods not adequately included, practical problems not fully explored, or a need to repeat a study with a new small qualitative sample. There are many types of deficiencies you can point out, and it is helpful to cite several of them. It is important as well for you to be thinking at this point about what qualitative research has to offer. Recall that qualitative research allows you to explore, to listen to the views of participants, to ask open-ended questions, and so forth (remember the characteristics of qualitative research mentioned in Chapter 1). The present literature may be deficient in several of these ways, and you could present in this section of the introduction a rationale for using qualitative research because past literature has been primarily quantitative or has not included these important qualitative components. In Figure 11.2, I refer to deficiencies in the study of adolescent smoking in terms of understanding the school content, the importance of peer groups, and schools as places where adolescents spend most of their time. I further clarify that many of the studies are quantitative and that we need qualitative research to understand the problem.

The Audience

The final section of an introduction refers to individuals and groups that profit from learning about or addressing the problem. I want you to think about the various audiences that may read your qualitative study. These may include fellow researchers, policy makers, practitioners in the field, leaders, graduate students, or committee members. In this final passage of the introduction, I would like for you to cite several audiences that will profit from reading your study. Be specific about what they will gain from your project, such as researchers' learning how interviews can go smoothly (or not), practitioners' understanding how people talk about a particular topic and the potential strategies they use to address the problem, and policy makers' adopting new laws or making decisions that will positively influence certain people. So talk about who will profit from your study. This brings the study home in importance to specific audiences, and perhaps your reader will be one of those individuals in the audiences you mention. You can see how I ended the introductory passage in Figure 11.2, where I refer to the importance of the study for researchers, school officials, and teachers.

The First Sentence of an Introduction

I mentioned that writing about the topic in the first few sentences begins a good qualitative introduction. I want to now narrow this to the first sentence. My friends in English composition call this the "narrative hook." Crafting good opening sentences creates reader interest and helps draw a reader into your study. It is useful to think about how to craft this sentence and the various ways it might be done. The opening sentence can convey:

- A personal statement about the researcher

- Past research conducted on your topic

- A timely issue

- Statistical information

- Information about a specific participant or site in your study

- A question

- References to give the opening sentence some scholarly weight

There may be other approaches as well, but these were a few first sentences I drew from existing qualitative studies in the literature that I often use in class. Here are some examples:

Example 1

A personal statement about the researcher in an article about people waiting for liver transplantation and a personal statement about the researcher's experiences:

> This study grew out of being ill at ease. (Brown, Sorrell, McClaren, & Creswell, 2006)

> I grew up in a small town of three thousand people located in the foothills of Virginia, the same place my parents were born and raised. (Ellis, 1993)

Example 2

A statement about the key participant in the study by the researcher:

> Vonnie Lee Hargrett celebrated his 29th birthday while I was writing this article in the summer of 1993 in the Florida city to which his parents had migrated from a rural part of the state. (Angrosino, 1994)

Example 3

A statement about past research on the topic:

> Past research has shown that outdoor recreation can aid in our deconstruction of gender and gender stereotyping. (Pohl, Borrie, & Patterson, 2000)

Example 4

A statement about a timely issue:

> Tobacco use is a leading cause of cancer in American Society. (Plano Clark et al., 2002)

Example 5

A statement that includes statistics:

> Incarceration rates for U.S. residents have increased 700% between 1970 and 2005 and are forecasted to climb an additional 13% in the next 5 years (Public Safety Performance Project, 2007). (Shivy et al., 2007)

SUMMARY

A good qualitative introduction consists of several ideas. It begins with a topic and includes in this topic a strong "narrative hook" to draw the reader into the study. It then moves into a specific problem or issue that needs to be addressed and into a discussion of the existing literature that addresses the problem. Deficiencies in this literature are noted next, and these deficiencies might include the lack of qualitative research and some of the strong elements that constitute qualitative research. Finally, the section ends with a statement about the potential audience that will profit from the study, and members of this audience can be drawn from different categories, such as researchers, policy makers, practitioners, and leaders.

ACTIVITY

Consider the key elements of a good introduction as found in Figure 11.2. Use these elements as a template for crafting your own introduction for your study. Make sure that in the end, the reader can clearly see that your project is addressing a problem.

FURTHER RESOURCES

In my book *Research Design: Qualitative, Quantitative, and Mixed Methods Approaches* (Creswell, 2014), I provide a detailed example of writing an introduction to a scholarly research study. I draw on a higher education article (Terenzini, Cabrera, Colbeck, Parente, & Bjorklund, 2001) to illustrate the components that go into a good introduction.

We can draw on resources from the writing community as to how to design good narrative hooks. You might consult the "Guide to Writing Introductions and Conclusions" from Gallaudet University (http://www .gallaudet.edu/tip/english_center/writing/ guide_to_writing_introductions_and_ conclusions.html), which discusses several models for opening sentences, such as a thesis statement, a story, specific detail, a quotation, an interesting statistic, or an opening question.

Visit study.sagepub.com/30skills for quizzes, eFlashcards, and more!

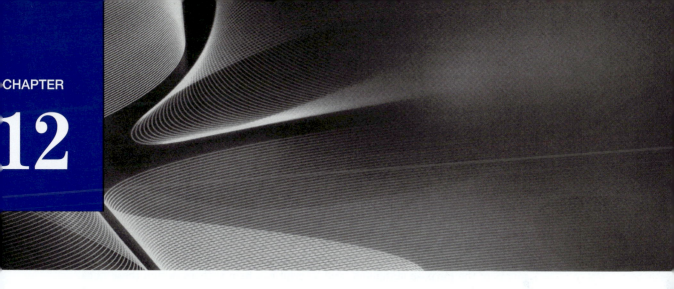

Scripting a Qualitative Purpose Statement and Research Questions

Skills

- Develop the skill of writing a good qualitative purpose statement.

- Develop the skill of writing a complete qualitative central question and sub-questions.

- Develop the skill of creating a clear, understandable central phenomenon for your purpose statement and research questions.

Why the Skills Are Important

Stanley Fish's (2011) book *How to Write a Sentence and How to Read One* is a helpful guide to writing research, especially the purpose statement. Fish tells us that we need to think about how sentences are put together: a "sentence is a structure of logical relationships" (p. 57). He adds that we should pay attention to the relationship of ideas rather than focusing on the parts of speech such as nouns, verbs, and direct objects. He asks, What are the "content's vehicles and generators" (p. 121) for carrying forward ideas in a sentence? What are the vehicles and generators and the logical parts of the structure of a purpose statement? This idea has led me to think about the use of "scripts" in which authors fill in the blanks around the key parts that belong in a purpose statement. "Scripts" can help authors design one of the most important statements in a qualitative research project—the purpose statement—and they can also be useful in the design of the research questions.

In this chapter you will find a "script" with the parts for writing a good purpose statement, and the logical order of the parts that carry forward ideas about the purpose or intent of your study. In short, this purpose statement needs to be carefully scripted so that it is absolutely clear and straightforward. I always say that if the purpose statement is fuzzy, the reader will be lost in the parts to follow in a research study. Second in importance, then, after the purpose statement would be the research questions that narrow the purpose down into questions to be answered in a study. These, too, need to be carefully designed to carry forward the key elements of the purpose statement, and a script can help authors design these questions. Embedded within both the purpose statement and the research questions is the core idea being explored in a study—the central phenomenon. Focusing on the nature of the central phenomenon, how to write it, and how to consistently use it are also important features of good qualitative studies.

Interrelating the Purpose, the Research Questions, and the Methods

The **purpose statement** is the overall objective or intent of the study. In some projects it is called the "study aim." It is the most important statement in your qualitative study. It is a statement that conveys the essence of a project. A **central question** is a single general question that reframes the purpose into a specific question. This central question is the broadest question that can be asked. It is unlike quantitative questions, in which authors try to narrow the questions down to specific variables that can be related. It is helpful to think about the qualitative central question by asking yourself, "What is the broadest question I can ask about my central phenomenon?" The *central phenomenon* is the core idea being explored in a qualitative study. It needs to be stated in a way that is not too broad (e.g., experiences of individuals) or too narrow (e.g., identity when at work). It needs to rest somewhere in the middle, such as the "cultural identity" of individuals. The central phenomenon is stated within both the purpose statement and the central question. The central question can then be made more specific by writing five to seven **sub-questions** that subdivide the central question into parts or topics. If you were to ask questions about your central phenomenon when you explore it, what subtopics would you ask participants in your study? These sub-questions then become the major questions used during your qualitative data collection procedures. They can become key questions asked during interviews, questions to reflect on yourself during observations, or questions to ponder as you examine documents, pictures, videos, photographs and other forms of audiovisual materials.

Purpose Statements

I have probably written more about the purpose statement than what you will find in most research methods books. My book *Research Design* (Creswell, 2014) devotes an entire chapter to the topic. I believe in providing a "script" for writing this statement, a "script" in which the researcher fills in blanks with his or her own study using a template. My approach is quite applied and practical. I have even suggested that there are certain elements to include in this statement.

Elements to Include in a Good Purpose Statement

Here are some key elements I find useful in developing a good qualitative purpose statement:

- Use *key words* to denote to the reader that your statement is the purpose statement. Start your statement by saying, "The purpose is . . . ." You could also talk about the "intent" or the "objective" of the study. In many proposals for funding, the word *purpose* is replaced by the words *study aim*. Regardless of the precise terminology, you might consider how you alert the reader that the most important statement in a project is coming.

- Use an appropriate *verb tense* in the statement. For research that will be completed, use the future tense; for research already finished, the past tense; and for an active, dynamic statement voice, use the present tense. All three are possible in qualitative research.

- Keep the statement *short and to the point*. This means eliminating unnecessary words and explanations.

- Use *nondirectional language* that opens up the responses from your participants rather than closing them down. Words such as *positive*, *successful*, *effective*, and *useful* close down the discussion rather than opening it up.

- Include the following *elements* in your statement:
  - Mention that your study is qualitative research. Once you decide on the appropriate qualitative design to use (see Chapter 30), you can insert the name of the design.
  - Use an action verb to convey how you will learn about your topic, such as *understand*, *describe*, *develop*, *discover*, or *generate*.

○ State the central phenomenon. The central phenomenon is the core idea you want to explore (e.g., being a professional, buckling under stress, tolerating ambiguity).

○ Indicate the participants in your study. Who will be providing data in your project? If you are gathering data from documents or audio-visual materials, these need to be specified.

○ Indicate where you will gather the data—the research site. If it is a virtual site, you could mention this fact. In some instances, it is wise to make the site anonymous (e.g., "a large public university in the Midwest").

○ Provide a general definition of your central phenomenon if the term or phrase is not self-evident to readers. You could provide a textbook definition, a rephrased definition, or the definition you plan to use that is acceptable in your field of study.

A Suggested Script for Writing a Qualitative Purpose Statement

The elements can be put together in a "script" in which you fill in the information on the basis of your study.

> The purpose of this _____ (*qualitative approach*) study is (*was, will be*) to _____ (*action verb*—understand, describe, develop, discover, *etc.*) _____ (*the central phenomenon being studied*) for _____ (*the participants*) at _____ (*the research site*). At this stage in the research, _____ (*the central phenomenon*) will be generally defined as _____ (*provide a general definition*).

Example 1

> Therefore, the purpose of this qualitative study [qualitative approach] was to generate a theoretical model that explores [action verb] what low-income rural families [research site] with young children do for fun [central phenomenon] from the perspective of mothers [participants]. (Churchill, Plano Clark, Prochaska-Cue, Creswell, & Ontai-Grzebik, 2007)

Example 2

> Accordingly, the purpose of this multi-site qualitative case study [qualitative approach] is to explore [action verb] how adolescents [participants] talk about tobacco use [central phenomenon] in their schools and in their lives [research site]. (Plano Clark et al., 2002, pp. 1265–1266)

You will note that in both of these examples, the central phenomena were not defined, as the authors felt that "do[ing] for fun" and "talk[ing] about tobacco use" were self-explanatory ideas not needing definition.

Research Questions

The research questions then narrow the purpose statement to specific questions the qualitative researcher will answer by collecting and analyzing data. In qualitative research we ask research questions rather than posing hypotheses. Hypotheses would typically narrow the scope of our inquiry, and in qualitative research we try to keep our questions as open-ended as possible so that multiple perspectives can emerge from participants. There are two types of research questions in qualitative research: the central question and sub-questions.

The Central Question

The central question is the broadest question that can be asked about the topic you are studying in your qualitative project. It is an interrogative statement in the form of a question, and it does not include directional words signifying a quantitative project, such as *positive*, *successful*, or *change*. It also does not compare groups or relate variables, as found in quantitative research. Often it uses language that is familiar to a wide audience and is not social or health science oriented, it repeats some of the wording found in the purpose statement, and it consists of logical parts. These logical parts are as follows:

> The central question subdivides into several sub-questions, and the sub-questions then form the core content for an interview or observation.

- The central question begins with a word such as *how* or *what*. Typically it does not begin with the word *why*, which suggests a quantitative cause-effect language.

- It states the central phenomenon, the core idea you want to explore in the qualitative project.

- It identifies the participants in the study, the people from whom the data will be collected.

- It may identify the research site or the place where the study will be undertaken. Sometimes this element is implied by the statement and left out.

An Ideal Order of the Central Question Elements

Because the central phenomenon is the key feature of a study, we need to highlight it up front in a research question. Also, participants reside in specific research sites, and so we might mention the participants first, followed by the site. This flow of ideas in a central question might look like this script:

Position			
(1)	(2)	(3)	(4)
What	Central Phenomenon	Participants	Site
What (*or how*) does the _____ (*central phenomenon*) mean for _____ (*participants*) at the _____ (*site*)?			

As you can see, the central question is quite simple and short in form.

Examples of Improving the Central Question

Example 1: Revising a Central Question—Making It Interesting

Original question:

> How first-year Chinese graduate students adjust at Midwest University? (X. Ma, personal communication, November 18, 2014)

Improved question:

> What are the coping strategies that first-year Chinese graduate students use to adjust in their first year at Midwest University?

The original question had the key components of a research question. What was needed for this central question was to make the project more interesting (see Chapter 3). For instance, we could shift the central phenomenon to cultural aspects of the students or the coping skills they use. The revised question takes coping strategies as the central phenomenon.

Example 2: Revising a Central Question—Clarifying the Central Phenomenon

Original question:

> How do ranchers use off-ranch information to make on-ranch decisions in the central Great Plans? (M. Siliwinksi, personal communication, November 18, 2014)

Revised question:

> How do ranchers in the Central Great Plains use information about the landscape to manage their own land?

Notice in the original question the ambiguity of the central phenomenon being explored. In the revision, the central phenomenon, "use information," is much clearer.

Example 3: Revising a Central Question—Adding the Central Phenomenon

Original question:

> How do employee resource groups operate? (S. Schlachter, personal communication, November 18, 2014)

Revised question:

> How do employee resource groups establish and maintain their social identity?

It is necessary to mention the central phenomenon in the research question, yet it was missing from the original question. The original phenomenon from the purpose was the "inner workings of the employee resource groups." Perhaps the central phenomenon is better clarified as the social identity of employee resource groups. The revised question adds this revised central phenomenon.

Sub-questions

Sub-questions then narrow the central question to specific aspects. I recommend that a small number of sub-questions, say five to seven, be written. I further suggest that qualitative researchers look closely at their central phenomena and ask themselves, "How can this central phenomenon be subdivided into several parts?" These parts, the sub-questions, then become the key questions asked during the data collection, such as the questions asked of interviewees or the questions researchers ask themselves as they observe. As shown in Figure 12.1, the central question subdivides into several sub-questions, and the sub-questions then form the core content for an interview protocol (see Chapter 15).

For example, the central question "What is the campus climate toward diversity?" (diversity is the central phenomenon) might be subdivided into several sub-questions, such as:

> "What are student attitudes on campus toward forming diverse social groups?"
>
> "How is diversity encouraged by the central administration?"
>
> "How is diversity encouraged in the undergraduate classes on campus?"
>
> "How is diversity encouraged by the campus police force?"

FIGURE 12.1   **Relationship of Central Question to Interview Questions**

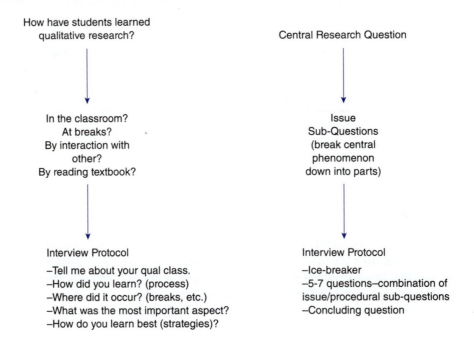

How have students learned
qualitative research?

In the classroom?
At breaks?
By interaction with
other?
By reading textbook?

Interview Protocol

–Tell me about your qual class.
–How did you learn? (process)
–Where did it occur? (breaks, etc.)
–What was the most important aspect?
–How do you learn best (strategies)?

Central Research Question

Issue
Sub-Questions
(break central
phenomenon
down into parts)

Interview Protocol

–Ice-breaker
–5-7 questions–combination of
issue/procedural sub-questions
–Concluding question

The Central Phenomenon

> The central phenomenon must be absolutely clear and consistently stated.

One of the most challenging parts of writing good purpose statements, central questions, and sub-questions is clarifying the central phenomenon in a study. Part of this challenge lies in understanding what you would like to explore or study in your project. It may take you several attempts to identify your central phenomenon, and the final version may result from sharing it with others, going back to the literature and reviewing key studies on your topic, or collecting some data, analyzing it, and determining what participants in your study actually talk about when you ask them questions. So, you may find yourself working backward from the themes or findings to clarify the central phenomenon in your study. Here are some suggestions for identifying the central phenomenon that may help:

- State your central phenomenon in two to three words or fewer, such as "professional development," "integration of technology," or "mothering." Make your central phenomenon as concise as possible.

- Realize that your central phenomenon may change during your study as you collect data and actually analyze them. It is more important that you end with a clear central phenomenon rather than start with one.

- Settle on a label (or name) for your central phenomenon, and then stay with it. Be consistent, and do not change the words of the central phenomenon throughout your project, as this will confuse the reader. Use the exact same name wherever the central phenomenon appears in your study (e.g., in the title, in the purpose statement, in your research questions, in your conclusion). In short, do not change the label (or name) of your central phenomenon in your study by the time you conclude the study.

Example of a Changing Central Phenomenon

Look at the following example that illustrates a changing central phenomenon in a study.
From the abstract of a study:

> The purpose of this study is to understand how college students interact in a diversity class taught by a White teacher.

From the introduction to the same study:

> The purpose of this qualitative study is to discover how students react to interactions to a White instructor teaching about diversity in a college classroom at a public four-year university in the Midwest.

Notice in this example how the central phenomenon in the abstract, "students interact," changed to "students react to interactions" in the purpose statement. This type of changing central phenomenon is confusing for a reader and leads to ambiguity about the central phenomenon being explored.

Other Ideas About the Central Phenomenon

Consider identifying a central phenomenon that is neither too broad nor too narrow, to help a reader understand your project. Examples of central phenomena that are too broad are "experience" and "perceptions." These broad examples do not communicate what you will be exploring. Examples of central phenomena that are too narrow are "eating bananas" and "sharpening pencils." These narrow examples illustrate ideas being explored that may not be conceptually interesting.

Furthermore, state only one central phenomenon. The use of the conjunction *and* is a tipoff that more than one central phenomenon is being presented (e.g., "What do emotion *and* attitudes mean for young teenagers?")

SUMMARY

It is important to write the central question clearly. A "script" can help that includes elements of the qualitative approach, an action verb, the central phenomenon, the participants, and the research site. The central question narrows the purpose down to a general question that will be addressed through the data collection. This central question is the broadest question that can be asked, and its general nature enables participants to share multiple perspectives. The central question further subdivides into sub-questions that are asked in a qualitative study. A small number of sub-questions subdivide the central phenomenon into its parts. The central phenomenon is the key core idea being explored in a study, and it is challenging to write in a simple and clear way.

ACTIVITY

1. Consider this central question:

   What does mothering mean to women who are adoptive parents?

   Identify the:

   Central phenomenon

   Participants

   Research site

2. Consider this central question:

   What is medical care to faculty/students at the Medical Center Sharing Clinic for underserved patients?

   Identify the:

   Central phenomenon

   Participants

   Research site

FURTHER RESOURCES

Consider the specific chapter on writing a purpose statement in:

Creswell, J. W. (2014). *Research design: Qualitative, quantitative, and mixed methods approaches* (4th ed.). Thousand Oaks, CA: Sage.

Visit study.sagepub.com/30skills for quizzes, eFlashcards, and more!

Collecting Data

PART

IV

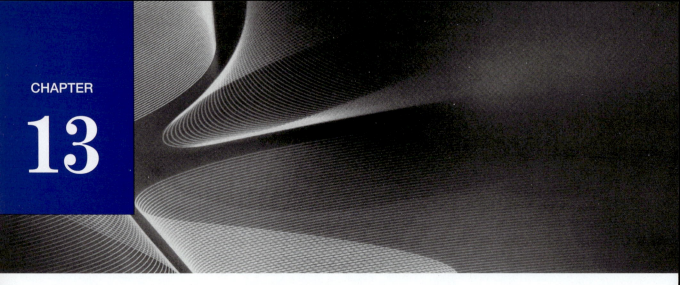

Understanding the Process of Qualitative Data Collection

Skill

Develop the skill of understanding the interrelated nature of the multiple steps involved in qualitative data collection.

Why the Skill Is Important

Individuals new to qualitative research often consider data collection to be simply conducting interviews or gathering observations. In fact, the process of qualitative data collection involves several steps that stretch from selection of the site to designing forms for recording information. A complete data collection plan or discussion includes many steps. At the end of this chapter you will have a checklist to help guide you through all of the steps, and the chapter also provides a reminder of the topics that need to go into a rigorous qualitative data collection section. At the center of data collection are, of course, the sources of the data you will gather. This is the beauty of qualitative research: It is built upon gathering many types of data, and the list of potential types has grown considerably in our digital age. In this chapter we will spend some time reviewing the types of data that might be collected and assessing the strengths and weaknesses of each form of data.

The Parts of Qualitative Data Collection

In my discussion of these parts, I have often used a wheel to illustrate the various elements that go into a good data collection procedure (Creswell, 2013). As I have worked with individuals designing qualitative studies for publication, my list of data collection procedures has expanded. Here are the parts I would encourage you to use in writing a complete qualitative data collection section for a dissertation, a project, or a journal article:

> The process of data collection in qualitative research consists of more than simply collecting different forms of data.

- Rationale for using qualitative research

- Research sites that will be studied

- Permissions obtained to study sites and individuals

- Recruitment strategies for encouraging people to participate in your study

- Purposeful sampling of participants

- Demographics of participants

- Reciprocity for participants

- Types of data collected

- Extent of data collection

- Use of protocols and data collection questions asked

Rationale

The methods might begin with a rationale for using qualitative research. Ten or 15 years ago, this was a required section for most qualitative projects. As people have become more and more familiar with qualitative inquiry, a rationale is needed less and less. The rationale would consist of mentioning the advantages of using qualitative research and drawing on the elements mentioned in Chapters 1 and 2, in which I review the characteristics of qualitative research. Unquestionably, qualitative research is used for exploration when we do not know the variables to measure or the questions to ask. It is also important when we need to listen to the actual words of a participant to obtain the best understanding of our central phenomenon. Because qualitative research takes place in a specific setting, often the setting where the research problem occurs, the context is most important. This might be referred to as the setting, context, or environment that surrounds a study. Qualitative research also enables us to present a complex portrait of a project and present the many different perspectives individuals might have on the topic.

Research Site

Next, going from the broad perspective to the narrow, I would mention the specific research site or place where the study will take place. I would describe this site and discuss why it has been selected as an ideal site to study the problem. Again, in describing this site, I like to discuss the broader picture and then narrow it. For example, in my ethnography of a soup kitchen you will find a discussion of the building and the land surrounding it, then on to the dining room, and to specific tables and individuals seated at the tables—a model of description from the broad to the narrow (Miller, Creswell, & Olander, 1998).

Permissions Obtained

Qualitative research takes place in the homes and workplaces of participants. It also focuses on difficult-to-research issues or emotional issues not amenable to measurement or precise assessment. Because of this, qualitative researchers take permissions quite seriously, and they often discuss the use of multiple permissions. Permission is needed from the institutional review board (IRB) at an institution or a company, from "gatekeepers" at sites where access is required to gather information, and from participants and possibly the parents of participants (when children are involved). Gaining multilevel permissions makes qualitative research challenging. In Chapter 7, I discussed the process of seeking approval from IRBs. During data collection, qualitative researchers need to provide participants with informed consent letters with which participants give approval for the provisions of the data collection and are guaranteed their rights. A sample consent form used during data collection is shown in Figure 13.1.

It is important to look closely at this form. It contains specific elements that need to go into an informed consent letter, such as:

- The right of participants to voluntarily withdraw from the study at any time

- The central purpose of the study and the procedures to be used in data collection

- Assurances of confidentiality for the respondents

- The known risks associated with participation in the study

- The expected benefits to accrue to participants in the study

- The signature of the participant as well as the researcher

Alternatively, these elements can be covered in a question-and-answer format for the IRB informed consent documents. In this format, each section poses a question from the participant's point of view. Covering the same elements listed previously,

FIGURE 13.1   Sample Human Subjects Consent-to-Participate Form

"Experiences in Learning Qualitative Research: A Qualitative Case Study"

Dear Participant,

The following information is provided for you to decide whether you wish to participate in the present study. You should be aware that you are free to decide not to participate or to withdraw at any time without affecting your relationship with this department, the instructor, or the University of Nebraska–Lincoln.

The purpose of this study is to understand the process of learning qualitative research in a doctoral-level college course. At this stage in the research, "process" will be generally defined as perceptions of the course and making sense of qualitative research at different phases in the course.

Data will be collected at three points—at the beginning of the course, at the midpoint, and at the end of the course. Data collection will involve documents (journal entries made by students and the instructor, student evaluations of the class and the research procedure), audiovisual material (a video of the class), interviews (transcripts of interviews between students), and classroom observation field notes (made by students and the instructor). Individuals involved in the data collection will be the instructor and the students in the class.

Do not hesitate to ask any questions about the study either before participating or during the time that you are participating. We would be happy to share our findings with you after the research is completed. However, your name will not be associated with the research findings in any way, and only the researchers will know your identity as a participant.

There are no known risks and/or discomforts associated with this study. The expected benefits associated with your participation are the information about the experiences in learning qualitative research, the opportunity to participate in a qualitative research study, and coauthorship for those students who participate in the detailed analysis of the data. If submitted for publication, a byline will indicate the participation of all students in the class.

Please sign your consent with full knowledge of the nature and purpose of the procedures. A copy of this consent form will be given to you to keep.

Signature of Participant

Date

John W. Creswell, Ed. Psy., UNL, Principal Investigator

Source: Adapted from Creswell (2013).

the informed consent headings in question format might be (Agency for Healthcare Research and Quality, 2009):

- Why are you doing this study?

- What if I say no to being in this study?

- What if I say yes now, but change my mind and want to quit the study later?

- What happens if I say yes to being in the study?

- How much times will it take?

- Who will see information about me?

- Could being in this study be bad for me in any way?

- Will being in the study help me in anyway?

- Will I be paid for being in the study?

- What if I have questions?

- What should I do if I want to be part of this study?

The question-and-answer format is sometimes favored by health sciences fields (visit the Agency for Healthcare Research and Quality's Web site at http://www.ahrq.gov for a sample) and by certain IRBs. I recommend that you investigate the informed consent requirements of your IRB in preparing the document.

These elements pertain to gaining permission from individuals. Equally important is seeking permission to have access to research sites. It is important that "gatekeepers" or individuals responsible for permitting you to enter the site be aware of what your presence at the site will require. Bogdan and Biklen (1992) suggested that researchers inform individuals at sites on the basis of the following information:

- Why was the site chosen for study?

- What will be done at the site during the research study?

- How much time will be spent at the site by the researcher?

- Will the researcher's presence be disruptive of activities at the site?

- How will the results be reported?

- What will the gatekeeper, the participants, and the site gain from the study (reciprocity)?

I often suggest that researchers address each of these questions in writing and supply the participants at the site with this useful information.

Recruitment Strategies

Qualitative researchers often have to recruit participants to be involved in qualitative projects. This recruitment may require placing ads in newspapers, contacting sites (e.g., support groups), sending out letters, or posting flyers about the project and asking for recruits. IRBs often require that researchers supply information about how their participants will be recruited to projects. The actual flyers or notices to be posted need to be filed with the IRB. Sometimes multiple recruitment strategies are used in qualitative research until the desired number of participants have agreed to be in a project.

An easy way to reach a larger number of people is through an invitation sent through e-mail or a Web-based service like a list server. Figure 13.2 provides an example of an e-mail invitation sent to recruit participants for a qualitative interview. Although the next section discusses sampling in more depth, it is worth noting that snowball or chain sampling can be a helpful way to recruit participants. Using these strategies, you find people who can direct you to other information-rich participants. You may find referrals from a gatekeeper, someone in a group of individuals likely to fit your criteria, or from your participants themselves (Rossman & Rallis, 2012). A closing interview question could ask who else you could talk to in order to learn more about the topic. Of course, these approaches require attention to ethics and the nature of the relationship with participants.

Purposeful Sampling

Purposeful sampling is the process of selecting participants for a qualitative project by recruiting individuals who can help inform the central phenomenon in a study. This is a different type of sampling from that found in quantitative research, where individuals (or groups or sites) are chosen because they are representative of a population or because they are available. It involves three components: making decisions

FIGURE 13.2   **Sample Interview Invitation Letter**

Dear [Insert Name]:

We are writing regarding a study of the skills needed to develop proficiency to conduct mixed methods research. Because of your recognized expertise in conducting and teaching mixed methods, I would like to invite you to participate in an individual interview in order to help us better understand these skills. The interview will last approximately 45 minutes and take place over the telephone.

Please find the attached informed consent form that contains information about the study and participation. If you are willing to participate, please contact Tim Guetterman at tcguetterman@gmail.com or John W. Creswell at jcreswell1@unl.edu. Tim will schedule a time to discuss the informed consent and conduct the interview.

Thank you for your consideration.

Sincerely,
Tim Guetterman, Research Assistant
John W. Creswell, Professor

about whom to select as participants (or sites), the sampling strategy to use, and the number of individuals for the sample.

It is important to select individuals for your study who have experienced the phenomenon you are exploring. This is a basic prerequisite of qualitative research. Next, the pool of individuals may be quite large, and you need to use a sampling strategy to select individuals. It is not enough to simply purposefully sample; you need to convey the specific sampling strategy you plan on using. Fortunately, there are several options from which to choose. I have identified these options in Table 13.1 and presented their overall purpose.

As you can see from Table 13.1, I begin with **maximal variation sampling**. It consists of determining in advance some criterion that differentiates the sites or participants, and then selecting sites or participants that are quite different on that criterion. This approach has the advantage of building into the sampling strategy differences in perspectives, an advantage in qualitative research when a core feature of the research is to present multiple perspectives of participants (see Chapter 1). Other sampling strategies frequently used are critical cases, which provide specific information about a problem, and convenience sampling, the choice of participants who volunteer or are available to engage in a study.

The sample size is determined by several factors: the complexity of the phenomenon being studied, the type of qualitative design you are using (see Chapter 30), the richness and extensive use of data, and the resources being used. When planning a study, it is helpful to examine similar studies and consider your resource constraints. When collecting your data, I recommend paying close attention to whether and when you begin to hear the same (or similar) data from participants over and over again. This notion is called saturation, and it provides a broad way to think about your sample size. In qualitative research, the idea is to explore a topic in depth. If data begin to repeat and you are not hearing new information, your sample size is likely adequate.

Demographics of Participants

Qualitative research has a sense of realism to it—this form of inquiry actually involves people in our projects. Thus, a good qualitative data collection section often includes a detailed personal profile of the participants in the study. This profile can assume the form of a table that includes gender, race, position, geographical location, and other factors about each participant. In this way, readers can obtain a detailed understanding of the demographic characteristics of the participants.

Reciprocity for Participants

For individuals in your study, qualitative research involves considerable time participating in interviews, sharing documents about their lives, or being observed in their homes or workplaces. Researchers need to give back to participants for their time. **Reciprocity** involves the researcher's giving back to the research subjects in some form, from a minor token of appreciation (e.g., money for a cup of coffee) to a major

TABLE 13.1 Typology of Sampling Strategies in Qualitative Inquiry

Type of Sampling	Purpose
Maximum variation	Documents diverse variations and identifies important common patterns
Homogeneous	Focuses, reduces, simplifies, and facilitates group interviewing
Critical case	Permits logical generalization and maximum application of information to other cases
Theory based	Find examples of a theoretical construct and elaborate on and examine it
Confirming and disconfirming cases	Elaborate on initial analysis, seek exceptions, looking for variation
Snowball or chain	Identifies cases of interest from people who know people who know what cases are information-rich
Extreme or deviant case	Learn from highly unusual manifestations of the phenomenon of interest
Typical case	Highlights what is normal or average
Intensity	Information-rich cases that manifest the phenomenon intensely but not extremely
Politically important	Attracts desired attention or avoids attracting undesired attention
Random purposeful	Adds credibility to sample when potential purposeful sample is too large
Stratified purposeful	Illustrates subgroups and facilitates comparisons
Criterion	All cases that meet some criterion; useful for quality assurance
Opportunistic	Follow new leads; taking advantage of the unexpected
Combination or mixed	Triangulation, flexibility; meets multiple interests and needs
Convenience	Saves time, money, and effort, but at the expense of information and credibility

Source: Miles and Huberman (1994, p. 28). Reprinted with permission from SAGE Publications.

step of support (e.g., in my ethnography of a soup kitchen, I became an advocate for the rights of the homeless to support agencies; see Miller et al., 1998). As you discuss your data collection, you need to identify how you plan to give back to participants for their time in your project.

Types of Data Collected

A centerpiece of qualitative data collection involves assessing the types of data you can collect and deciding which type or types are best for your study. It means weighing the advantages and limitations of each source of data. Furthermore, I routinely suggest that a hallmark of good qualitative research is the use of multiple sources of data (e.g., interviews and observations), and being creative about the selection of unusual sources (e.g., text messages). The use of multiple sources of data in a project, as mentioned in Chapter 3, can add to the conceptual interest of a qualitative project and make it interesting.

The types of qualitative data fall into four categories: observations, interviews, documents, and audiovisual materials. Each source of data has both advantages and limitations, as shown in Table 13.2.

TABLE 13.2   **Types of Qualitative Data Collection: Advantages and Limitations**

Data Collection Types	Options Within Types	Advantages of the Type	Limitations of the Type
Observations	• Complete participant— researcher conceals role • Observer as participant—role of researcher is known • Participant as observer—observation role secondary to participant role • Complete observer— researcher observes without participating	• Researcher has firsthand experience with participant • Researcher can record information as it occurs • Unusual aspects can be noticed during observation • Useful in exploring topics that may be uncomfortable for participants to discuss	• Researcher may be seen as intrusive • Private information may be observed that researcher cannot report • Researcher may not have good attending and observing skills • Certain participants (e.g., children) may present special problems in gaining rapport
Interviews	• Face to face—one-on-one, in-person interview • Telephone—researcher interviews by phone • Focus group (and online focus group)— researcher interviews participants in a group • Online interviews (e.g., e-mails, chat rooms, bulletin boards, instant messaging)	• Useful when participants cannot be directly observed • Participants can provide historical information • Allows researcher control over the line of questioning • Allows questioning over a long period of time • Encourages open exchanges • Cost and time efficiency	• Provides indirect information filtered through the views of interviewees • Provides information in a designated place rather than the natural field setting • Researcher's presence may bias responses • Not all people are equally articulate and perceptive • Privacy may be an issue with online contact • Technical skills needed for online data collection

Data Collection Types	Options Within Types	Advantages of the Type	Limitations of the Type
Documents	• Public documents, such as minutes of meetings, or newspapers • Private documents, such as journals, diaries, or letters	• Enables a researcher to obtain the language and words of participants • Can be accessed at a time convenient to researcher—an unobtrusive source of information • Represents data that are thoughtful in that participants have given attention to compiling them • As written evidence, it saves a researcher the time and expense of transcribing	• Not all people are equally articulate and perceptive • May be protected information unavailable to public or private access • Requires the researcher to search out the information in hard-to-find places • Requires transcribing or optically scanning for computer entry • Materials may be incomplete • The documents may not be authentic or accurate
Audiovisual materials	• Photographs • Videotapes • Art objects • Computer software • Film	• May be an unobtrusive method of collecting data • Provides an opportunity for participants to directly share their reality • It is creative in that it captures attention visually	• May be difficult to interpret • May not be accessible publicly or privately • The presence of an observer (e.g., photographer) may be disruptive and affect responses

Sources: This table includes material from Merriam (1998), Bogdan and Biklen (1992), and Creswell (2014).

Certainly, more and more forms of qualitative data have become available because of the Internet and digital means of gathering data. In my books on qualitative research, I have included a "compendium" of sources of qualitative data, and I keep adding to this list as time goes by. Most recent entries relate to collecting digital information. My most updated list is shown in Figure 13.3.

Extent of Data Collection

Often we will see in qualitative studies the authors mentioning the extent of their data collection (e.g., "During this project I gathered 30 observations over a 6-month period, 15 interviews, and over 100 documents"). Comments such as these illustrate the extent and depth of the data collection. Sometimes researchers will put into their studies tables that list the various forms of data and the amount of information collected. I find it useful to highlight this information. It helps emphasize the rigor and time-consuming nature of qualitative research.

FIGURE 13.3   A Compendium of Data Collection Approaches in Qualitative Research

A Compendium of Qualitative Data Sources

Observations

- Conduct an observation as a participant
- Conduct an observation as an observer
- Conduct an observation shifting positions from participant to observer (and vice versa)

Interviews

- Conduct one-on-one interviews
- Conduct a focus group interview
- Conduct online interviews: e-mail, chat rooms, Internet conversations, list servers

Documents

- Keep a research journal during the study
- Have a participant keep a journal or diary during the research study
- Collect personal letters from participants
- Analyze public documents (e.g., official memos, minutes, records, archival material)
- Examine autobiographies and biographies
- Have participants take photographs or record videos (i.e., photo elicitation)
- Conduct chart audits
- Review medical records

Audiovisual Materials

- Examine physical trace evidence (e.g., footprints in the snow)
- Video or film a social situation or an individual or group
- Examine photographs or videos
- Examine Web sites' main pages
- Collect sounds (e.g., musical sounds, a child's laughter, car horns honking)
- Collect e-mails or electronic messages
- Gather phone or computer text messages
- Examine possessions or ritual objects
- Gather tweets
- Collect Facebook messages

Source: Adapted from Creswell (2013).

Use of Protocols

The data collection section also mentions the protocols for collecting and recording data. A **protocol** is the means for recording the qualitative data and for asking questions. Typical protocols are observational protocols (see Chapter 14) and interview protocols (see Chapter 15). Researchers also include copies of these protocols, for they convey the types of information being gathered in a study. Frequently, a complete data collection method section will end with a list of the specific questions that will be asked during the data-gathering stage, such as the interview questions, or the questions observers might ask themselves as they observe a site. These may be mentioned in the protocols.

A Checklist for Qualitative Data Collection

Here is a checklist for making sure that you have identified all of the important components in qualitative data collection when you prepare a plan for a qualitative study or present a completed journal article for publication. You might review this list after you have planned your qualitative study or when you submit your qualitative article for publication to make certain that you have covered all of the important bases in data collection.

FIGURE 13.4   **Checklist for a Complete Data Collection Methods Section in Qualitative Research**

_____ Discuss the rationale for qualitative research

_____ Discuss the site(s) that will be studied

_____ Identify permissions that have been granted (include something about IRB permissions)

_____ Discuss the type of purposeful sampling to be used (inclusion criteria)

_____ Indicate how participants will be recruited to the study

_____ Identify the number of participants

_____ Provide a table of the demographics of participants

_____ Indicate how the participants will benefit from the study (reciprocity)

_____ Indicate the types of data to be collected (perhaps a table of data collection?)

_____ Indicate the extent of data collection

_____ Mention the use of protocols (interview, observations, records) used to record the data and the questions asked

SUMMARY

Qualitative data collection proceeds through a series of topics, and including all of them will provide a rigorous qualitative study. It begins with stating a rationale for your use of qualitative research in your project. Then, you need to mention the research site and permissions at different levels to gain access to the site and individuals. Also, you need to discuss the recruitment strategies for enrolling participants in your study. This is followed by your purposeful sampling strategy, in which you identify the specific type of purposeful sampling you plan to use (e.g., maximal variation sampling). It is helpful then to also mention the demographics of your participants so that readers can gain a realistic picture of the participants and sites in your project. Next, discuss how you plan to reward participants for engaging in your study and the incentives you will use. The types of qualitative data are varied, and you need to select from among the types, and weigh the advantages and disadvantages of each type. I suggest that you be creative and use unusual types of data that will help create interest in your project. Once you have selected the types of data, create a table that illustrates the extent of your data collection by listing the forms and the participants. Include information about the protocols that will be used in your project, whether these are observational or interview protocols. These protocols should state the specific questions you will be asking of participants or yourself as you gather data.

ACTIVITIES

1. Write down your data collection methods for your project. Include something about every topic. Make sure that all components in this chapter are addressed, and use the checklist at the end of the chapter as a guide to ensure that you have drafted a complete data collection methods section.

2. In this chapter I have discussed the elements that go into a good informed consent form that participants review and sign before they participate in your data collection. Draft a sample informed consent form that you might use for a qualitative project.

FURTHER RESOURCES

For a review of different types of qualitative data that could be collected, see:

Creswell, J. W. (2013). *Qualitative inquiry and research design: Choosing among five approaches* (3rd ed.). Thousand Oaks, CA: Sage.

For a sample informed consent form in question-and-answer format, see:

Agency for Healthcare Research and Quality. (2009, September). *The AHRQ informed consent and authorization toolkit for minimal risk research*. Retrieved from www.ahrq.gov/funding/policies/informedconsent/icform1.html

Visit study.sagepub.com/30skills for quizzes, eFlashcards, and more!

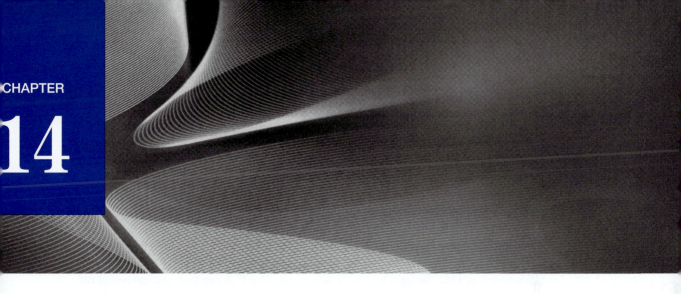

Conducting a Good Observation

Skill

Develop the skill of conducting a good observation.

Why the Skill Is Important

Observations may be an ideal form of qualitative data when individuals cannot express themselves in interviews, when they are unable or unwilling to be interviewed, and when the qualitative inquirer can actually visit the site where the central phenomenon is being expressed or talked about. Observations can also be a good adjunct to interviewing because they enable a researcher to compare the codes and themes from the observation with findings from the interviews. This triangulation of data sources is important to check the accuracy of the interpretations made by the researcher. Observations can also yield detailed information that may not be divulged during discussions or in written documents. Much more has been written about interviewing and using focus groups, so less is typically known about how to conduct a good observation. Still, as you add it to your sources of qualitative information to collect, you need to know the type of observing you will do, how you go about the process of observing and recording information, and the challenges in conducting a good observation.

Observation as a Developed Skill

Observation is one of the key tools for collecting data in qualitative research. I see it as a skill that can be developed. I think about individuals and occupational groups that are good at observing. Police and private detectives come to mind; they often have highly developed observational skills. As police ride in their cruisers, they become highly proficient at watching in all directions, noticing unusual behavior, and seeing accidents that have just occurred. My cousin's husband was a private detective for many years. He talks about how he observed the veins popping out on the necks of individuals he was interrogating to determine whether they were telling the truth. Once, as I sat on the porch of a motel looking out at Washington, D.C., he said to me, "Did you see that?" A car had just careened off the road and up onto the sidewalk about a block away. He had both "heard" and "seen" the accident before I had any indication that it had occurred. Children also come to mind as good observers. My wife tells me that in the garden at the elementary school where she is master gardener, the children can spot a bug on a leaf much more quickly than can their parents. Children often have a keen sense for observing.

Observation has long been a primary form of data collection for qualitative researchers. It is the act of noting a phenomenon in the field through the five senses of the observer, often with an instrument, and recording it for scientific purposes (Angrosino, 2007). The observations are based on finding a place or site where you can learn about your central phenomenon. You may observe and note the physical setting, participants, activities, interactions, and conversations, as well as your own behaviors during the observation. Good observers use all of their senses, including sight, hearing, touch, smell, and taste. When you observe, it is difficult to write down everything you see. Typically, qualitative observers start with broad observations and then narrow their view to information that will answer their research questions.

The Nature of Observing

According to Hatch (2002), "the goal of observation is to understand the culture, the setting, or social phenomenon being studied from the perspectives of the participants" (p. 72). **Observing** involves locating a site, developing a protocol for recording information, focusing in on events, looking for activities that help inform the central phenomenon, determining the appropriate role as an observer, recording "descriptive" and "reflective" **field notes** on the observation protocol, and slowly withdrawing from the site by respecting and thanking those observed for their time and your presence at the site. These components can flow into a series of steps that I would recommend.

Steps in the Process of Observing

Step 1: Select the Research Site

Decide on and select a *site* where you can best understand your central phenomenon. Obtain the required permissions needed to gain access to the site. Several levels of permissions might be needed, and gatekeepers can help with this process.

Step 2: Develop the Observational Protocol

Design an observational *protocol* as a method for recording observational notes in the field. Include in this protocol both "descriptive" (e.g., notes about what happened) and "reflective" (i.e., notes about your experiences, hunches, and learnings) notes. Make sure to provide appropriate identification information on the protocol, such as the date, place, and time of observation (Angrosino, 2007). In Figure 14.1, I provide a general example of the types of information that would go into an observational protocol.

In Figure 14.2, I illustrate an observational protocol using one I developed when I observed a visiting scholar (Professor Harry Wolcott) come to my class and make a presentation about qualitative research. You can see in this example both "descriptive" and "reflective" notes as well as a drawing of the classroom site.

Step 3: Focus the Observation

At the site, quietly observe without writing for a few minutes. Think about what catches your attention. Look at the ordinary and the unordinary. Take in the entire scene. There will be much in the environment to see. Then, *focus* in on one aspect that will help you understand your central research question and the central phenomenon. I consider this starting broadly and then zooming in on one aspect. Start with some aspect that is not complicated or complex, but simple.

FIGURE 14.1   **A General Model for an Observational Protocol**

Header: Time, Place, Observer	
Descriptive Notes	**Reflective Notes**
• State here the questions you will ask yourself • Often these are your sub-questions • They may also include chronologies • You can set times as well • Basically, you are describing what you see	• These are notes for yourself • They may include what problems/highlights you are experiencing as you observe • They could also be preliminary themes — your first pass at what you are learning as you observe

FIGURE 14.2   **A Sample Observation Protocol Including Descriptive and Reflective Notes**

Length of Activity: 90 Minutes	
Descriptive Notes	**Reflective Notes**
General: What are the experiences of graduate students as they learn qualitative research in the classroom?	
See classroom layout and comments about physical setting at the bottom of this page.	*Overhead with flaps: I wonder if the back of the room was able to read it.*
Approximately 5:17 p.m., Dr. Creswell enters the filled room, introduces Dr. Wolcott. Class members seem relieved.	*Overhead projector not plugged in at the beginning of the class: I wonder if this was a distraction (when it took extra time to plug it in).*
Dr. Creswell gives brief background of guest, concentrating on his international experiences; features a comment about the educational ethnography "The Man in the Principals Office."	*Lateness of the arrival of Drs. Creswell and Wolcott Students seemed a bit anxious. Maybe it had to do with the change in starting time to 5 p.m. (some may have had 6:30 classes or appointments to get to).*
Dr. Wolcott begins by telling the class he now writes out educational ethnography and highlights this primary occupation by mentioning two books: *Transferring Qualitative Data* and *The Art of Fieldwork.*	*Drs. Creswell and Wolcott seem to have a good rapport between them, judging from many short exchanges that they had.*
While Dr. Wolcott begins his presentation by apologizing for his weary voice (due to talking all day, apparently), Dr. Creswell leaves the classroom to retrieve the guest's overhead transparencies.	

Seemed to be three parts to this activity:
(1) the speaker's challenge to the class of detecting pure ethnographical methodologies,
(2) the speaker's presentation of the "tree" that portrays various strategies and substrategies for qualitative research in education, and
(3) the relaxed "elder statesman" fielding class questions, primarily about students' potential research projects and prior studies Dr. Wolcott had written.

The first question was "How do you look at qualitative research?" followed by "How does ethnography fit in?"

SKETCH OF CLASSROOM

Source: Creswell (2013).

Step 4: Determine Your Role

Determine what observer role you will assume. This role can range from that of a complete participant (going native) to that of a complete observer. Consider also how your role may change during the observation. I especially like the procedure of being an outsider initially, followed by becoming an insider over time. There are four types of observational roles that you can assume:

- Complete participant: The researcher is fully engaged with the people he or she is observing. This may help greater rapport with people being observed (Angrosino, 2007).

- Participant as observer: The researcher is participating in the activity at the site. The participant role is more salient than the researcher role. This may help the researcher gain insider views and subjective data. However, it may be distractive for the researcher to record data when he or she is integrated into the activity.

- Nonparticipant/observer as participant: The researcher is an outsider of the group under study, watching and taking field notes from a distance. He or she can record data without direct involvement with activity or people.

- Complete observer: The researcher simply observes without attracting notice. It may require sitting at the back of a room or in a spot where he or she cannot be easily noticed. The researcher does not say anything but simply records field notes.

Step 5: Record Field Notes

Record what you are observing on your observational protocol. This is called recording *field notes*. What do you record? First consider the "descriptive" side of your observational protocol. Here are some options (and often multiple approaches are used), and you might place prompts down the page under the "descriptive" side of your protocol to reflect the following:

- Write down prompts that relate to the five senses: what you see, what you hear, what you touch (literally), what you taste, what you smell. You might record what you "feel" or the movement going on around you.

- Develop a chronology of what happens. You can indicate the times when events occur by looking at your watch. This chronology simply lists the events in the order in which they occur.

- Use your sub-questions as a guide and list them down the page. While in interviews we ask people to respond to our questions; in observations, on the other hand, we ask ourselves the questions, and then answer them by recording what we observe in response to these questions.

- Draw a picture of the setting.

- Write a story about what you see happening in terms of your central phenomenon. This approach places you one step further toward writing your narrative.

- On the "reflective" side of your observation protocol, consider taking notes about any problems, issues, and concerns you have about observing and taking field notes. These notes may become important in writing about your methods, ethical issues, and limitations in your final report. Also consider listing themes—these are the broader constructs you will derive as you analyze qualitative data. They are phrased as two- to four-word labels, and they help us organize the narratives we will write. They become the headings in our qualitative report in the "findings" section.

Step 6: Slowly Withdraw

After observing, *slowly withdraw* from the site, thanking the participants for their time and letting them know, if they ask, that they will receive an abstract of the summary of the findings in the study (obtain their e-mail addresses to send this).

Additional Helpful Guidelines for Observing

Here are some helpful guidelines for writing your "descriptive" and "reflective" notes:

- Try to capture detail. Writing in a detailed way is not easy and it takes practice.

- If you have time, write in complete sentences. If time is limited (after all, you do not want to disturb the site too much), take brief notes, and immediately following the observation, sit down and write out your notes in a more complete fashion.

- Realize that you can talk to participants in the setting if they will engage you. In this way you can record conversation in your field notes. This dialogue can be a useful way to bring quotes into your final narrative.

- Following your observation, write up your "descriptive" notes into a narrative—a paragraph or two—that describes what you saw and perhaps some potential larger themes that emerge from your observation. In qualitative research, the activities of data collection, data analysis, and interpretation (written narrative) often occur simultaneously, and they are not separated activities as is often the case in *quantitative* research.

Challenges in Observing

Observing takes patience and being able to anticipate and adjust to several challenges that will likely arise during the observational period. For beginning researchers, a common reaction is to be overwhelmed by the amount of information available at the observational site. It is helpful to begin observing by simply looking around, without taking notes. After a while, you need to focus your observation on activities, people, and events that help you explore your central phenomenon. Also, new researchers struggle with the dual tasks of observing and taking notes. I find it helpful to take notes in short phrases, and then, after leaving the observational situation, to spend time recording longer field notes and filling in details. Sometimes new researchers encounter people who do not like being observed. In this situation, I move to a different place in the room and shift my observation to another person or event. New qualitative inquirers need to be reminded to take detailed notes so that complete sentences can be transferred from the field notes directly into the qualitative report. Beginning researchers are often curious about whether they can observe in a public space without obtaining the consent of individuals. I see no problem with this as long as the space is truly public and my observations would not disrupt the activities going on.

New researchers should be aware of the potential deception of people being observed (Hammersley & Atkinson, 1995), and, if possible, have the participants complete an informed consent form. Studies may involve different degrees of deception. At one end is minor deception that arises when we do not share all of the details with participants (Rossman & Rallis, 2011). For example, not sharing the full details of our conceptual framework or assumptions might be considered a minor form of deception. A similar form arises if the purpose of inquiry evolves throughout the study. Of course, it also might be considered sparing participants unnecessary details. At the other end, deception can be more intentional, such as misleading participants about the true intent of the study. This form of deception is particularly relevant to observations. Often, when individuals know they are being observed, they change their behavior. For example, when researchers are focused on a sensitive topic, such as sexist interactions, individuals might behave differently if they are aware of the true focus. As Rossman and Rallis (2012) noted, the potential benefit of the study might outweigh the need to disclose the true purpose. However, before engaging in this form of deception (i.e., assuming a covert role as a researcher), I recommend you carefully consider the ethical implications and consult with experienced researchers to determine whether deception is worth the risk. In addition, it will be necessary to describe your plans and rationale for deception in the institutional review board submission.

FIGURE 14.3   A Checklist for Conducting an Observation

_____ Did you gain permission to study the site?

_____ Do you know your role as an observer?

_____ Do you have a means for recording your observation—an observational protocol?

_____ Do you know what you will observe first?

_____ Will you enter and leave the site slowly, so as to not disturb the setting?

_____ Will you make multiple observations over time?

_____ Will you develop rapport with individuals at the site?

_____ Will your observations change from broad to narrow during your observation?

_____ Will you take limited notes at first?

_____ Will you take both descriptive as well as reflective notes?

_____ Will you describe in complete sentences so that you have detailed field notes?

_____ Did you thank your participants at the site?

_____ Did you refrain from intentionally deceiving participants during the observation?

Observation Checklist

Figure 14.3 is a checklist you might use to make sure that all parts of your observation are completed.

SUMMARY

Observations are an important qualitative source of data collection, and it is especially helpful to collect data when individuals are unable or unwilling to be interviewed and when detailed information about the central phenomenon needs to be collected. Observing is the process of gathering unstructured, open-ended, firsthand information by watching people and places at a research site. It involves the steps of selecting a site, developing a protocol or instrument for recording information, starting slowly by taking in the scene and then focusing on information helpful in exploring your central phenomenon, assuming one or more observational roles, recording information as descriptive and reflective notes, and then slowly redrawing from the site. Observing can be challenging and overwhelming in terms of the amount of information, the dual tasks of writing and observing, the need to write detailed notes, and the use of observing public spaces and the potential for deceiving people.

ACTIVITY

I recommend that you practice conducting an observation. You might try the following. To learn how to observe, I have new researchers identify a public setting where they can practice applying an observational protocol and recording field notes. My favorite site is the campus "climbing wall," where I ask that students in my class simply observe individuals climbing. This seems like a physical activity to which many people can relate. I first have students design an observational protocol. They then go to the climbing wall in the activity center and receive permission to observe. They start slowly and then focus on one aspect of the climbing experience. They start taking field notes. I remind them to have conversations with climbers. Sometimes my students will actually become participants and put on the climbing straps and practice climbing. After about half an hour, they conclude their observation. They type up their field notes and share them with other individuals in the class. This activity introduces many of the challenges facing observers that I have identified, such as observing people who may not want to be observed, learning how to write detailed notes, becoming overwhelmed by the amount of activity going on in a high-stimulus environment, and balancing observing with note taking.

FURTHER RESOURCES

Angrosino, M. V. (2007). *Doing ethnographic and observational research*. Thousand Oaks, CA: Sage.

Visit study.sagepub.com/30skills for quizzes, eFlashcards, and more!

Designing and Administering an Interview Protocol

Skill

Develop the skill of conducting a good qualitative interview.

Why the Skill Is Important

Interviewing is a popular form of collecting data in qualitative research. It consists of asking open-ended questions of participants. The central part of the interview should be the research sub-questions being asked during the study. Interviewing enables individuals to provide personal perspectives to interviewers. It allows interviewers to ask follow-up questions (i.e., probes) to obtain detailed views. An interview can be one-on-one, in which participants may be free to share in-depth personal perspectives. Interviews can yield useful information to answer research questions, but they need to be conducted in a good, rigorous way, with detailed procedures in place. Often the interviewer becomes a learner and not only the "expert." The process begins with understanding the types of interviews available, learning the steps involved in conducting an interview, developing a complete interview protocol for gathering information, and adhering to good practices.

Types of Interviews

In Chapter 13, I reviewed the types of qualitative data collection and pointed out the advantages and disadvantages of each type of data. The qualitative researcher needs to weigh the advantages of each type of interview. *One-on-one* interviews should be used when the personal perspectives of participants are needed and they are not likely to share these perspectives in a group setting. In a one-on-one interview, the researcher can watch the body language of the participant, hear directly the inflections of his or her voice, and establish a personal connection with the participant that may enhance his or her willingness to open up. The disadvantages of this approach are that the researcher needs to have access to a location where a personal interview can be conducted. *Telephone or cell phone interviews* are ideal when participants are located at some geographic distance from the interviewer. The disadvantages of this approach are the cost of telephone calls, and the need for participants to have access to telephones or cell phones. Also, in this form of interviewing, the researcher cannot see the facial expressions of the participants and therefore may lose some insight into what the participants are saying. However, an alternative is to use video calls, such as Skype, FaceTime, and Google+ Hangouts. These services are becoming popular ways to conduct interviews at a distance while also enabling interviewers and subjects to see each other. However, it is important when recording from these sources to be aware of potential wiretap laws that may be in force. **Focus groups** represent a popular way to conduct interviews. These groups typically include about six individuals, and the synergy of a focus group encourages people to speak up, and ideas can expand because multiple individuals weigh in on topics (Krueger & Casey, 2009). Focus groups are not useful when the topic is sensitive, because individuals will not likely share their personal perspectives. Also, the logistics of recording information need careful attention so that transcriptionists can identify individuals who are speaking. I typically conduct focus groups by beginning with each person mentioning in order his or her first name so that a transcriptionist can identify individuals by the sound of their voices. *Open-ended Internet interviews* are another way to gather qualitative data. These interviews use an interview protocol, and individuals respond in writing to open-ended questions. They can also be conducted "live" with one of the software programs that enable individuals to have conversations on the Internet and record the information. This approach is useful when participants are geographically dispersed. It requires that participants be familiar with the Internet and be comfortable providing information through an Internet connection. It also requires that individuals provide permission to be interviewed.

How will you decide which form is best for your qualitative data collection?

- First consider one-on-one interviews. These will likely yield the most information.

- If geographical distance is a problem, consider Internet or telephone (or cell phone) interviews as a way to reach individuals.

- If time and resources are problems, consider using focus groups, because you will be able to reach more individuals than through one-on-one interviews.

Steps in Conducting a Qualitative Interview

There are several steps taken in conducting a good interview. I will present these steps, and although they may not be taken in the precise order in which I mention them, this list represents the order I typically use.

Step 1: Decide Whether Interviews Are Appropriate

I first decide whether interviews are appropriate for my qualitative study. People are accustomed to participating in interviews. Interviews net useful detailed information and are a hallmark of good qualitative research. Interviews are not useful when individuals are reluctant to speak and share ideas, and when the central phenomenon is sensitive to explore and the researcher needs to examine documents or simply observe. Qualitative interviews are typically unstructured and open ended. Some would refer to them as good conversations.

Step 2: Choose the Type of Interview

I next decide on the type of interview to conduct by weighing the pros and cons of the various types. The types I have mentioned are one-on-one interviews, telephone or cell phone interviews, focus groups, and Internet interviews.

Step 3: Invite Participants

On the basis of my purposeful sampling strategy (see Chapter 13), I next contact prospective participants and invite them to interviews. I send out an informed consent letter for them to review and sign prior to the interviews. Also, in my invitation letter I mention the topics I will ask participants about so that they know the questions in advance. I will mention how they will profit from the interview and any incentives they will receive as a result of their participation. If permissions are needed for their participation, I will write to "gatekeepers" and seek permission to involve the people in the interview process. I will also suggest a quiet location for the interview and inform each participant that the interview will be audio-recorded. Also, I will tell the interviewee the approximate length of time for the interview.

Step 4: Develop an Interview Protocol

At this point, I design an interview protocol, a tool for listing the questions I will ask and for recording some of my thoughts as the interview proceeds. A format for designing this protocol will be discussed in the next section of this chapter.

Step 5: Arrange the Audio Equipment

Prior to the interview, I will need to organize the audio equipment for recording the interview. If possible, I audio-record the interview regardless of the type of interview (e.g., one on one, focus group). I find high-quality digital recording devices to use, such as a dedicated digital audio recorder or a smart phone. To conduct and record an interview, I need to have good microphones.

Step 6: Arrange for a Quiet Setting for the Interview

Having a quiet location free of all audio distractions is important for an interview. Sometimes compromises need to be made because individuals want interviews to take place in their workplaces or at their homes. This is understandable, but I try to encourage participants to consider quiet locations for their interviews. Also, consider the privacy of the location both for ethical reasons and for encouraging the participants to talk.

Step 7: Conduct the Interview

Before the interview begins, I will check my audio equipment to make sure that it is working properly. My interviews are typically short. They do not run much longer than about half an hour in length. This length will yield about 20 pages of single-spaced text, and it will respect the time of the interviewee. In the interview, I use good procedures of asking questions, dressing appropriately, and maintaining courtesy (see the additional comments to follow in this chapter). I keep the interview to the length I have mentioned in advance to the interviewee. I also encourage the interviewee to stay on topic during my questioning.

Step 8: Follow-up After the Interview

After the interview I check to make sure that I obtained a good audio recording of the interview. I also write a note to the interviewee thanking him or her for participating, and I honor the follow-up the interviewee requests (e.g., a copy of the abstract of the final study). In some cases, I will ask for follow-up interviews to clarify points or to expand on participants' ideas. I also need to send the audio recording on to my transcriptionist to begin the process of developing a text copy of the interview so that I can begin the process of data analysis.

Parts of an Interview Protocol

The interview protocol should be about two pages in length. There should be some spaces between the questions for the interviewer to write short notes and quotations in case the audio-recording device does not work. The total number of questions should be somewhere between 5 and 10, although no precise number can be given. The protocol should be prepared in advance of the interview, and used consistently in all of the interviews. It is helpful for the interviewer to memorize the questions so that a need does not exist to read verbatim the protocol. The interview protocol consists of several important components. These are basic information about the interview, an introduction, the interview content questions with probes, and closing instructions.

Basic Information About the Interview

This is a section of the interview where the interviewer records basic information about the interview so that the database can be well organized. It should include the time and date of the interview, where the interview takes place, and the names of both the interviewer and interviewee. The project length of the interview could also be noted, as well as the file name of the digital copy of the audio recording and transcription.

Introduction

This section of the protocol provides instructions to the interviewer so that useful information is not overlooked during a potentially anxious period of conducting the interview. The interviewer needs to introduce himself or herself, and to discuss the purpose of the study. This purpose can be written out in advance and simply read by the interviewer. It should also contain a prompt to the interviewer to collect a signed copy of the informed consent form (alternatively, the participant may have sent the form to the interviewer). The interviewer might also talk about the general structure of the interview (e.g., how it will begin, the number of questions, the time that it should take), and ask the interviewee if he or she has any questions before beginning the interview. Finally, before the interview begins, some important terms that will be used in the interview may need to be defined.

Opening Question

An important first step in an interview is to set the interviewee at ease. I typically begin with an ice-breaker type of question. This is a question where I ask participants to talk about themselves in a way that will not alienate them. I might ask them about their jobs, their roles, or even how they spent the day. I do not ask personal questions (e.g., "What is your income?"). People like talking about themselves, and this open-ended question should be framed to set a relaxed atmosphere.

Content Questions

These questions are the research sub-questions in the study, phrased in a friendly way to the interviewee. They essentially parse the central phenomenon into its parts—asking about different facets of the central phenomenon. Whether the final question would be a restatement of the central question is open to debate (see Chapter 12). Hopefully by answering all of the sub-questions, the qualitative researcher will have a good understanding as to how the central question has been answered. For all of the content questions, I recommend asking open-ended questions to encourage interviewees to talk. These questions typically begin with the word *what* or *how*. In contrast, a closed-ended question that suggests a "yes" or "no" answer will not net much information.

Using Probes

These content questions also need to include probes. **Probes** are reminders to the researcher of two types: to ask for more information, and to ask for an explanation of ideas. The specific wording might be (and these words could be inserted into the interview protocol as a reminder to the interviewer):

- "Tell me more" (asking for more information)

- "I need more detail" (asking for more information)

- "What is an example of that?" (asking for more information)

- "Could you explain your response more?" (asking for an explanation)

- "What does 'not much' mean?" (asking for an explanation)

Sometimes beginning qualitative researchers are uncomfortable with a small number of questions, and they feel that their interviews may be quite short with only a few (5 to 10) questions. True, some people may have little to say (or little information to provide about the central phenomenon), but by including probes in the interview, it will expand the time of the interview as well as net useful information.

Example of a Content Question

A content question would ask:

> "How does your family support your Latina student in college through praise for their work?" (Probes: *Tell me more* about what praise means to you. Please *explain further* how you give praise while the student is both away from home and on the college campus.)

Follow-Up Questions

A useful final question might ask "Whom should I contact next to learn more?" or "Is there any further information you would like to share that we have not covered."

These follow-up questions essentially provide closure for the interview and show your curiosity in learning more about the topic of your interview.

Closing Instructions

It is important to thank the interviewee for his or her time and respond to any final questions. Assure the interviewee of the confidentiality of the interview. Ask if you can follow up with another interview if one is needed to clarify certain points. One question that may surface is how the interviewee will learn about the results of your project. It is important to think through and provide a response to this question, because it involves your time and resources. One convenient way to provide information to interviewees is to offer to send them an abstract of your final study. This brief communication of results is efficient and convenient for most researchers.

A Sample Interview Protocol

In Figure 15.1 you will see a sample interview protocol I used in my qualitative case study of a gunman on a college campus (adapted from Asmussen & Creswell, 1995).

FIGURE 15.1   Sample Interview Protocol

Interview Protocol Project: University Reaction to a Gunman Incident

Basic Information About the Interview

Time of interview:

Date:

Place:

Interviewer:

Interviewee:

Position of interviewee:

Recording/storing information about interview:

Introduction

☐ Introduce yourself

☐ Discuss the purpose of the study

☐ Get informed consent signature

☐ Provide structure of the interview (audio recording, taking notes)

☐ Ask if interviewee has questions

☐ Define any terms necessary

Interview Content Questions

1. What has been your role in the incident? (ice breaker)

    Probes: Tell me more. Please explain.

2. What has happened since the event that you have been involved in? (content question)

    Probes: Tell me more. Please explain.

3. What has been the impact on the university community of this incident? (content question)

    Probes: Tell me more. Please explain.

4. What larger ramifications, if any, exist from the incident? (content question)

    Probes: Tell me more. Please explain.

5. To whom should we talk to find out more about campus reaction to the incident? (follow-up question)

    Probes: Tell me more. Please explain.

Closing Instructions

☐ Thank the individual for participating

☐ Assure individual of confidentiality

☐ If needed, request further interviews

☐ If asked, comment on how interviewee will receive results of the study

Source: Adapted from Asmussen and Creswell (1995).

Additional Interviewing Ideas

Here are some additional ideas that will help you develop a good interview:

Dress for the Occasion

Make the interviewee feel comfortable by dressing appropriately for the interview. This will require that you consider what the *interviewee* might wear to the interview and dressing in a way that complements the dress of other people in the room.

Use Lapel Microphones

In one-on-one interviews, I always use label microphones—one for myself and one for the interviewee—so that I can obtain a clear recording of the interview. Also consider carefully where you will conduct the interview, so that undue noise does not interfere with your recording. When conducting an interview via the telephone or a video call, it is particularly important to test the sound quality and positions of the microphones. Try out the audio-recording equipment in advance. Your backup if the equipment does not work is to record a few notes on your interview protocol form.

Consider Your Role as Interviewer

Ask questions in a natural way. Try not to read each question from your interview protocol but to memorize the basic content of each question. In this way, your questioning will seem natural. Also, give participants time to answer your questions. I feel that it is quite acceptable to have some silence during an interview while the interviewee is thinking. Your role as an interviewer should be to be a good listener and to say very little. Withhold stating your evaluation (positive or negative) during an interview. The intent of this process is to learn from the participant, not to share your own views. If you must convey your personal stance, you might save this information for a time after the formal interview is completed. When you use the protocol, you might develop some shorthand version of taking notes—brief ideas. I find it useful to take down key quotations as they occur during the interview. Of course, it is important to maintain eye contact with your interviewee, and you need to balance taking notes with maintaining good contact. Finally, on your protocol, you might put in a box instructions to the interviewee, such as the purpose of the study, requests to be audio-recorded, and requests to complete the informed consent form. These boxes will be important reminders of information you need to share with interviewees. Also, the closing instructions can be placed in a box. These boxes clearly separate your instructions from the content of the interview, which is helpful visually when you are proceeding through the interview process.

An Interview Checklist

Figure 15.2 is a set of key questions you might ask yourself (or write about in your project description) if you are conducting an interview.

Challenges in Conducting Interviews

To conduct a good interview, you need practice, so I would recommend that you engage in a pilot interview to hone your skills in interviewing. A common challenge to new researchers is to schedule an interview that is too long—more than half an hour. This typically occurs because the researcher does not realize how much information can be conveyed in a short interview. Interviewers also have access to interviewees, and they want to make the most of the situation. A short interview is not only a courtesy to a busy interviewee, it will also yield extensive information when transcribed. Another challenge is getting interviewees to speak and talk about the central phenomenon. This may well be the case with young children (e.g., middle

| FIGURE 15.2 | Checklist of Questions for Conducting a Good Interview |

_____ Who will participate in your interviews?

_____ What type of interviews will you conduct (e.g., one on one, focus group, telephone)?

_____ Have you arranged a setting for your interview that is comfortable and quiet?

_____ Have you developed an interview protocol with all of its parts?

_____ Are your interview questions open ended and not leading?

_____ Do your questions reflect the sub-questions in your study?

_____ Do you have probes listed in your interview protocol?

_____ Do you have audio equipment, has it been tested, and is it in good working order?

_____ Do you have consent from the participants to engage in the interview?

_____ Will you listen closely and talk less during the interview?

_____ Will you keep your participants focused and provide concrete details?

_____ Will you withhold your own opinions with the participant?

_____ Will you exit the interview in a courteous way by thanking the participant?

school children I interviewed mainly used the word _like_ over and over without saying much more). But interviewers do not realize the power of probes to get people talking. If good probes are in place, individuals will start speaking and explaining ideas. Furthermore, if a good "ice breaker" is used, the interviewee should feel comfortable and be willing to share information. Certainly a pilot test of the interview protocol can provide some indication of whether it will yield information from interviewees. Another challenge for the interviewee is withholding personal opinions and keeping the interviewee on track with the questions. Certainly, the interviewer has opinions about the topic as the interview proceeds, but a comment can be made such as "After the interview is over, I want to return to that topic and share my own perspective." Keeping the interviewer on track with questions is important. Realize that interviewees often will be answering Question 3 when you ask Question 1. However, they may divert each question to their pet topic or a topic that occupies their thinking that day. In one interview I conducted, the individual had spent most of the day on budget hearings, and this person turned each question I asked into a budget-related issue. To keep the individual on track with my questioning, I had to frequently remind the interviewee about the overall purpose of my interview.

SUMMARY

Interviews with open-ended questions represent a major form of data collection in qualitative research. They yield important detailed information from individuals, and they consist of different types: one-on-one interviews, telephone or cell phone interviews, focus groups, and Internet interviews. Each type has its advantages and drawbacks. In conducting an interview, the qualitative researcher goes through several steps: deciding whether an interview is appropriate, determining the type of interview to be used, inviting participants, developing an interview protocol, arranging the audio equipment and the site for the interview, conducting the interview, and following up after the interview. The interview protocol is a central part of this process, and it consists of basic information about the interview, an introduction, interview content questions with probes, and closing instructions. Interviews can be challenging, and it is useful to schedule short interviews, use "ice-breaker" questions and probes to encourage participants to speak, withhold interviewer commentary throughout the interview, and keep the participant focused on the central phenomenon of the study.

ACTIVITY

Design a good example of an interview protocol. Assume this scenario: Your purpose in conducting the interview is to learn how your interviewee best learns qualitative research in a classroom. Be sure to do the following:

1. Include a header.
2. Write out sections on basic information about the interview and introduction instructions.
3. Write the first question as an ice breaker.
4. Write four or five questions that are sub-questions built from your central question. Include probes for each question.
5. Write a question asking about (a) whether you have left anything out and (b) to whom you should talk to learn more.
6. Write closing instructions.

Administer the interview. Divide into pairs. Test out your interview protocol by conducting an actual interview. The length of time of the interview should be approximately 15 to 30 minutes.

FURTHER RESOURCES

There are many good books available on interviewing. I tend to rely on these books:

Brinkmann, S., & Kvale, S. (2014). *Interviews: Learning the craft of qualitative research* (3rd ed.). Thousand Oaks, CA: Sage.

Holstein, J., & Gubrium, J. F. (Eds.). (2003). *Inside interviewing: New lenses, new concerns*. Thousand Oaks, CA: Sage.

James, N., & Busher, H. (2009). *Online interviewing*. Thousand Oaks, CA: Sage.

Rubin, H. J., & Rubin, I. S. (2011). *Qualitative interviewing: The art of hearing data* (3rd ed.). Thousand Oaks, CA: Sage.

Visit study.sagepub.com/30skills for quizzes, eFlashcards, and more!

Collecting Data With Marginalized Populations

Skills

- Develop the skill of being able to define a marginalized group.

- Develop the skill of using strategies to address challenges and collect accurate data with marginalized groups.

Why the Skills Are Important

Data collection is the process of systematically gathering information on an issue of interest. Regardless of your discipline, accurate data collection is essential to maintaining the integrity of research. Consequences of improperly collected data include an inability to answer research questions, distorted findings, compromised decisions for public policy, and harm to participants.

There are many benefits to conducting research with marginalized populations. The collected information may be used to improve policies, develop educational programs, or address health disparities. However, collecting these data requires acknowledging power imbalances that may occur with different societal groups. The needs of marginalized populations are nuanced and diverse; therefore, researchers must carefully consider all procedures and analyses involving participants. It is imperative to understand how challenges in working with marginalized groups shape how data are collected, interpreted, and acted upon. Understanding these concerns and how to appropriately address them will ensure that you are prepared to develop a research project and collect accurate data with a marginalized target population.

Marginalized Groups

The term *marginalized population* has been defined as any group that is excluded from mainstream social, economic, cultural, or political life (Cook, 2008). This can include numerous subgroups of individuals and exclusion due to race, religion, political or cultural group, age, gender, financial status or health condition, or some combination of these attributes. Whether a group is marginalized is both context specific and subjective. **Marginalized groups** may also be labeled as sensitive, underresearched, or hidden populations.

When we consider issues of equality, we may be tempted to focus on the degree of marginalization of these groups compared with others. For example, it may be possible to identify general inequalities between individuals with diagnosed mental illnesses and those without these diagnoses, or between individuals with a certain level of education and those lacking an education. However, this can lead to generalizations about the homogeneity of each group and incorrect assumptions about individuals within these groups. This focus on the group should be avoided, and it is therefore necessary to recognize that inequality exists as a result of multiple factors. These factors may include (but are not limited to) geographical location, ethnicity, age, socioeconomic status, and gender. For example, issues of old age, disability, and mental health may function in this way, with each representing a "cross-cutting factor" (Rogers et al., 2012). It is important for you to note that there is often convergence among factors across the life span, with factors combining to exaggerate existing inequalities. You must understand these combinations to understand and focus on the issues faced by populations in relation to the different aspects of inequality they experience.

Concerns in Collecting Data From Marginalized Groups

Working with marginalized populations offers myriad opportunities. However, there are challenges in collecting data from such groups. Challenges related to sampling and access, mistrust, culture and language, and ethical concerns will be discussed, as summarized in Table 16.1.

Sampling and Access

When you work with marginalized populations, you may experience challenges in sampling. These groups often share characteristics that can make sampling from the population difficult. First, there is an untrue belief that members of a marginalized group represent a homogeneous population. Because the size and boundaries of the population of interest are typically unknown, it may be difficult for you to obtain a

| TABLE 16.1 | Recommendations to Address Concerns in Collecting Data From Marginalized Groups |

Concern	Overview of Concern	Practical Recommendations to Address Concern
Sampling and access	Recruitment and access to participants and areas of interest may prove challenging	• Invite community members to serve on research team • Spend time in community prior to recruitment • Communicate benefits for participation
Mistrust	A lack of trust for researchers and the research process may result in poor participation or unreliable data	• Establish partnerships with community gatekeepers • Personally contact participants whenever possible • Return to the community to present research findings
Culture and language	When population culture or language is left unattended, researchers may perpetuate issues of mistrust and collect inaccurate data	• Have a community member review all protocols • Ensure that all forms are available in participants' first language • Have a representative from the group of interest aid in data collection
General ethical concerns	Issues of coercion, breaches of privacy, and challenges with obtaining informed consent may undermine the purpose of the study	• Establish community advisory boards to guide development of privacy protocols and determine appropriate incentives • Tailor informed consent forms to be culturally relevant • Include participants' relatives or other stakeholders in the informed consent process

purposeful, representative sample (Shaver, 2005). It must also be considered that members of the population of interest may feel threatened by their acknowledgment of group membership. This may be due to participation in stigmatized or illegal activities, or it may be a result of prior persecution. Either way, participants may refuse to cooperate with research efforts to protect their privacy.

> When studying a marginalized group, careful attention should be paid to issues of access, mistrust, culture, language, and ethical aspects of the group.

Mistrust

One of the greatest barriers for researchers is a lack of trust from members of marginalized groups (Jones, Hadder, Carvajal, Chapman, & Alexander, in press). This mistrust may stem from cultural misunderstandings, prior misdiagnoses of issues, or financial constraints. This lack of trust for researchers and the research process may lead participants to give unreliable responses to questions about themselves and the community to which they belong. Participants may provide what they deem the socially acceptable answer, resulting in unreliable data. It should be understood that members of the target population may be distrustful of any nonmembers, and this lack of trust may lead to a refusal to cooperate in an effort to protect their and other group members' identities.

Culture and Language

Working with marginalized groups may mean that participants have difficulty communicating in your language. Participants may lack terms for key concepts, or important information may be lost in translation. This can ultimately lead to misunderstandings in the data that have serious implications for the project and community as a whole. When instruments used in data collection require an understanding of the English language, it is impossible for non-English-speaking individuals to participate in the research activities (Jones et al., in press), ultimately affecting your ability to apply what you learn to other disadvantaged groups. In addition, members of non-English-speaking communities may attribute meanings to researchers' body language, gestures, and inflections. Inadequate understanding of how culture can play a role in interpreting all aspects of interactions can reduce the accuracy of the data collected throughout the research process.

When cultural issues are left unattended in the research process, the researchers are unable to address the study problem thoroughly and effectively. A lack of understanding and appreciation of the customs, beliefs, and values held by marginalized groups will jeopardize access to the groups of interest. When care is not taken to thoroughly consider culture, all aspects of the qualitative research design will be significantly flawed.

General Ethical Concerns

Researchers can encounter ethical issues at any and all stages of research (see Chapter 7). Ethical concerns stem from many issues, including those related to integrity, confidentiality, and human subjects protection (Shamoo & Resnik, 2009). In conducting research with marginalized populations, discussions surrounding ethical concerns have focused on undue inducement, maintaining participant privacy and confidentiality, and ensuring informed consent. One concern is that monetary reimbursement for study participation to economically marginalized individuals could be considered coercion and ultimately call into question the principle of voluntary participation (Davidson & Page, 2012).

Although privacy is an ethical concern in any research project, membership in marginalized populations may involve stigmatized or illegal behavior. Thus, protection of privacy and confidentiality is of upmost importance. When individuals belonging to marginalized groups participate in research projects, consider that obtaining informed consent may take longer than with other groups. This challenge has been demonstrated in research efforts with homeless individuals with mental illnesses (Rogers et al., 2012). During the consent process, it is critical that researchers ensure that each individual understand what participation in the study implies.

Addressing Potential Concerns

These concerns should be considered during the development of a qualitative research study. Thorough considerations should be given to researcher reflexivity, community involvement, research protocols, and informed consent and ethics before undertaking a study with a marginalized population.

Reflexivity

In qualitative research with marginalized populations, it is imperative that researchers engage in this process of self-reflection to understand how personal biases may affect the research project. In-depth reflective processes will challenge assumptions, reveal theoretical orientations, uncover social and cultural biases, and call personal behaviors into question. Using reflexive strategies can allow you to improve the rigor of a qualitative study by considering previously unaddressed cultural nuances. This process can therefore lead to improved trust with participants and increased reliability and validity of the findings.

Community Involvement

When you study hard-to-reach or marginalized populations, use combined purposive, snowball, and respondent-driven sampling techniques to obtain participants (Benoit, Jansson, Millar, & Phillips, 2005). In gaining access, you may find that members of marginalized groups may respond more positively to "insiders" who are involved in the research process. An example of this practice can be seen in research efforts with inmates at a state prison (Freshwater, Cahill, Walsh, Muncey, & Esterhuizen, 2012). As a result of the helpful role insiders play, there has been a rise in calls for **community-based participatory research** (CBPR), an action-oriented research method in which members of the population of interest are engaged in all phases of the research. Although there are challenges associated with engaging in this type of research process, including lengthened timelines and negotiations with community partners, the benefits are numerous. Collaborating with community members provides you with access to the population, which can address access concerns. Additionally, these partnerships enhance the research team's understanding of perspectives of members of the marginalized population, which can improve the reliability of the data that is collected (Rogers et al., 2012).

I would suggest that CBPR is appropriate when you seek to understand the experiences of groups involved in, affected by, or excluded from certain activities, especially when the experience is markedly different from that of the researcher (also see Reid, 2004). Therefore, CBPR fits well in research with marginalized populations. Engaging in this type of research can relieve concerns related to access and cultural misunderstandings, as the participants are treated as the true experts with regard to the topic of interest.

Transparency is an additional key aspect in conducting research with marginalized groups. You might make all essential parts of their research visible to participants and community partners, whether or not a CBPR approach is used. Transparency can be achieved by discussing the research design process with participants, engaging in member checking, and returning to the field to present findings.

Protocols

The development of detailed protocols ensures that proper steps are taken to address trust and ethical concerns. For example, protocols helped gain trust and respect in research work conducted with sex workers (Shaver, 2005). Protocols should also ensure that researchers take the time to thank and say goodbye to everyone involved in the project. Although this may seem a minute detail, it provides additional opportunities for building trust. Protocols should also take language into consideration and have options for participants to communicate in their first language. If you cannot communicate in this language, any and all efforts should be made to have a trained member of the research team serve as a translator. Above all, when collecting data from marginalized groups, you need to maintain dual professional roles as both an expert and a learner. Your privileged role justifies the asking of sensitive questions. But as a learner, you need to always respect the needs of participants.

Informed Consent and Ethics

You can take several steps to ameliorate ethical concerns. During the informed consent process, it should be made clear that participation is voluntary. To achieve this, it may be necessary to include participants' relatives or other stakeholders in the decision making about whether to participate in the study. When working with certain subgroups, you should also be prepared to address concerns related to potentially unethical previously conducted research. Researchers studying drug addiction have encountered these problems (Fisher et al., 2008).

Detailed and culturally sensitive informed consent processes are essential; however, this alone cannot solve ethical concerns associated with collecting data from marginalized populations. It has been suggested that the ethical concerns associated with working with marginalized groups can be addressed, in part, through work with community advisory boards (CABs), which advise the research design and implementation (Davidson & Page, 2012). These CABs are instrumental in addressing key ethical concerns, including the definition of appropriate compensation for study participation and the implementation of privacy protocols to ensure participant confidentiality.

Finally, it is important to consider that there is an intersection between culture and ethics. Each group has its own definition of "ethical" practices based on societal and cultural beliefs that may differ from that of the researcher. Therefore, the issue of ethics should be constantly reexamined throughout your research within the context of the specific group being explored (Hudson & Taylor-Henley, 2001).

SUMMARY

The skills introduced in this chapter are to learn to define a marginalized group and to use strategies to address challenges and collect accurate data. Conducting research with marginalized populations affords numerous benefits but presents several challenges as well. Careful attention should be paid to issues of access, mistrust, culture, language, and ethical aspects of the research. Through researcher reflexivity, community involvement, and detailed study protocols, these challenges can be addressed, and accurate data can be collected and used to benefit the population and the research community.

ACTIVITIES

1. Identify a group of interest related to your area of research that would be considered a marginalized population. Choose a sample of individuals who will force you to get out of your own skin and ethnic or racial orientation.

2. Engage in researcher reflexivity and reflect on how your personal experiences, theoretical orientation, and cultural background may influence your research with this sample.

FURTHER RESOURCES

Cook, K. (2008). Marginalized populations. In L. Given (Ed.), *The SAGE encyclopedia of qualitative research methods* (pp. 496–497). Thousand Oaks, CA: Sage.

Davidson, P., & Page, K. (2012). Research participation as work: Comparing the perspectives of researchers and economically marginalized populations. *American Journal of Public Health, 102*(7), 1254–1259.

Jones, R. T., Hadder, J., Carvajal, F., Chapman, S., & Alexander, A. (in press). Conducting research in diverse, minority, and marginalized communities. In F. Norris, S. Galea, M. Friedman, & P. Watson (Eds.), *Research methods for studying mental health after disasters and terrorism*. New York: Guilford.

Visit study.sagepub.com/30skills for quizzes, eFlashcards, and more!

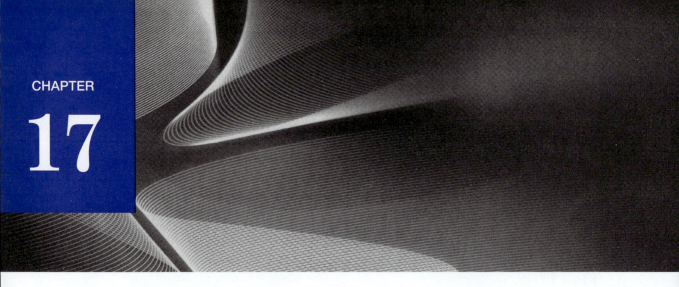

Being Culturally Aware in Global Qualitative Research

Skills

- Develop the skill of being culturally aware when conducting qualitative research in countries around the world.

- Develop the skill of addressing challenges when conducting global qualitative research.

Why the Skills Are Important

In recent years, there have been calls to increase research efforts that focus on addressing global health disparities and improve our understanding of diverse populations. Global research investments have provided remarkable insights in the past 20 years, resulting in an emergence of a globalized knowledge base in addition to a globalized economy (Hall, 2015). This is characterized by interconnections at multiple levels, including internationalization of activities of for-profit education service firms and cultural competency trainings offered by nonprofit agencies.

The trend toward global research will continue, advanced by economic globalization and technology. Now more than ever, it is imperative that researchers understand the challenges associated with conducting global qualitative research in order to effectively address the research questions at hand and to conduct culturally sensitive research. Researchers must take steps to tailor qualitative studies appropriately. In doing so, these researchers will be equipped to work both abroad and domestically as the United States population continues to become more diverse.

Key Concepts in Conducting Global Qualitative Research

Successful global research has four prerequisites (Trostle, 1992), including:

- Having individuals and teams with appropriate research skills and abilities

- Having an adequate support system in place to conduct the research

- Conducting research relevant to national policies

- Applying findings to both national and global research agendas

To ensure that these prerequisites are met, you can develop a sense of general **global cultural awareness**, which includes building country-level expertise, understanding methodological orientations in a country, and becoming knowledgeable about preferred data collection methods used by researchers in the location where research is to be conducted. Global cultural awareness also entails understanding policy platforms that may influence research agendas and tailoring the qualitative research design appropriately.

> Global qualitative researchers build country-level expertise, understand methodological orientations, use country-specific data collection methods, and respect policy platforms.

Cultural Competency

Global awareness has been defined as knowledge of the world and one's interconnectedness with others (Dower, 2002). Building global awareness requires knowledge of cultures, languages, and world issues as well as experience abroad. Individuals who portray global awareness bring a worldview related to ethnorelativism to their research. Ethnorelativism is the idea that cultures can be understood only in relation to one another and that behaviors can be understood only within a cultural context (Olson & Kroeger, 2001). As suggested by Bhattacharya (2013), we need to interrogate border crossing and colonizing discourse, and come to terms with our own lenses of resistance and critique. An important point to consider is that cultural competence is an ongoing developmental process that requires many experiences and contexts in which to integrate cultural competence constructs (Smith-Miller, Leak, Harlan, Dieckmann, & Sherwood, 2010). One way you can build cultural awareness is to participate in cultural competency training, which may include working with interpreters, improving on cross-cultural communication and understanding the intricacies of conducting research in a specific location.

Building Country-Level Expertise

An element of global cultural awareness is spending considerable amounts of time building specific country-level expertise (Thornton, 2014). This includes establishing an in-depth understanding of the current research agendas in the area. By becoming educated on the area's research priorities, investigators can ensure that their qualitative projects align with and work toward established research goals. Fielding (2013) commented on the "globalization of methods" around the world. He recommended that we need to push back against the "methods establishment" and to look outside of the academy for emerging methodologies such as cyberactivism, cyberresearch, and indigenous methodologies in the world community.

To aid in these efforts, you should take time to establish and maintain collaborative relationships with researchers who represent the location being researched. In building country-level expertise, you need to understand what topics or issues are off limits prior to establishing a research agenda, and you must also recognize differential definitions of topics for discussion. It is important to consider that topics can be sensitive for various reasons, and what is considered sensitive in everyday culture varies from country to country and region to region (Thornton, 2014). For this reason, it is especially important to allow individuals the option to opt out of answering questions or being observed if they feel uncomfortable.

When developing a global qualitative study, you must also recognize differential definitions of topics for discussion. Take, for example, an investigation of child maltreatment in India (Maiter, Alaggia, & Trocmé, 2004). In this study, cultural awareness was critical, as parents of different ethnic groups used different methods to discipline their children, including some that may be frowned upon by members of other cultures. It is important to have a comprehensive understanding of how a phenomenon may be received and interpreted in the geographical location of interest.

Global Research Policies

Another aspect of global cultural awareness is that understanding and acknowledging research policies within the country conditions and then creating research platforms that are grounded within these specific principles (Adams, Burke, &

Whitmarsh, 2014). It is also important to understand how international politics may affect how your research (or research proposal) is received. Note that this does not necessarily require an understanding of culture, but more so an understanding of how individuals in the local research communities may perceive your research methods and topic of interest.

I recommend that you understand and appreciate what is currently being done and working well as far as research is concerned in the country of interest. It is imperative to understand what the leading research institutes in the specific country are embracing as their research agendas and their methodologies to build policy platforms. If your topic is not perceived as important, or if qualitative research is not currently being used, you may have a challenging road ahead. Collaborating with local researchers and studying country-specific journals can help you understand what research is being done in the country where you plan to research.

Methodological Orientation and Data Collection Methods

Qualitative researchers looking to implement a global research agenda must then consider what research methods are emphasized in the country of interest. For example, in South Africa, there are increasing demands for qualitative research studies, whereas in China and Thailand, quantitative methods are preferred. Which is deemed more acceptable in the country you wish to explore? The qualitative researcher must have a firm understanding of this issue, as it will shape the interactions with investigators and collaborators. It is important, however, to consider that the preferred methodology may vary depending on the specific field of study. Whereas quantitative methods may still dominate in the fields of business and marketing, qualitative methods may be preferred in the social sciences, such as social work, mental health, and education.

In designing research protocols, it is also imperative that qualitative researchers do not habitually apply Western methods before thoroughly understanding the phenomenon and location of interest (Yang, 2000). As suggested by Denzin and Giardina (2013), epistemology must precede the practice of research. Cultural awareness means varying data collection and analysis methods as needed, on the basis of the country where the data are collected. In some countries, researchers may find that certain forms of data collection are prohibited, while in others, there are forms that are simply preferred over others. For example, in Africa and India, face-to-face interviews are strongly preferred over other forms of data collection (Thornton, 2014), and in South Africa, photovoice is becoming increasingly popular. It is the researcher's responsibility to investigate these elements of the location of interest and design a qualitative study that takes these nuances into consideration.

Qualitative Study Designs and Procedures

Qualitative researchers who work in countries with limited resources are likely to find numerous opportunities to build partnerships and explore myriad research topics. However, they may also be met with challenges related to recruitment, data collection, and dissemination of findings. Therefore, it is necessary to tailor the research design appropriately to meet the needs and fit the requirements of the location and population being explored.

I recommend that you ensure that the research questions, recruitment strategies, data collection methods, and all other aspects of the study are tailored to the language, culture, and other social nuances of the country of interest. This cannot occur without first becoming an expert in the location being explored and building collaborative partnerships with investigators who represent the area. That being said, global qualitative research may require a significant time commitment, even lengthier than nonglobal qualitative research.

Recommendations for the Global Qualitative Researcher

There are several steps qualitative researchers should take to address the discussed challenges in conducting global qualitative research and build cultural awareness. A checklist, shown in Table 17.1, has been created to guide the global qualitative researcher in the development and implementation of a new project. Although this list is not all inclusive of the steps necessary to building cultural awareness, new global qualitative researchers will find themselves well on their way after advancing through these steps.

TABLE 17.1   **Checklist for Building Global Qualitative Cultural Awareness**

_____ Participate in general cultural competency training.

_____ Interrogate your own lenses of resistance that may lead to a colonizing discourse.

_____ Begin collaborative communications with several investigators in country of interest.

_____ Explore the research topic within the context of the country of interest to determine how research may be received.

_____ Consider possible differential definitions of key topics in research projects.

_____ Become well versed in primary research methods in the country of interest.

_____ Understand the most used data collection and analysis methods in the country of interest.

_____ Become knowledgeable about the research platforms of the leading local research institutions.

SUMMARY

The skills introduced in this chapter are to develop cultural awareness in global qualitative research and address challenges in global qualitative research. Although there may be several challenges associated with conducting global qualitative research, the potential benefits are many. By building country-level expertise, understanding methodological orientations, using country-specific data collection methods, and respecting policy platforms, qualitative researchers can tailor their research designs appropriately. The resulting research has the potential to improve global public health and reduce knowledge gaps within our newly globalized economy.

ACTIVITIES

1. Identify a country in which you might like to conduct a qualitative study. Spend some time exploring this location's preferred research and data collection methods. Examine articles in international journals, study dissertation studies reported in English, collaborate with scholars from another country, and determine what research issues are being explored in policy reports.

2. Consider one of the qualitative research papers you have recently read. How might you recommend that the author modify this study to best suit the country of interest you identified in Activity 1?

FURTHER RESOURCES

Deardorff, D. K. (2006). Identification and assessment of intercultural competence as a student outcome of internationalization. *Journal Studies in International Education, 10*(3), 241–266.

Denzin, N. K., & Giardina, M. D. (Eds.). (2013). *Global dimensions of qualitative inquiry*. Walnut Creek, CA: Left Coast.

Dower, N. (2002). Global ethics and global citizenship. In N. Dower & J. Williams (Eds.), *Global citizenship: A critical introduction* (pp. 146–157). New York: Routledge.

Trostle, J. (1992). Research capacity building in international health: Definitions, evaluations and strategies for success. *Social Science & Medicine, 35*, 1321–1324.

Visit study.sagepub.com/30skills for quizzes, eFlashcards, and more!

Analyzing and Validating Data

PART

V

Coding Text Data

Skill

Develop the skill of coding a text file.

Why the Skill Is Important

Most people are not skilled in how to take text data and make sense of them. They are used to counting numbers and using statistics. What they often do not realize is that text data are dense data, and it takes a long time to go through them and make sense of them. They are also not aware of the interpretive nature of qualitative data analysis, in which the researcher needs to make an interpretation of what is contained in the text. They further are not aware of how to make an assessment and then to place that information into a qualitative report. The skill of how to code text data is central to qualitative research because much of our data are text, such as the text found in open-ended interviews, the text in field notes from observations, and the text in documents. Thus, it is important to know the steps involved in coding text data, making sense of them, and then using the interpretations in our qualitative research reports.

The Overall Process of Qualitative Data Analysis

Coding is taking transcribed text data and making sense of them. It is one step in the overall process of conducting a qualitative analysis (see Creswell, 2013, for the data analysis spiral). It can be done by hand, where you mark up the text with colored pens and highlighters. It can also be assisted by qualitative software (see Chapter 21).

The first step in analysis is to have the text database available. This means transcribing the interview and developing a database; it also means taking your field notes from observations and creating a text file of them, or scanning a document file and creating a digital copy of the document. These steps all involve *preparing the data* for data analysis. The next step would be engaging in the *general procedure of data analysis*. I typically think about this step as involving first reading through the database slowly, making marginal notes about what people were saying or what I observed them doing. Once I am satisfied that I have a general understanding of the database, I then begin the process of *coding* the data. This involves determining what is being said and assigning a code label to a text passage. I then group similar codes together to build evidence of support for broader categories of information, called *themes* (see Chapter 20). These themes are sometimes interrelated to tell a story, and they become the headings in my findings in a qualitative report. Throughout this process, I will use a *qualitative software program* to help me store, analyze, report, and visualize the codes and themes (see Chapter 21). Once my analysis is complete I will then seek to *validate* my interpretation, through a number of potential procedures (see Chapter 22). I will typically use two or three validation procedures to help establish the accuracy of my interpretation. In addition, I will use *multiple coders* in a process called intercoder agreement to see if multiple individuals coding separately all arrive at similar codes of the data (see Chapter 23). A final aspect of data analysis consists of *reflexivity*, in which I am conscious of how my background and personal experiences shape my interpretation of the database (see Chapter 26). A checklist, as shown in Figure 18.1 for the entire process of data analysis, can assist in making certain that you have addressed the important components of data analysis in your methods discussion.

FIGURE 18.1   **Checklist for Writing a Complete Data Analysis Methods Section**

_____ Discuss preparing the data (transcriptions)

_____ Indicate the general procedure of data analysis (reading through the data and taking notes, coding the data, description, developing themes, interrelating the themes)

_____ Discuss the use of qualitative data analysis software to help analyze the data (e.g., MAXQDA)

_____ Discuss the use of multiple coders (i.e., intercoder agreement) if used in the study and how this process was accomplished, with percentage agreement stated

_____ Discuss validity strategies (e.g., member checking, triangulation, disconfirming evidence, peer debriefing, external audit, prolonged engagement in the field)

_____ Discuss reflexivity—how the researchers' experiences and role will influence the interpretation of the findings

When you are preparing your final qualitative manuscript for publication, go through this checklist to make sure that you have a complete qualitative data analysis discussion. Also, use the checklist to assess the inclusion of important elements in a plan or proposal for a study. One aspect of the checklist is the element of coding, a central feature of qualitative data analysis, and a skill that all qualitative researchers should master. For purposes of the present discussion, I will focus on the important step of coding.

From the Raw Data to Codes

As shown in Figure 18.2, the overall process of qualitative data analysis is inductive, working from the raw data up to the codes. I begin the coding process with a text file composed of my interview transcripts, my observation field notes, or my scanned documents. After I prepare the data for analysis, I then read through the data to get a general sense of them. At this point I am recording memos in the margins of the text. I then go through my text, line by line, bracket a segment of text, and then assign a code label or term to the text segment. These codes then become evidence for description and themes presented in the findings in my report. Thus, in summary, the steps involve exploring the database, coding the data and assigning labels to the codes, aggregating the codes into description and into themes, making an interpretation of the themes, and then validating the information. Also, as seen in Figure 18.2, the aspects of this process are interactive, whereby one influences the other, as well as simultaneous, and multiple steps are being enacted at the same

FIGURE 18.2   **Data Analysis From the Raw Data to Codes**

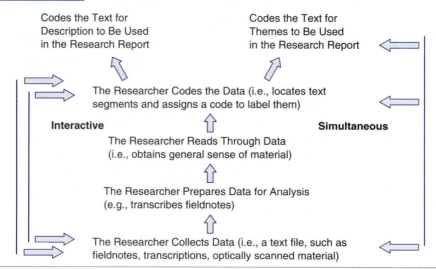

Source: Adapted from Creswell (2015).

time. For heuristic purposes, it is helpful to see it as a "bottom-up" process from the raw data to the codes.

From the Raw Data to Themes

Figure 18.3 addresses how to move from the raw data into the themes. We can reconceptualize the coding process as starting with raw data that becomes funneled down into themes. Basically, the themes report the major findings in a study. They are composed of codes and evidence for the codes. Several codes will go into building a theme, and the themes are distinct categories of information that do not overlap. These themes will be the headings in the findings section of a qualitative report. It is helpful to see a visual of how the process of coding from the raw data into the themes occurs.

As shown in Figure 18.3, building themes is a process beginning broadly, with many pages of text that the qualitative inquirer reads through. The next step is to divide the text into segments. In my first pass through a text database, I typically work with large "chunks" of data, such as paragraphs of information. In this way, I can engage in "lean coding," a process of forming a smaller number of codes rather than a larger number of codes in my analysis process. I try to code all of my text data (whether a small database of a few pages or a large one of thousands of pages) into about 30 to 50 codes. I then look for overlap and redundant codes and start to

FIGURE 18.3   **From Many Pages of Text to Themes**

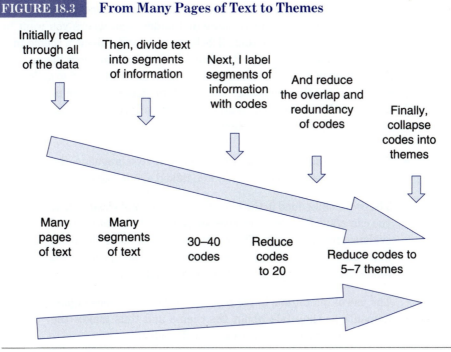

Source: Creswell (2013).

reduce the number to, say, 20 codes. These 20 codes then collapse further into about five to seven themes that become the major headings in my findings section of my qualitative report.

The Nature of Coding

Coding is the process of analyzing qualitative text data by taking them apart to see what they yield before putting the data back together in a meaningful way. Through coding, the researcher develops diverse evidence for themes. This means that in analyzing the data, the researcher does not simply report long passages from transcripts but actually analyzes what the participants are saying.

There are three types of data analysis: conventional, summative, and directed. In conventional data analysis, the coding categories are derived directly from the data. In summative data analysis, the process involves counting and comparisons. The directed approach starts with a theory as a guide to the analytic process (Hsieh & Shannon, 2005). I will focus on conventional coding because this is the practice that is typically used in many qualitative data analyses.

Working Backward From a Theme Passage to Understand Coding

One procedure I have found helpful in qualitative data analysis and in coding text data is to work backward, that is, to visualize and understand where you want to end up with your analysis. The end point, I believe, is to write about a theme in a "findings" section of a research study. It is helpful, therefore, to see a theme passage, a specific write-up of a theme, and to consider what elements need to go into it. Examine, for instance, the theme passage about "safety" found in one of my journal articles (Asmussen & Creswell, 1995), as shown in Figure 18.4. As you examine this example of a theme passage, note the following:

- The heading for the theme is phrased in in vivo language, the words of the actual participants who talked about "safety."

- The codes embedded in the passage (which are italicized so that you can easily find them) provide specific but different forms of evidence for the theme. These different codes make the point that "safety" is a complex issue with many perspectives—a fundamental idea in good qualitative research.

- The use of quotations in the passage shares the voices of participants as they talk about the theme and thus makes the discussion "come alive" with practical vitality.

FIGURE 18.4   **Theme Passage That Illustrates Coding**

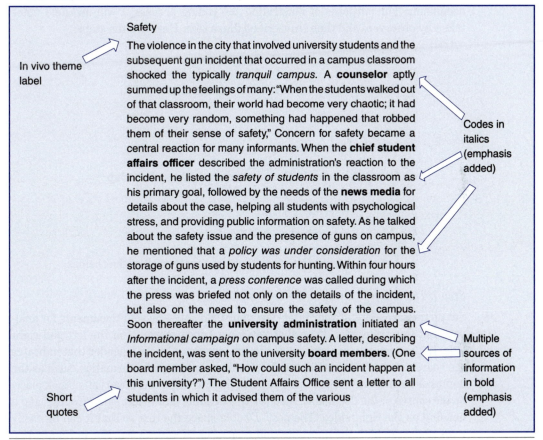

Source: Adapted from Asmussen and Creswell (1995, pp. 582–584).

- The use of multiple sources of data helps build the codes and, in turn, the evidence for the theme. The use of multiple sources in the passage (which are bolded) also shows that the evidence is built from several sources of information, and, in this case, many different individuals (students, board members, etc.) talked about this issue. These varied sources then indicate that it is an important issue to highlight as a major theme in the study.

The Process of Coding

I will take you through the steps involved in coding a text database. I will use the example of my qualitative students going to the "climbing wall" at the student recreation center and observing and taking field notes of their experiences. Instead of observational field notes, your text database might be interview transcripts or documents. For purposes of illustrating the coding process, I will use field notes taken by observers and then transcribed into a text. Here are the steps:

- Set up your transcript for easy coding.

- Read through each text to get a general sense of it.

- Code each text.

- List all of the codes.

- Group the codes to eliminate redundancy and overlap.

- Write a theme passage.

- Create a conceptual map of the themes.

- Develop a narrative story that ties together all of the themes.

Step 1: The Setup

Set up the transcript of your interview, your field notes, or your documents for analysis. Set this transcript up so that you have 1-inch margins on the left and right side. In this way, you can write notes in the margins. Create a header that indicates the source of the information, the date, and any additional information, such as the names of the interviewers or interviewees, the site where the observation took place, or the source of the document. Also, write a heading on the left side, "Codes," and a heading on the right side, "Themes." Double-space the text so that it can be easily read, and state both the questions and responses (if interviews). See in Figure 18.5 an example of a transcript set up for processing.

Step 2: Read Through Each Text

Read through all of your text to get a sense of what individuals are saying or doing. Record a few notes in the margins. Ask yourself, "What are people saying or doing?"

Step 3: Code Each Text

Start coding all of the text documents, as shown in Figure 18.6. Start with one that is the shortest or easiest to access. Coding means that you will draw a bracket around the text segment, and assign a code label. Use large "chunks" of data, such as paragraphs, to code the first time through your text. This is "lean" coding. For your entire text database, assign no more than about 20 to 30 codes. You can expect to not use all of the data. We "winnow" the data and do not use all of them because

FIGURE 18.5   Sample Observational Field Notes Setup for Coding

Codes	#1 Observation at the Climbing Wall by John	Themes
	As I walked into the gym, I was bombarded with the smell of old gym shoes, a smelly locker that had seen the many wins and losses of a team. Around me was a juxtaposition of sights. The old wood floors and brick foundation of the gym did not fit with what was inside; badminton nets, an open view of different workout rooms, and lastly, a climbing wall. The climbing wall was separated by two activities: instruction and climbing. To the left of the wall, an instructor was giving a tutorial, with a typed handout, on how to use the necessary equipment to climb. The new climbers were asked to read a portion of the handout, as the instructor provided a visual demonstration of the equipment. The new climbers asked questions regarding the handout and the demonstration. This process continued for some time; a detailed process, yet very relaxed and informal. Another instructor came in, wearing jeans and a tank top. She asked the instructor giving the lesson what was going on. Once she heard his response, she laughed, looked around and went about her business getting her phone out, texting someone, while standing against the mat observing the wall and the instruction going on in front of her. The lesson continues to go on, even with her interruption.	

FIGURE 18.6   Sample Text for Coding With Code and Theme Headings

Codes	#1 Observation at the Climbing Wall, December 2014, by John	Themes
	As I walked into the gym, I was bombarded with the smell of old gym shoes, a smelly locker that had seen the many wins and losses of a team. Around me was a juxtaposition of sights. The old wood floors and brick foundation of the gym did not fit with what was inside; badminton nets, an open view of different workout rooms, and lastly, a climbing wall. The climbing wall was separated by two activities: instruction and climbing. To the left of the wall, an instructor was giving a tutorial, with a typed handout, on how to use the necessary equipment to climb. The new climbers were asked to read a portion of the handout, as the instructor provided a visual demonstration of the equipment. The new climbers asked questions regarding the handout and the demonstration. This process continued for some time; a detailed process, yet very relaxed and informal. Another instructor came in, wearing jeans and a tank top. She asked the instructor giving the lesson what was going on. Once she heard his response, she laughed, looked around and went about her business getting her phone out, texting someone, while standing against the mat observing the wall and the instruction going on in front of her. The lesson continues to go on, even with her interruption.	Physical space New climbers Interruption

there is so much available. This is in contrast to quantitative research, where the investigator tries to save as much data as possible from the database. You can certainly code a text segment with multiple codes, but ask yourself, "What is the main idea being conveyed?" and assign a single code. This code label typically consists of one to three words.

There are different types of code labels that you can apply. The best code label would be in the exact words of the participant or words you heard when you observed. These are called "in vivo codes." In this way, you start to build codes and later themes that resonate with your participants. Other types of code labels would be a term you make up on the basis of your personal experiences (e.g., *stressed out*) or a good social science or health science label based on theory (e.g., *efficacy*). Still, "in vivo codes" are best because they move you toward the voices of participants, which you want to reflect in your realistic final report.

It is helpful to think about the different types of codes you can use. I would definitely use the code label *quotes* to capture those sentences or phrases I want to use later in my qualitative report. Look especially for short quotations or short phrases you can directly use in your report to capture the essence of the voices of participants. I also assign *expected codes*, codes for what I hope to find either through my rational thought or through material I have read in the literature. I also assign surprising or *unexpected codes*. These are codes that come as a surprise and something I did not expect to find. I may also assign *unusual codes*, or codes with information that is not only unexpected but represents an unusual way that an interviewee or a participant I observed talked or acted (e.g., retriggering).

I also write down "themes" that occur to me as I code under the "theme" section on the right-hand side of my text. These must be seen as tentative themes, and I may change them or not use them; some picture of the emerging themes is helpful even during the process of coding a text.

I proceed through each interview, observation, or document and code each one. See in Figure 18.7 how I coded the text segment.

Step 4: List All of the Codes

I next place codes on a piece of paper or in a file as follows and simply list them:

Physical structure

Individual climbers

Men/women

Disappointment

Teamwork

Use of the facility

FIGURE 18.7   Coded Text Using "Lean" Coding

Codes		Themes
Quote	The Ree Center at UNL is a busy place. One of the attractions here is the Climbing Wall, which is a vast structure with colorful holds to make the way to the top and imprints of fossils on the sides. The climbing wall is located in a gym with basketball hoops and people playing badminton, while others climb. When the class arrived, there were two people climbing with music playing in the background – music from a CD player as well as the noise of sneakers squeaking across the floor to hit the birdie flying. The spotters are encouraging the men climbing, and interestingly enough it is all men who are there for the first 30 minutes. Eventually a woman makes her way into the group, yet nothing seems to change. You can see that the ones climbing are straining, yet at the same time they make it look simple, as if it's just an easy climb to the top and back down again. When they are on the floor, though, the sweat shining on their foreheads becomes evident. Once at the top, there is a noticeable victory for each of the climbers. Yet when something is missed there appears to be a feeling of disappointment. For example, one climber came down and said, "Damn, I missed the orange one." There is also a general trust in the spotters, the people holding the ropes. If they let too much rope go, or not enough, it could be dangerous. So, then what is the meaning of the climbing wall? It seems as if it means trust, strength, community, exercise. and accomplishment.	

Codes (left column, in order):

Quote

Physical structure

Individual climbers

Men/Women

Disappointment

Quote

Teamwork

Use of the facility

Importance of wall/closeness

Quote

Going over the top

Themes (right column):

Achievement Victory

Meaning of climbing wall

Main text:

The Ree Center at UNL is a busy place. One of the attractions here is the Climbing Wall, which is a vast structure with colorful holds to make the way to the top and imprints of fossils on the sides. The climbing wall is located in a gym with basketball hoops and people playing badminton, while others climb. When the class arrived, there were two people climbing with music playing in the background – music from a CD player as well as the noise of sneakers squeaking across the floor to hit the birdie flying. The spotters are encouraging the men climbing, and interestingly enough it is all men who are there for the first 30 minutes. Eventually a woman makes her way into the group, yet nothing seems to change. You can see that the ones climbing are straining, yet at the same time they make it look simple, as if it's just an easy climb to the top and back down again. When they are on the floor, though, the sweat shining on their foreheads becomes evident. Once at the top, there is a noticeable victory for each of the climbers. Yet when something is missed there appears to be a feeling of disappointment. For example, one climber came down and said, "Damn, I missed the orange one." There is also a general trust in the spotters, the people holding the ropes. If they let too much rope go, or not enough, it could be dangerous. So, then what is the meaning of the climbing wall? It seems as if it means trust, strength, community, exercise. and accomplishment.

Ask the check-in person how many people use the climbing wall at the recreation center at UNL a day, and you may be told about 10. Ask the front-desk person, and he may tell you about 15. When asking a random 15 people in the exterior locker area how many have climbed it, only I may have climbed it. Yet when you ask one of the guides at the wall, they'll tell you about 50 people climb per day.

Depending on how close you are to the wall, literally, may affect how important the wall is to you, for those who are nearest know best what it means: it means that if you really want to know the wall, you have to have climbed it – several times, several different ways, even spit over the top, as one of the guides did as he climbed a particularly difficult trail. You won't find the check-in person having ever spit over the top.

Importance of the wall/closeness

Going over the top

Quotes

Step 5: Group the Codes

After I go through all of my codes for all of my observations (an extensive list of about 20 codes), I then group the codes to eliminate redundancy and overlap:

Physical structure—wall as a piece of art—closeness of the wall

Process of climbing the wall—checking-in—to really know the wall—going over the wall

Trust—teamwork—buddy-system

Individual climbers—diverse climbers—instructor

Motivation (to climb)—disappointments

Through this process, I hope to have variety in my codes to capture the range of interests of what I observed. I am now beginning to reduce the codes down into broad themes. For example, I might create a table such as Table 18.1, where the codes have now become themes.

In the cells of this table I now have five different groups of codes to write about. I have now developed themes. Notice that I have collapsed my codes into five themes. Now, I am curious about whether the themes might be arrayed in some order that makes sense, so that in my final qualitative narrative, I can tell a story that unfolds in my qualitative report.

Step 6: Write a Theme Passage

This step involves writing a theme passage that includes the codes as evidence for the theme, gives specific quotations to provide a realistic description of the situation, uses multiple sources of information, and cites different people. Remember the theme passage on "safety" from my gunman case study that illustrates how this passage should look (see Figure 18.4 again). These themes then become components with the theme label as a heading in the "findings" section of a qualitative report.

Step 7: Create a Conceptual Map of the Themes

A good qualitative strategy is to consider how the themes might be interrelated to tell an overall story about the phenomenon under study. Sometimes, I develop a con-

TABLE 18.1   Diverse Types of Codes Organized Into Themes

What I Would Expect to Learn	What Is Surprising to Learn	What Is Unusual to Learn
Physical description of the wall Process of climbing	Trust/teamwork Motivation	Individual climber stories

FIGURE 18.8 **Moving From Themes to Narration in Data Analysis**

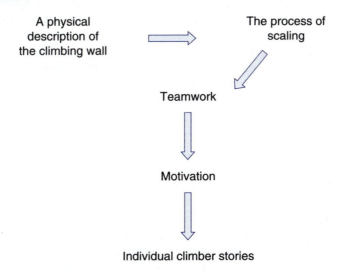

cept map and array the themes into a logical flow of reporting them in the findings, as shown in Figure 18.8.

Step 8: Develop a Narrative Story

Finally, I might develop an overall storyline for my qualitative report. I can use the concept map to help organize the sequence of themes in this overall story. On the basis of my concept map, the themes could be tied together and presented in the "conclusion" section of my qualitative report or at the end of my "findings." Here are several examples of overall stories based on the climbing wall database.

Example 1: A Summary for the Conclusion Section

What does it mean to climb the wall? The climbing wall is in a multi-purpose gymnasium in the University student recreation center. The air has a dusty smell. The wall's purpose is for individuals to practice scaling an artificial cliff in hopes that the skills developed will transfer to the out-of-doors. The wall itself is "massive," about 50 feet high. It is made of an odd "spongy feeling" material. A mat at the bottom protects climbers if they fall. Music plays in the background because "music chills." Different sized handhold rocks dot the wall, and one is shaped as a human skull, as if it provides a not-so-subtle tribute to a fallen climber. Different routes up the wall are color-coded (red, purple, green, orange, pink, blue, grey, and black) with strips of paper marking varying degrees of difficulty. These routes are named: "Yearning," "Snake and Ladder," "Wild Yet Roasty," and "We Love U Gaston." There are several climbers practicing their climbs. I am reminded metaphorically of Spiderman crossing and contorting legs and arms in unnatural ways. Some see the wall as a conquest; some plan their attack much like an animal deliberating before attacking its prey. To others it may be an intricate dance as next steps up the wall are carefully planned. These climbers can be distinguished by their colorful dress, their hair color, their age, their physical appearance ("there are no plus sizes") and their style for going up the wall. How do they go up the wall? They don equipment such as harnesses, shoes, and chalk bags in belly-pouches. They team with a spotter, they stretch and look closely at the wall plotting their best, smart approach, they elongate their bodies pulling and pushing themselves up, they sometimes lose control and dangle in the air, they sweat, they persevere and reach the top, and quickly repel down. The trip up and down takes about 20-30 minutes. Why do they do this? Some saw it as fun, others as reaching a goal, making a conquest, as a thrill, or as exercise. It was like life itself, "starting something, accepting the risks, choosing a path, sometimes slowing down, and finally reaching the top."

Example 2: Another Summary for the Conclusion Section

One of the most memorable Halloween day experiential learning opportunities for me was the observation about "The Climbing Wall." This wall was located in a smelly old gym with wood floors and a brick foundation. The wall had colorful holds that climbers used to make their way to the top. These holds were of different sizes. A wide mattress was at the bottom of the wall, and music played, a mixture of rock and jazz. The wall is an art object. The process of climbing began with having instruction, finding a buddy to hold the safety rope, looking at the wall, putting on shoes that fit tightly, grabbing strong holds, controlling the legs from shaking, sometimes looking down, hitting the bar at the top, and maybe spitting on it, and then rappelling down quickly. If you are lucky, instructors will go up with you and provide guidance. This climb involves trusting helpers, reaching the top, and being afraid of an accident. Experienced climbers such as Sebastian can tell you about it or someone I dubbed the "Spiderman." It provides a "bond that transcends life," and one climber said, "for a millisecond, I had the world in my hands."

How did I create these summaries? First they are summaries of the major themes in the study. I went back and reread the transcripts and used the codes and themes I had come up with. In this process I added more codes and refined a few. I also found as I wrote out the summary that the logical order of my themes began to change some: I wanted to bring the metaphors in earlier, and they seemed to relate to the individual climber's theme. I also wanted to incorporate a few quotations to give the summary a more realistic feel. I kept the summary reasonably short, and my intent was to provide an overview of the experience for readers that they would find as the first passage in the "conclusion" section of a study or at the end of the "findings" section.

SUMMARY

Data analysis consists of more than simply analyzing the data. It also includes preparing the data, proceeding through the general steps of data analysis, coding the data and thematic analysis, using a qualitative software program, validating the accuracy of the qualitative report, using multiple coders, and then being reflexive in your account. The procedure involves moving from the raw data (e.g., text or images) on to codes, and then to aggregate at a larger level, the themes. In the end, many pages of text are reduced to five to seven themes that are reported in the findings of a qualitative project. When coding, it is helpful to work backward from the themes to coding to see how the process works. Coding basically involves reviewing the transcript or observational notes, bracketing a segment of text, and then assigning a code label to the text segment to indicate what the participant is saying. From this point, the qualitative researcher aggregates the codes into a small number of themes, writes a theme passage, organizes the themes into a sequence (concept map) to tell a story, and then writes an overall narrative for the study.

ACTIVITY

Take text data from an interview, observational field notes, or a document. Code the text data, develop a list of the codes, look for redundancies or overlaps, develop a conceptual map, and then write a conclusion section for a qualitative report including the codes as evidence for broad themes.

FURTHER RESOURCES

Examine the following book and article to see different approaches to coding and the analysis of data:

Bazeley, P. (2013). *Qualitative data analysis: Practical strategies.* London: Sage Ltd.

Hsieh, H.-F., & Shannon, S. E. (2005). Three approaches to qualitative content analysis. *Qualitative Health Research, 15*(9), 1277–1288.

Visit study.sagepub.com/30skills for quizzes, eFlashcards, and more!

Coding Images and Pictures

Skill

Develop the skill of being able to code an image or a picture.

Why the Skill Is Important

While many think of qualitative research as concerned with text-based data, more broadly it is an approach that uses open-ended data. For some studies, qualitative researchers have available images and pictures as open-ended data. As visual methodology has garnered more interest from researchers in general, qualitative researchers are also realizing the value of visuals to understanding human lives and society. Simply, visual data are part of our everyday lives.

For the researcher, images offer a record to refer back to in a way that is not possible with field notes and a reliance on memory. Images provide powerful visual records of real events—capturing cultural events for future generations and providing snapshots of visual phenomena, such as home or work surroundings. Images capture nonverbal behavior, such as facial expressions and body language. As qualitative researchers, it is important to understand the use of images in qualitative research and how to analyze and code them. Knowing how to collect and analyze images will give you an additional tool to understand your central phenomenon.

Types of Qualitative Image Data

Photographs, videos, film, and drawings are all types of qualitative image data. Here, I will use *images* to refer generally to any of these types of visual data. Each type of image has unique characteristics. Photographs capture a moment or an event in extraordinary detail. Videos and film portray moving images, may include audio, and preserve temporal events in sequence (Knoblauch, Tuma, & Schnettler, 2014). These characteristics can bring further depth to the data. Drawings give the researcher the potential to create something or to create something with participants through their artwork. The artwork then offers another instance of collecting open-ended data. Drawings can be particularly useful when working with children. Of course, what a drawing portrays may be less obvious to outsiders who are not involved in its production.

Images usually arise from one of three methods. Sometimes researchers gather existing images to study, and sometimes they generate images themselves, such as recording a video at a research site. Sometimes participants generate images. These three methods have led to several ways to collect image or picture qualitative data.

- Participants might receive *disposable cameras* (or their cell phones) to carry with them to take photographs of the phenomenon under study (e.g., their community). This data collection procedure reflects a participatory approach, which brings the participants' insights further into the research process.

- Qualitative researchers have used **visual elicitation** as a popular approach to participatory visual research (Prosser, 2011). The researcher uses a visual image, such as a photograph, in a research interview to stimulate (i.e., elicit) a response, generating dialogue. An advantage of participant involvement is that images not only record events, they also evoke responses (and data) from the participants. According to Prosser (2011), a photograph can act as an "ice-breaker" (p. 484) when a power difference exists between the researcher and participant.

- *Photovoice* is a popular form of photo elicitation that has three goals: (a) to allow participants to document the strengths and concerns of their community, (b) to promote critical dialogue, and (c) to influence policy makers (Wang & Burris, 1997). For example, collaborating with a researcher, participants might receive disposable cameras with instructions to photograph meaningful scenes. The researcher then collects the photographs and uses them in a facilitated group discussion. Individuals in the discussion then reflect on the images they produced. Often, local participants receive training and serve as the discussion facilitators because of their unique understanding. In addition to producing rich data, a major aim of photovoice is to bring about change in communities by influencing policy makers.

- A *drawing* might be used as a qualitative data source as in the participatory reflection and action technique (Chambers, 2007). Drawings can be especially useful when interviewing children who are still developing verbal communication skills. The intent is for the image to evoke a response. Regardless of the type of image, discussing topics through an intermediary object tends to reduce pressure that participants feel. They tend to be able to discuss strong emotions and sensitive topics more easily.

Potential Concerns When Using Images

Although images can be a useful source of rich qualitative data, you should be aware of the potential disadvantages. Photography is both a product of culture and something that contributes to the culture of a society through what it captures. Some argue that because photographic data are interrelated with society, we should be cautious when using photographs for analysis, as they are a product of societal forces, capturing a moment in time (Bogdan & Biklen, 2006). A photo does not represent change or fine details surrounding an event. In addition, a photograph itself is a selective representation of the world because the photographer (researcher, participant, or professional photographer) decides what to sample. It is important for you to be aware of this caveat to not extend interpretation beyond the actual data. Furthermore, generated photographs can engrain your position as an outsider, distancing you from participants.

Ethical concerns with images also arise. You might ask whether the use of images is necessary to the project and be cognizant of privacy invasion, as image data preserve a permanent record of events. Some qualitative researchers argue that the use of photographs and videos of individuals does not respect anonymity (e.g., Marshall & Rossman, 2011). If you propose the use of video and photographs, additional details must be added to informed consent documents. In particular, participants need to know that their images are being recorded, and participants need the opportunity to consent to the recording. You often need to explain the circumstances and develop procedures to ensure that digitized images do not spread without authorization. When using visual elicitation methods, it is also important to identify the potential harm that may result as participants capture photos or videos in the community. Will the participants experience animosity as a result of what they do or do not capture? It will be particularly important for you to discuss with participants what is appropriate to photograph or video-record.

Analyzing Images

The process of coding involves aggregating qualitative data into a small number of units of information. These units are known as *codes* and are assigned meaningful labels. These codes are then grouped into broader units of information known as *themes* (as discussed in Chapter 18). Coding images follows the same general process, but we have different options for how to divide the data into smaller units, and the options depend on the type of data. For one, images might be considered a form of observation, whereby the researcher is observing the image (Marshall & Rossman, 2011) and assigns codes to the entire image. Another approach is to attach codes to aspects and areas of the image. Finally, when using visual elicitation methods, the researcher codes the transcript of the discussion.

Coding Images as Observations

As mentioned, one option is to treat an image (e.g., photograph, drawing) as an observation and record notes about the image. The notes then become the data source for the coding process. However, the researcher can also code the image itself by looking for unique features, contrasts, the presence or absence of something, or something about the shot itself (e.g., camera angle or perspective). The researcher can tag these features by hand-coding a paper copy of the image or by using a computer-assisted qualitative data analysis software application. Regardless of the technique, the process consists of eight steps:

> **Step 1:** Prepare your data for analysis. If hand-coding, print each image with a wide margin (or affix it to a larger piece of paper) to allow space to assign the code labels. If using a computer, import all images into the application.
>
> **Step 2:** Code the image by tagging areas of the image and assigning code labels. Some codes might involve meta-details (e.g., the camera angle).
>
> **Step 3:** Compile all of the codes for the images on a separate sheet.
>
> **Step 4:** Review the codes to eliminate redundancy and overlap. This step also begins to reduce the codes to potential themes.
>
> **Step 5:** Group codes into themes that represent common ideas.

Step 6: Assign the codes and themes to three groups: expected codes and themes, surprising codes and themes, and unusual codes and themes (see Chapter 18). This step helps ensure that the qualitative "findings" will represent diverse perspectives.

Step 7: Array the codes and themes into a conceptual map that shows the flow of ideas in the "findings" section. The flow might represent presenting the themes from a more general picture to a more specific picture.

Step 8: Write the narrative for each theme that will go into the "findings" section of a study or for a general summary that will go into the "discussion" section as the overall findings in the study.

A Semiotic Approach to Image Analysis

One common interpretive framework for image coding is semiotic analysis. When using semiotic analysis, Penn (2000) recommended dividing the coding task into two aspects after selecting the image. The first aspect involves describing what the image denotes (i.e., what it signifies). For example, when coding a picture to describe a person, the researcher might code gender, color, facial expressions, position, clothing, and other noteworthy elements. The second aspect focuses on the connotation—the higher level significance ascribed to the image. In other words, when determining connotation, the researcher asks, "What does this image mean?"

The process of **semiotic analysis** consists of five interrelated procedures (Spencer, 2011) that encompass image context, textual features, intertextual references, anchor, and connotation. You might begin by paying attention to the *context* of an image. Consider where the image came from, who took the photograph, where the photographer was positioned, and the setting. The next step is to describe what the image denotes. The focus of determining what an image denotes is to determine the overt *textual features* found in the image. For example, think about an image of a classroom in session. It might be important to describe what students look like, what they are wearing, what positions they are in, and what they are doing (e.g., are they interacting or focused on the teacher?). The next step is to identify the *intertextual references* that relate the image to other genres or uses of visual codes. Here, it may be helpful to think about the image relative to other images or outside contexts. Returning to our image of students in the classroom, some questions might be the following: How does one image compare with others from other classrooms? What influences of the discipline or subject are present? What other outside influences can we see? It is then important to *anchor the image* with any text that may be present. Drawings often include text, but photographs often have signs and other text in the background. The analytic question here is, What do the visual and linguistic elements communicate together? The final procedure of semiotic analysis is to identify the *connotation* of the image. In light of the previous procedures, this one ascribes the overall meaning of the image. Of course, the entire semiotic analysis process is iterative rather than linear, and you may revisit steps as the analysis proceeds.

Analysis of Video and Film

Researchers might gather existing video or films to conduct an analysis. The first task is then determining what material to select—the sampling. Analysis of videos requires a special approach because videos contain images and sound. Rose (2010) recommended first transcribing the audio into text, followed by creating a two-column version of the transcript (see Table 19.1 for an example). One column contains the verbal transcriptions with time points, and the second contains the visual features. Noting time points preserves the temporal aspects of the video. The visual aspects recorded depend on the unit of analysis. Potential units of analysis include scene changes, persons involved in the scene, and camera shots. For example, when the unit of analysis is the camera shot, the researcher might note the background, camera angle, and people in the scene for each shot.

Visual Elicitation Data Analysis

Using photo elicitation methods, participants take photographs and participate in a facilitated group discussion. Similarly, the researcher may empower the participants to select scenes to photograph and use the resulting images as a discussion point to elicit conversation. The goal of the discussion is to identify main issues, themes, or theories that arise through the discussion (Berg, 2004). It is a facilitated discussion in which participants describe the photos as a group. Wang and Redwood-Jones (2001) provided a framework for discussion that they termed "SHOWeD": "These questions were set around the mnemonic 'SHOWeD': What do you *S*ee here? What is really *H*appening? How does this relate to *O*ur lives? *W*hy does this problem or strength *e*xist? What can we *D*o about it?" (p. 562). The researcher may use this framework as a basis but should remain flexible as the discussion evolves. The general idea is that the ensuing group discussion will clarify meaning and ultimately

TABLE 19.1   Example Two-Column Transcription for Analysis of Video

Audio	Visual Features of the Image
Enter the verbatim transcription with time points, depending on the unit of analysis. For example:	Note visual features for the corresponding time points. For example:
1:00: transcribed text	1:00: background, camera angle, people in scene, etc.
2:00:	2:00:
3:00:	3:00:

lead to richer data. In their study of community development workers in Uganda, Bananuka and John (2015) noted that the photographs elicited "deep, reflective and authentic discussions" (p. 10).

As a photovoice researcher, you then analyze data arising through the discussion. This requires recording and transcribing the discussion. Coding and analysis then follow the typical technique to analyze the text of the transcript. A thematic text analysis involves identifying segments of text that have meaning and assigning codes to those segments. In the write-up, you should note which photographs were selected for discussion and why. With appropriate permission, you might consider including some of the photographs in the findings section to better convey the study to the reader.

SUMMARY

The skill introduced in this chapter is to develop an understanding of the types of and analysis procedures for visual data that may be useful in qualitative research. Photographs, videos, film, and drawings represent types of visual data. These forms of image data represent a powerful tool to capture records in today's visual world. These types of data can be collected by gathering existing images, having the researcher generate images, and having participants develop images. Such data collection involves the participants' taking pictures, using pictures as elicitation in an interview, using the pictures to generate dialogue about the pictures, or having participants draw pictures. In all of these data collection procedures, potential drawbacks and ethical concerns need to be observed. Analyzing images depends on the type of data collected. Analysis might take the form of observational techniques, semiotic approaches of describing what the images denote and the significance of the images, analysis of images and sound in videos, and video elicitation approaches.

ACTIVITIES

1. Go to this Web site: http://www.nytimes.com/ interactive/2010/11/07/sports/20101107-nyc-marathon-faces.html?emc=eta1. Practice coding photographs of runners at the finish line of the 2010 New York City marathon. Go through all 99 pictures and develop 5 to 10 code words that describe what you see. Collapse these code words into themes and then write a short passage about the evidence you have gathered from the pictures. Title the short passage to tell the story of the faces from the 2010 marathon.

2. A science education colleague of mine asked students to "draw a science teacher." (see Thomas & Pedersen, 2003; Thomas, Pedersen, & Finson, 2001). Code the following two pictures using the eight steps of coding visual data advanced in this chapter.

FURTHER RESOURCES

For further information on images and video in qualitative research, see:

Prosser, J. (2011). Visual methodology: Toward a more seeing research. In N. K. Denzin & Y. S. Lincoln (Eds.), *The SAGE handbook of qualitative research* (4th ed., pp. 479–496). Thousand Oaks, CA: Sage.

Two references discuss using pictures to understand science teacher preparation:

Thomas, J. A., & Pedersen, J. E. (2003). Reforming elementary science teachers preparation: What about extant teaching beliefs? *School Science and Mathematics, 103*(7), 319–330.

Thomas, J. A., Pedersen, J. E., & Finson, K. (2001). Validating the Draw-a-Science-Teacher-Test Checklist (DASTT-C): Negotiating mental models and teacher beliefs. *Journal of Science Teacher Education, 12*(4), 295–310.

For photovoice, Wang and Burris (1997) provided an excellent introduction:

Wang, C., & Burris, M. A. (1997). Photovoice: Concept, methodology, and use for participatory needs assessment. *Health Education & Behavior, 24*(3), 369–387.

Additional discussion and specific strategies for analysis of video and film can be found in:

Rose, D. (2000). Analysis of moving images. In M. W. Bauer & G. Gaskell (Eds.), *Qualitative research with text, image and sound: A practical handbook* (pp. 246–262). London: Sage Ltd.

Visit study.sagepub.com/30skills for quizzes, eFlashcards, and more!

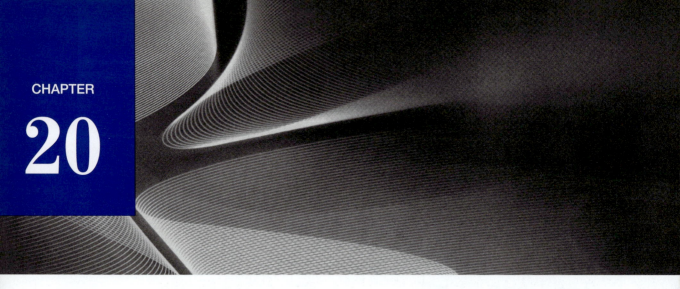

Developing Theme Passages

Skill

Write themes that capture the evidence for participants, codes, and quotations into your findings.

Why the Skill Is Important

Themes are the major findings in a qualitative study. Qualitative data tend to be dense data, and we cannot use all the information we gather. Consequently, we take the data, such as transcripts of interviews, and collapse them into codes during our qualitative data analysis. However, in a qualitative database, especially a large one consisting of many pages of text, we will have many codes, and these cannot all be reported in the findings of a study. We must collapse the codes into themes. These themes represent the "findings" in a qualitative study, and as I have mentioned earlier, we identify a small number of themes (say five to seven) and write passages about each one of them. The most popular form of analyzing text data is a thematic analysis (Kuckartz, 2014), although others may be found in the literature, such as analyzing data into a priori evaluative categories, or into typologies. A thematic approach will be taken here, and the challenge now becomes how to actually write a theme passage. Thus, it is important to learn about several aspects of this theme passage—how it relates to the overall data analysis procedure, what components go into it, and an illustration of what a final theme passage in a qualitative study looks like.

Four Levels of Evidence in Qualitative Data Analysis

A theme in a qualitative study presents evidence for the central phenomenon in the study. In qualitative data analysis, the raw data provide information you have gathered to help explain your central phenomenon. These data are then coded through the process of reading through the text (or viewing the pictures) and assigning code labels to the text or images. This process I described in Chapters 18 and 19. I further encouraged you to consider "lean coding" and to come up with a small number of codes, such as 20, regardless of the size of your database. These codes are then collapsed into themes, a label is affixed to each theme, and the theme then becomes a subheading in the "findings" section of your qualitative study. Sometimes these themes are related to one another to form a chronological storyline (Plano Clark et al., 2002). These themes might be further aggregated into dimensions or combined into a figure that provides an explanation for the central phenomenon. These dimensions or figures are often found in the discussion section of a qualitative study. In short, the process flows inductively from the data to larger dimensions or figures, with the evidence being collapsed into smaller and smaller units of information during the process of data analysis (see Figure 18.3 for a visual of this process). Thus, I see the evidence you gather collapsing into four levels, as shown in Figure 20.1: the raw data, the codes, the themes, and larger dimensions or figures.

> A good theme passage in a study contains a theme label, multiple codes, quotations, and multiple sources of information.

Elements to Write Into Themes

The basic idea of writing a theme passage is to present the complexity of a theme on the basis of evidence collected during a study. I see this theme passage as having several components:

FIGURE 20.1   Four Levels of Evidence Used in Qualitative Data Analysis

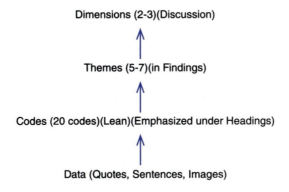

Dimensions (2-3)(Discussion)

↑

Themes (5-7)(in Findings)

↑

Codes (20 codes)(Lean)(Emphasized under Headings)

↑

Data (Quotes, Sentences, Images)

- A theme label that is clear and conceptually interesting

- Multiple codes that provide evidence for the theme

- Quotations that offer the voices of participants and add realism to the theme passage

- Views from multiple participants in the study (or from multiple sources of information)

It should be helpful to first see a complete theme passage with these parts. Recall that in Chapter 18, I provided an example of a theme passage with these parts that related to the theme of "safety" from my study of a campus reaction to a gunman (Asmussen & Creswell, 1995). In Figure 20.2, I change the illustration but convey similar parts that I mentioned earlier and then elaborate on each part. This passage on tobacco use by adolescents was found in the "findings" of a journal article (Plano Clark et al., 2002).

Theme Labels

A theme label is similar to a code label and perhaps more important because it needs to stand on its own in the findings section of a study and be easily understood by readers. The themes become subheadings in the findings section of a qualitative report. The best theme label would be an "in vivo" label—a short phrase mentioned by one of the participants. A theme label would not be the same as the central phenomenon being explored; indeed, the themes help explain or show evidence for the central phenomenon. This theme label could be placed in a findings section surrounded by quotation marks to signal to a reader that the theme represents the exact words used by participants in a study. This label should be short and easily understood by readers. It could have two parts, with the first consisting of words from a participant and the second based on the overall meaning of the words. It should not be so broad that its meaning is lost, for example, "Personal Experiences." Think about conveying to readers conceptually interesting theme labels in your study. Here are a few examples of what I have found to be interesting labels that would encourage me to read on in a project. These examples illustrate a two-part theme label, the use of questions, and a label that creates reader interest:

Example 1

Theme labels in a pilot study exploring the cultural construction of egg donation through women donor narratives (K. Brockhage, personal communication, December 2014):

- "Why would you want someone else to have your child?" The importance of genetics

- "Everything was natural except for a small, little scientific procedure" Discourses that reinforce nontraditional conception and motherhood

FIGURE 20.2   **Example of a Theme Passage in the Findings Section of a Journal Article**

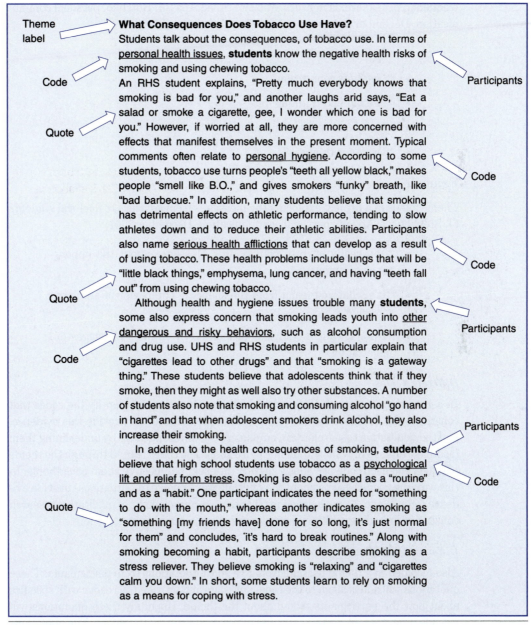

Theme label →

What Consequences Does Tobacco Use Have?
Students talk about the consequences, of tobacco use. In terms of personal health issues, **students** know the negative health risks of smoking and using chewing tobacco.

Code

An RHS student explains, "Pretty much everybody knows that smoking is bad for you," and another laughs arid says, "Eat a salad or smoke a cigarette, gee, I wonder which one is bad for

Quote

you." However, if worried at all, they are more concerned with effects that manifest themselves in the present moment. Typical comments often relate to personal hygiene. According to some students, tobacco use turns people's "teeth all yellow black," makes people "smell like B.O.," and gives smokers "funky" breath, like "bad barbecue." In addition, many students believe that smoking has detrimental effects on athletic performance, tending to slow athletes down and to reduce their athletic abilities. Participants also name serious health afflictions that can develop as a result of using tobacco. These health problems include lungs that will be "little black things," emphysema, lung cancer, and having "teeth fall out" from using chewing tobacco.

Quote

    Although health and hygiene issues trouble many **students**, some also express concern that smoking leads youth into other dangerous and risky behaviors, such as alcohol consumption and drug use. UHS and RHS students in particular explain that

Code

"cigarettes lead to other drugs" and that "smoking is a gateway thing." These students believe that adolescents think that if they smoke, then they might as well also try other substances. A number of students also note that smoking and consuming alcohol "go hand in hand" and that when adolescent smokers drink alcohol, they also increase their smoking.

    In addition to the health consequences of smoking, **students** believe that high school students use tobacco as a psychological lift and relief from stress. Smoking is also described as a "routine" and as a "habit." One participant indicates the need for "something

Quote

to do with the mouth," whereas another indicates smoking as "something [my friends have] done for so long, it's just normal for them" and concludes, "it's hard to break routines." Along with smoking becoming a habit, participants describe smoking as a stress reliever. They believe smoking is "relaxing" and "cigarettes calm you down." In short, some students learn to rely on smoking as a means for coping with stress.

Participants

Code

Code

Participants

Participants

Code

Source: Plano Clark et al. (2002).

Example 2

Theme labels in a pilot study exploring the virtual climate among individuals who frequent a pro–anorexia nervosa Web site called Ana (M. Butchko, personal communication, December 2014):

- "In it to win it"
- "Need for connection"
- "Feeling and thinking 'fat'"
- "Love/hate relationship with Ana"
- "Drive for thinness"

Example 3

Theme labels in a project exploring the messages from advisers to doctoral students (J. Stephenson-Abeetz, personal communication, December 2001):

- "You really have to plan it out": Messages about the importance of timing
- "It's what you learn from the silence": The power of ambient messages
- "I don't want my advisor to look down on me": Messages of negotiation

Different Codes

In a good theme passage, the reader should be able to easily identify the codes that constitute the evidence for the themes. Multiple codes often provide this evidence, and the qualitative researcher can emphasize the different codes by underlining them (as I have done in my illustration in Figure 20.1). The codes thread through the theme passage, and each code provides a slightly different perspective about each theme. In this way, the reader learns about the multiple ways people (or situations) provide evidence for a theme. As we learned in Chapter 1, a core element of qualitative research consists of providing multiple perspectives about a central phenomenon.

Different Quotations

Also included in a theme passage would be short quotations from participants. These quotations will add realism to the theme passage and provide the reader with specifics about how the participants talked about the theme. Hopefully these quotations will provide different perspectives and add to the complexity of the theme. The quotations need to be short, and typically I include short phrases instead of complete sentences or paragraphs. These quotations are set in quotation marks to highlight that they are the words of participants. I try to draw in quotations from different individuals to add variety. Sometimes the quotations can be arrayed one after another to illustrate different perspectives, as shown in this example where team members commented on how face-to-face meetings affected the workings of a team (K. James, personal communication, December 2011):

> "Group meetings were good and needed to be more. When you're alone in your office it is easy to get distracted so face-to-face is much more effective."

> "Continue funding for future projects so that face-to-face opportunities are a possibility and a necessity."

> "Face-to-face is always the best. It allows for ideas to be bounced around better."

During the process of reviewing transcripts, I try to identify quotations that will illustrate the codes and then the themes. In observing, I like to capture what people are saying and keep in mind the use of the quotations to provide detailed evidence for my themes.

Different Individuals

In Figure 20.1, I also included perspectives from different individuals or different sources of data. If a qualitative project unfolds with the collection of multiple data sources, I try to include evidence from each data source in the theme passage. Information from interviews, from observations, from documents, and from visual materials will be included in my theme passage. These multiple sources of information will also provide multiple perspectives for my theme passage.

A Table That Organizes Themes, Codes, and Quotations

Because there are many codes in a qualitative project and they are aggregated into themes and illustrated with quotations, qualitative researchers often present in their "findings" sections tables that show an overview of the interrelationship among these three aspects of research. In Table 20.1, I provide an illustration of a sample table that a student developed in a pilot project on the motivation of college-age students to drink alcohol (C. Temmen, personal communication, December 2014).

In this table you can identify multiple codes for each theme and several examples of quotations that accurately reflect the codes and themes.

TABLE 20.1	An Illustrative Table for Presenting the Themes, Codes, and Quotations in a Qualitative Findings Section

Themes	Codes	Examples of Quotations
Drinking to socialize	Social environment	"I drink about half the time I'm in a big social environment. Like a house party I'll usually drink, besides that it doesn't matter."
Drinking to relieve stress	Week activities	"It was such a stressful week because we had been planning and there was more alcohol than I thought there would be."
Drinking to relax	Before sleep	"I'll have a gin and tonic or something before I go to bed sometimes. It really helps. It's relaxing."
Drinking because of curiosity	Finding out for myself	"I am gonna find out for myself. So I did."
Drinking to feel a sense of community	Connections	"You kind of have like this weird connection with everyone else that you're with."

SUMMARY

Qualitative themes are the results or findings in a study that present evidence for the central phenomenon. The process of deriving themes comes from analyzing the raw data (e.g., interview transcriptions, observational field notes), collapsing the raw data into a reasonable set of codes (say 20), aggregating the codes into a small number of themes (say five to seven), using the themes in a findings section as subtopics (or subheadings), and then possibly further grouping the themes into dimensions or figures. The elements that go into a good theme passage are a theme label that is conceptually interesting, multiple codes to provide evidence for the theme, specific quotations to further add information about the theme, and the views of different sources of information (participants, observations, and so forth).

ACTIVITY

Look at a theme passage in a published qualitative journal article. Underline the following elements: the codes, the participants, and the quotations. Reflect on whether the theme label is interesting and would encourage you to read about the theme.

FURTHER RESOURCES

Bazeley, P. (2013). *Qualitative data analysis: Practical strategies*. London: Sage Ltd.

Kuckartz, U. (2014). *Qualitative text analysis: A guide to methods, practice and using software*. London: Sage Ltd.

Visit study.sagepub.com/30skills for quizzes, eFlashcards, and more!

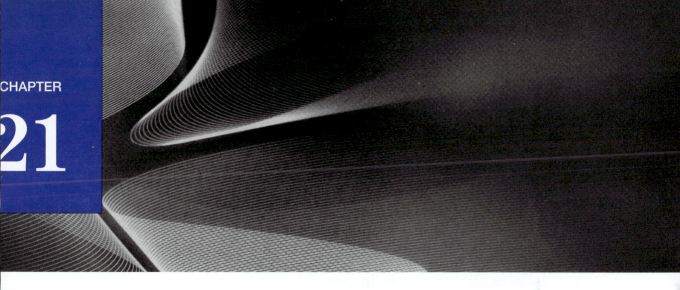

Using a Computer Software Program for Data Analysis

Skill

Use qualitative software to store, organize, and assist in your qualitative data analysis and report writing.

Why the Skill Is Important

Qualitative data analysis (QDA) software has been around since the late 1980s. Several commercial programs exist. The use of these programs by qualitative researchers has been extensive, and new features develop each year so that these programs have grown in capability and utility. They improve over the traditional method of creating transcripts or field notes and then manually marking passages with pen and paper or with colored markers. In one of my early qualitative projects, I collected about 200 interviews that each lasted about 1 hour. I ended up with several thousand pages of transcripts. We then used scissors to cut the typed transcripts into segments, pasted them on three-by-five index cards, and then posted the cards on the four walls of a large room. I had 10 qualitative researchers helping me in this process. To this day, I am not sure I understood the information in our database. I wish I would have had QDA software to help store and sort through the database.

QDA programs are useful for storing your database, finding relevant evidence in the database for the codes and themes, analyzing how different participants spoke about different topics, and visualizing your information in concept maps. Furthermore,

QDA programs help you keep your data organized, help locate material, and provide useful concept maps.

these programs are not expensive to purchase, and they are relatively easy to learn to use. In order to use them, you need to know what programs are available, how they relate to your data analysis procedure, how they might assist you in developing various parts of your qualitative study, and possible steps you might take in conducting analysis using one of the programs. Because specific QDA software quickly becomes obsolete, and new features appear frequently, this discussion will not focus on specific software packages or on screen shots and procedures used within a program. Instead, I will provide a general overview of QDA software that you can use in analyzing your qualitative data and writing your report.

Using QDA Software in the Data Analysis and Report Writing Phases

The processes of data collection, data analysis, code and theme development, and writing are all interactive processes. You may be engaged in all of these steps simultaneously as you conduct your study. It is helpful, however, to consider where QDA software fits into the process of research. As I discussed in earlier chapters, you will collect qualitative data and prepare them for analysis. This analysis process consists of exploring the database to gain a general sense of it, coding the database by tagging segments of text (or images) and assigning code labels, combining the codes into themes, and then reporting the themes as headings in the findings of your qualitative report. QDA software helps in the data analysis and report writing phases of your research. Examine Table 21.1. In this table, you can see that the software program will help you in the coding process, the codebook development phase (and intercoder agreement checks; see Chapter 23), and the report writing processes of developing a storyline, finding useful quotations, summarizing information and building theories, and assembling a geographical location profile for participants.

Should You Use QDA Software?

I recommend that you use a QDA software program to assist in your data analysis. The software does not do the analysis for you—it simply assists in the process. QDA software is useful even if you have an extremely small qualitative database, such as 100 pages of text. It helps you store your data so that you can easily find them. It provides an easy way to search a large database and find useful quotations and evidence for your codes and themes. It enables you to diagram a concept map that links your codes and themes. It allows you to relate your themes to geographical locations. In addition to managing the large volume of qualitative data, QDA software can help you work with a team of researchers. It is easy to collaborate with others by dividing documents (or images) among multiple individuals using the same codebook. You can then compile everyone's analysis to write the report.

TABLE 21.1   Uses of QDA Software in the Qualitative Research Process

Process of Qualitative Research	How the QDA Program Helps You	What Phase of the Qualitative Research Process This Helps
Coding process	Counts the frequency of use of words	Identifying important words to be selected for codes
	Creates a list of codes and organizes the codes into themes (or categories)	Continually reviewing your codes and the evidence being built for your themes Writing notes (i.e., memos) about your coding Limiting your codes in "lean coding" Establishing headings for your themes in the findings of your study
	Identify phrases useful for "in vivo" coding	Identifying phrases that then can be created as codes in the code list
	Work with a team of coders	Splitting data among multiple coders and easily bringing coded data back together
Code and theme evidence	Search and retrieve all text that relates to a code	Providing multiple perspectives on a code for your qualitative write-up
Codebook development	Write memos and comments helping define a code	Developing a qualitative codebook (see Chapter 23) that includes codes and their definitions
Intercoder agreement	Numbers the lines of the text so that multiple coders can compare coded segments	Finding text and codes during intercoder agreement checks Calculating intercoder agreement
Comparing groups	Search and retrieve information about subgroups	Comparing how different subgroups (e.g., gender, age, location) speak about codes or themes
Writing the storyline	Develop a concept map of your codes or themes	Identifying a storyline that links your codes Seeing the progression of codes from an interview or observation Developing a theoretical model
Providing rich quotations as evidence	Identify, search, and retrieve phrases that are useful quotations	Inserting quotations into theme passages as additional evidence Seeing the breadth of quotations across participants and data sources
Theory building Summarizing cases	Creates memos of various types	Developing a theory or case summaries (Kuckartz, 2014)
Developing a geographical profile	Link your codes to geospatial locations	Linking how people speak about a code or theme in different geographic areas

Note: QDA = qualitative data analysis.

I realize that some researchers are hesitant to use QDA software (as mentioned by Hesse-Biber & Leavy, 2006). It does require learning how to use a new computer program, although QDA software is not difficult to learn through the demonstration copies you can get online. It places between you and the database a physical object—the computer—that may seem like an interfering third party in your data analysis. In our digital world, however, we are all becoming used to computers, laptops, e-readers, and phones that stand between the physical world and us. It may seem like QDA software structures your data analysis too much and interferes with the creative process at work. This structure may make it seem like you are using quantitative research processes. For some graduate advisers, for some editors of journals, and for some reviewers for conferences, this structure is seen as providing rigor to your qualitative research.

Major Software Programs Available

As shown in Table 21.2, there are several QDA packages from which to choose. These programs have all emerged during the past 25 years, and they have been developed in different countries, such as the United States, Germany, and Australia. A demonstration copy of a program can be obtained online, and I would recommend that you select a software program and download the demonstration copy to try out the features of the program. Some of the companies produce videos to accompany the demonstration copies. Today, most of these programs are formatted for both the PC and Mac platforms. Some even have mobile versions that work on tablets and phones. Costs vary among the programs, although the pricing structure is somewhat similar across the different products, and discounts are available for graduate students. Most of the programs will accept text data files as well as video or image files, and their Web sites provide overviews of the major features of the programs.

How Do You Choose a QDA Program?

Several factors go into your choice of qualitative software (Creswell & Maietta, 2002). First and foremost, you need to be comfortable with the program after you try out the demonstration copy. This means that you need to be at ease with the features of the program, the documentation available for the program, and the tasks the program will accomplish. You can look at Table 21.2 and see some of the capabilities of the programs you might need in coding and writing your qualitative report. Beyond this, you can look into costs, the programs that are popular on your campus, and what programs faculty and faculty advisers use. You might order one of the specific books aimed at the use of a specific software program and read through the details about how to use the program. However, having offered these points, I must admit that all of the software programs provide generally similar features. In

TABLE 21.2   **Alternative QDA Software Programs**

Computer Program	Company	Demo/ Free Trial	Platform	Text/Image Analysis	Key Features
ATLAS.ti 7	ATLAS. ti Scientific Software Development GmbH (http:// atlasti.com)	Yes (unlimited with maximum of 10 documents and 50 codes)	Windows/ Mac/iOS/ Android	Yes	The first QDA tool to create a platform for the universal exchange, storage, and processing of QDA data Exports complete data to virtually any application Supports an open, universal data format and publishes its data structure
Dedoose	UCLA and the William T. Grant Foundation (http://www .dedoose.com)	Yes (1-month free trial)	NA	Yes	Explicitly aimed at facilitating rigorous qualitative and mixed methods research; Web based, low cost, and collaborative nature Many interactive data visualizations
Ethnograph 6.0	Qualis Research (http:// qualisresearch .com)	Yes (unlimited with up to 3 projects and 3 data files)	Windows	No image analysis	Analyzing text-based qualitative data Straightforward, easy to use
Hyper RESEARCH	ResearchWare, Inc. (http://www .researchware .com)	Yes (unlimited with up to 7 cases and 75 codes)	Windows/ Mac	Yes (text, images, audio, and video)	Easy-to-use interface Flexible methodologies Multilingual text support Code mapping Multimedia capabilities
MAXQDA 11	VERBI GmbH (http://www .maxqda.com)	Yes (1-month free trial)	Windows/ Mac/iOS/ Android	Yes (text, images, audio, and video)	Document input Coding Personal attributes Searching Creating maps License exchange

(Continued)

TABLE 21.2   (Continued)

Computer Program	Company	Demo/ Free Trial	Platform	Text/Image Analysis	Key Features
NVivo 10	QSR International (http://www .qsrinternational .com)	Yes (1-month free trial)	Windows (full support)/ Mac (partial support)	Yes (Windows— text, images, audio, and video)	Importing, creating and editing a wide range of data Transcription services Capturing and analyzing online data
QDA Miner Full 4.1	Provalis Research (http:// provalisresearch .com/products/ qualitative-data-analysis-software/)	Yes (QDA Miner Lite 1.3, Windows only, partially functional)	Windows/ Mac (virtual machine solution or Boot Camp is needed)	Yes	On screen coding and annotation of texts and images Memoing and hyperlinking Geotagging and time tagging Statistics and visualization Mixed methods and QDA software
Qualrus	Idea Works, Inc. (http://www .qualrus.com)	Yes (unlimited, fully functional, the project cannot be saved)	Windows	Yes (text, images, audio, and video)	Quick learning curve Unparalleled coding efficiency Powerful scripting language

Note: NA = not available; QDA = qualitative data analysis.

my research office, we use MAXQDA because it has good documentation, support, available videos, and the concept mapping feature.

What Are the Steps in Using QDA Software?

When I use QDA software, I generally follow the steps outlined below. These may work for you or may need to be modified.

Step 1: Consider the Output of the Program to Place in My Qualitative Report

I first consider how I am going to use the results of the software program in my qualitative project. I will refer to Table 21.1 to explore ways I can use the output from the program.

Step 2: Identify What Is a "Document"

Typically I look across documents in my database to form codes and themes. Thus, each interview would be a document, or each observation or written note or letter would be a document. I will be asking myself, What are the codes and themes that cross all of these documents? I may want to peer into one document by itself, so each interview, for example, would constitute a document.

Step 3: Name My Project and Enter the Documents

Once I have decided on specific QDA software, I need to provide a name for my project. Once that is done, I need import my documents. These may be text documents or image (photo or video) documents. If I have conducted 30 interviews, I will import into the program 30 documents.

Step 4: Provide Characteristics for Each Document

I think about the individual providing each document (or the site or place where I obtained the document). I would add into the program the characteristics of each document, such as, for an individual interview, the demographics of the interviewee (such as gender, age, and education background), geographic location of the interview, duration of the interview, and so forth. Later I may want to compare women and men with respect to a theme, and I could ask the software program to give me only information about women and the theme, and then only about men and the theme. In other words, I may want to cross-tabulate demographic information with themes or with codes. This requires setting up information in the program for each document.

Step 5: Coding the Documents

I pull up each document one by one and go through the document bracketing text or pictures and assigning code labels to the text or picture segments. This begins to create my codebook, and I can start grouping my codes into themes so that I have a list of codes and themes. As I go through each of my documents, I am trying to add to my code list when I find new information that I code differently than the codes on my list. I see this as a process of developing initially, say, 30 to 50 codes that can be reduced to about 20. I may go through the database several times and check and record new codes, but basically I am using "lean" coding procedures. I would also organize these codes around five to seven themes in my list. With the software, you can add a memo to the code that includes a description of the code or theme or any other notes you have. You can later retrieve just this information to insert into your report.

Step 6: Retrieve Information About Each Code

In my write-up of my project, I want to provide multiple codes to support a theme, and multiple forms of evidence to support a code. You may recall that this process was modeled in Figure 20.2, where I presented a theme passage and pointed out the multiple codes in it. I will thus use the retrieved information about each code in my actual write-up of the final study.

Step 7: Pull Out Quotations for My Research Narrative

As I code my text or image documents, I will create a special code for "quotations." Every time I find a passage—typically a short passage—that provides useful quotable material, I will code the passage with my "quotations" code. In this way, I can retrieve all of the passages I have coded as "quotations" and see if they can be inserted into my qualitative report as additional, specific evidence for themes.

Step 8: Comparisons of Personal Characteristics and Codes

At this point I may be curious as to how different types of people or different observations led to differences in describing the codes or themes. So I will identify, for example, all women to see how they reported on a code and how men all responded to the same code.

Step 9: Map the Relationships Among Codes or Themes

At this point I can place my codes and themes into a concept map to see how they are interrelated. Perhaps the map might show a chronological development of the codes as the interviews progressed, or a linear unfolding of themes as I explored the topic with participants. I am quite partial to visual diagrams for my qualitative projects, and I often like to include more in my studies than simply a report of the themes. So I often look at my themes and see if they can be better presented in a chronology over time.

Many other features of software programs can be used, such as writing memos, or writing summaries as you proceed to make sense of your codes and themes. Special topics relate to using visual materials, using hyperlinks, different types of visualization in the mapping features, running frequencies on the use of words, working with teams, and conducting reliability checks (i.e., intercoder agreement, to be discussed in Chapter 23) with multiple coders. In these steps that I have indicated, these are basic procedures that have worked well for me.

SUMMARY

Qualitative data analysis software enables you to organize and store your data, search through a database and locate evidence that supports codes and themes, and conceptually map the relationships among your codes or themes. A QDA program is helpful during the data analysis and the report writing phases of conducting qualitative research. I would recommend that you use a software program, regardless of the size of your database. There are several commercial software programs available, and they provide similar features that might be used on a PC or a Mac. I recommend that you choose a software program after working with the demonstration copy so that you can see firsthand the features of the program. You might also consider what software is used at your site, and your comfort level with all aspects of the software. Once you have selected a QDA software program, you might follow some steps in conducting your analysis. My steps include starting at the end—where and how you plan on using the computer output, then identifying what constitutes a "document" in your study, entering the documents in the software, attaching to each document some characteristics of it that might be compared later with your themes, coding the documents and retrieving segments of information as well as quotations to be used in your final report, and then developing a visual map of the codes or themes that can represent a diagram in your final project.

ACTIVITY

Select a software program and use it to analyze one document (preferably a text document) on a topic of your choice. Go through the nine steps I have suggested for you to use. Identify specifically how you will use the output for the coding process and for writing the final report based on Table 21.2.

FURTHER RESOURCES

For a good discussion of qualitative computer software see:

Hesse-Biber, S. N., & Leavy, P. (2006). *Emergent methods in social research*. Thousand Oaks, CA: Sage.

Silver, C. & Lewins, A. (2014). *Using software in qualitative research: A step-by-step guide* (2nd ed.). Thousand Oaks, CA: Sage.

For books on specific QDA software programs, see:

For MAXQDA:

Kuckartz, U. (2014). *Qualitative text analysis: A guide to methods, practice and using software*. Thousand Oaks, CA: Sage.

For NVivo:

Richards, L., & Morse, J. M. (2012). *Readme first for a user's guide to qualitative methods* (3rd ed.). Thousand Oaks, CA: Sage.

Bazeley, P., & Jackson, K. (2013). *Qualitative data analysis with NVivo* (2nd ed.). London: Sage Ltd.

Visit study.sagepub.com/30skills for quizzes, eFlashcards, and more!

Implementing Validity Checks

Skill

Use multiple validity checks in your qualitative project.

Why the Skill Is Important

Unquestionably, qualitative research is "interpretive" research, where the inquirer makes a personal interpretation of information. With open-ended research questions, and the generation of text data, the researcher needs to make sense of the data, and to code and provide code labels that seem to characterize the text of information. Alternatively, a researcher may read through a document and assign codes or examine field notes taken during an observation and again assign codes. Because the process of asking questions and analyzing the data requires a personal interpretation, the qualitative researcher needs to pay close attention to validating the findings. Often people will trust the conclusions of a study if they know that the results are accurate and resonate with the participants in a study. In this way, qualitative research becomes more than simply the personal interpretation of the author.

What Is Validity in Qualitative Research?

In *quantitative research*, validity means that good underlying measures are gathered (i.e., construct validity), that the measures represent a good sampling of measures from the universe of possibilities (i.e., content validity), that the information has statistical use (i.e. statistical conclusion validity) and practical use (i.e., consequential validity), that inferences drawn are meaningful (i.e., construct validity), and that results can be generalized to other settings and populations (i.e., external validity). In quantitative research, validity is a centerpiece of doing good, rigorous research. In *qualitative research,* on the other hand, validity means something different. In short, it means that the findings are accurate (or are plausible). You can assess this accuracy through the eyes of the researcher, through the views of participants, and by readers and reviewers of studies (Creswell & Miller, 2000). Over the years, a number of qualitative validity lenses have developed, such as Lincoln and Guba's (1985) evaluative criteria of credibility, transferability, dependability, and confirmability. Others advance terms such as *ironic validity* (Lather, 1993, p. 21). Richardson (1994) likened validity to a prism in which the crystals reflect external light as well as refract within themselves. In brief, validity has multiple perspectives. Novice researchers can understandably be lost in all of the terms and approaches that have surfaced in recent years.

Types of Validity in Qualitative Research

Amid these perspectives, the stance I have taken (and it still seems to hold) is that validity lenses (i.e., researcher, participants, readers, and reviewers) differ depending on the philosophical orientation of the researcher. I think of validity as establishing the accuracy of the account. If researchers are more postpositivist, they will engage in more systematic and rigorous approaches, such as triangulation, member checking, and auditing. Individuals with more of a constructivist orientation will use disconfirming evidence, prolonged engagement, and thick, rich description. Those inquirers taking a more partici-

> Use multiple validity strategies to assess the accuracy of your interpretations.

patory or critical perspective will embrace research reflexivity, collaboration, and peer debriefing. These validity procedures arrayed against worldview or paradigm assumptions are shown in Table 22.1.

The Researcher's Lens

Researchers check the accuracy of a qualitative account. *Triangulation* refers to building evidence from different sources to establish the themes in a study. The term comes from military navigation at sea, where sailors drew on different sources or points of information to determine their ship's bearing. These sources can be from different sources of information (Denzin, 1978), such as from interview transcriptions and typed field notes. The sources can also be from different individuals providing interview information. It can also be from different investigators and from different theories. In qualitative research, triangulation naturally occurs during the process of coding, in which the inquirer looks across different sources of information, such as documents, and finds evidence for themes.

TABLE 22.1	Different Lenses and Philosophical Assumptions in Qualitative Research		
Philosophical Assumption and Lens	**Postpositivist or Systematic Assumptions**	**Constructivist Assumptions**	**Critical/Participatory Assumptions**
Researcher	Triangulation	Disconfirming evidence	Researcher reflexivity
Study participants	Member checking	Prolonged engagement in the field	Collaboration with participants
Report readers and reviewers	External audit	Thick, rich description	Peer debriefing

Source: Adapted from Creswell and Miller (2000, p. 126).

The researcher may also look for *disconfirming evidence*. The process involves having the researcher first establish a theme, and then look through all of the evidence for exceptions to this theme. This is evidence that presents an alternative explanation for a theme. It should not overwhelm the theme (or the theme may not work), but it adds an exception to the body of evidence that provides support for the theme. The importance of disconfirming evidence is that it helps establish a realistic (and accurate) picture of the theme. Evidence for a theme is more realistic because typically all evidence does not point toward a theme—there is usually some information that suggests a contrary picture of the theme. In practice, the qualitative researcher writes the disconfirming evidence into a theme passage as a minor part of the theme passage.

Researchers can also reflect on how their experiences and backgrounds have an impact on shaping their accounts. By sharing these biases and beliefs, the accounts become more accurate. This is called *reflexivity*, and I devote an entire chapter to it (Chapter 26). At this point, however, we need to acknowledge that a qualitative account becomes more valid if we know the biases and beliefs the researcher brings to the study and how these biases and beliefs shape the researcher's interpretation. This account can be written into a methods section, typically in a passage headed "role of the researcher."

The Participants' Lens

Another important validity check can come from the participants in the study—the individuals being studied. One approach to learning about the participants' views is through *member checking*. Member checking is when the researcher takes back to participants their themes or entire stories and asks the participants whether the themes or stories are an accurate representation of what they said. The information taken back, thus, is not the interview transcriptions or the field notes, but rather broader summary statements about the data, such as the themes or the discussion of the overall story. The way the researcher can use this strategy is typically through a focus group led by the researcher, who asks open-ended questions to determine if the themes or stories are accurate. One-on-one interviews may also be conducted. Regardless of the method, the questions can focus on whether the account is accurate, what themes are missing, and what participants disagree with. If the account is not found to be accurate, then the researcher revises the themes to better portray the views of the participants.

Another way to learn if the account is accurate with participants is to use extended or *prolonged engagement in the field*. The idea here is that the more time the researcher spends in the field, the more accurate will be the inquirer's account. How much time will vary from study to study, but if the researcher has the opportunity to spend several months in the setting being studied, the codes, themes, quotations, and overall storyline will be enhanced. There is no magical amount of time for involvement in the field, and the time may depend on the researcher's time, the amount of time allowed by participants, and financial and scheduling factors. In the methods discussion, qualitative researchers often report on the extent of their data collection and especially on the amount of time they spend with participants. Staying in the field for a lengthy time provides an opportunity to check codes, themes, and the story with participants and to modify them, if needed.

In much qualitative research, the investigators check in with participants and involve them in key decisions in the research process. Thus, another strategy to help establish the accuracy of a study is to *collaborate with participants*. This collaboration can stretch from minimum involvement to extensive involvement in all phases of the research process. The idea is to build support for the study and the use of its findings. Collaboration may include asking participants to help form the research questions to be asked of people, assisting in the analysis of the text or image data, or reflecting on the findings and forming recommendations for action. At a more formal level, this collaboration may be called "community-based participatory research" or involving the participants as "co-researchers" in a project.

The Readers' or Reviewers' Lens

A final form of validity comes from when a reviewer or reader feels that the qualitative account is accurate. A qualitative inquirer may hire someone to conduct an external audit of all aspects of a project, thus providing an "outside" review of the accuracy of the study. In Chapter 24, attention will be paid to the process of conducting an audit. But for purposes of this discussion, validity is enhanced when someone outside of a project looks closely at it and helps determine that the information is accurate and that the study is done in a rigorous way. The way this works is for the researcher to hire an individual to conduct an audit of the entire project. This external auditor reviews all materials from the study, from the design of the project to the final results. After concluding this audit, the auditor compiles a report of the accuracy of the study, and this report may be filed (e.g., in an appendix in a dissertation) for others to review.

Also provided for the reader is a detailed, *rich description* of the setting, the people, and the themes in a qualitative report. This discussion has the effect of transporting readers into an actual setting, where they can smell, feel, and hear people. This transporting provides an accurately felt rendering of a study. Thick, rich description is an element of good writing style in qualitative research, and it will be covered more extensively in Chapter 27 on the literary elements of research. We see these rich descriptions when the author provides a small slice of interaction, discusses the settings of the action, or brings interactions among two or more people through dialogue or quotes. This level of detail helps readers actually experience the central phenomenon the researcher is exploring.

Also, for readers and reviewers, we compile our qualitative reports and then have individuals familiar with the subject area or qualitative researchers examine our accounts. *Peer debriefing* is a final strategy that can be used in a study. A peer review or debriefing is the review of a project by someone who is familiar with the research or the central phenomenon being explored. This peer can provide support, play devil's advocate, play challenger, and help refine the study. The peer can ask hard questions and realize that given his or her role as a peer, you might be accommodating of criticism. In practice, these peers may be fellow students or researchers. They may be individuals just like the participants in the study. These peers then write a report summarizing both the strengths and the potential weaknesses of a study so that the researcher can improve the project.

What Validity Strategies Should You Use?

I have reviewed eight different validity strategies and provided names for them so that they can be easily cited. As a general rule, I recommend using two or three strategies in a qualitative project, and you might consider first implementing the easy strategies to conduct and then incorporating, if possible, the more difficult time-consuming procedures. The easy ones to conduct would be triangulation of different data sources, conducting a member-checking analysis by forming a focus group, finding the resources to spend prolonged time in the field and reporting this extensive time, searching for negative case evidence to put into your theme discussion, providing a detailed description of your themes so that the reader is transported to your study site, and clarifying your own personal biases through a passage on reflexivity. More difficult to conduct—and involving other people—would be peer auditing, external auditing, and obviously collaborating with participants. These involve the time, the possible expense, and the expertise of others, adding to the labor involved in conducting qualitative research.

SUMMARY

Many types of qualitative validity exist, and they often present a confusing array of terms and meanings. My approach is that qualitative researchers do need to establish the accuracy (or validity) of their accounts, and that they can do this by using multiple strategies in their projects. These strategies can take different lenses: that of the researcher, the study participants, or the audience for the study.

Researchers could triangulate information, check their reports with participants (i.e., member checking), spend a lengthy time in the field gathering data, report disconfirming evidence for themes, write detailed descriptions of the setting or themes, and clarify their biases in interpretations through reflexivity. They can also conduct more labor-intensive strategies, such as engaging a peer in an audit or having a person outside their project conduct an external audit.

ACTIVITY

Select one of the forms of validity and indicate how it would be implemented in your project.

Discuss what the validity assessment entails, how it would be conducted, what it would bring to your project, and how it might be accepted by study participants.

FURTHER RESOURCES

Often researchers turn to the traditional perspectives on validity established by Lincoln and Guba (1985). These involve credibility, transferability, dependability, and confirmability. An article that addresses these criteria is the following:

Shenton, A. K. (2004). Strategies for ensuring trustworthiness in qualitative research projects. *Education for Information, 22*(2), 63–75.

Also you might look at the article by Creswell and Miller (2000) in which the typology of worldview by lens for validity is discussed in some detail:

Creswell, J. W., & Miller, D. L. (2000). Determining validity in qualitative research. *Theory Into Practice, 39*(3), 124–130. doi:10.1207/s15430421tip3903_2

Visit study.sagepub.com/30skills for quizzes, eFlashcards, and more!

Conducting Intercoder Agreement

Skill

Use intercoder agreement to have an additional coder check the accuracy and reliability of your interpretation.

Why the Skill Is Important

Intercoder agreement provides a means for checking the consistency between two or more researchers as they code a database. Thus, it provides a reliability check in qualitative research. It also adds to the sophistication and rigor of qualitative database analysis because more than one individual's coding scheme is taken into consideration. Thus, it serves as a crosscheck of your coding because someone else is also coding the data and providing his or her interpretation. After all, qualitative data analysis is a highly interpretive process in which you identify appropriate text segments and assign codes that make sense to you.

What Is Intercoder Agreement?

Intercoder agreement is when one or more additional coders analyze a qualitative database, provide codes for the database, and compare the results of coders for the amount of agreement on the codes. This procedure essentially provides a "reliability" check during qualitative data analysis and adds to the rigor of the interpretive process under way in analyzing a qualitative database. Two or more researchers are likely to have different interpretations of the same data and code somewhat differently. It is important then to monitor and discuss codes as part of the analysis process (Richards & Morse, 2013). Kuckartz (2014) recommended attending to intercoder agreement whenever multiple coders are used. For those coming from a quantitative background or seeking to publish their qualitative studies in a field that has been largely quantitative, this reliability check adds credibility and rigor to the qualitative data analysis. Many computer-assisted qualitative data analysis software packages include reliability features whereby you can calculate agreement among different coders. Alternatively, there are procedures that qualitative inquirers have used to conduct intercoder agreement, and you can study their procedures and implement them in your own project.

> Use intercoder agreement to check the consistency of coding text or image data.

Procedures for Conducting Intercoder Agreement

Step 1

You need to find one or more additional coders, individuals who understand qualitative research and coding, to participate in the intercoder agreement process. Many projects involve only one additional coder, although I was involved in a U.S. Department of Veterans Affairs project in which we had four coders (see the third example below).

Step 2

Create a codebook of codes through an initial coding of the database. The basic idea of a qualitative codebook is to have an agreed-upon set of codes and their definitions. Although there is no single way to develop a codebook, I like the codebook organization scheme advanced by Guest, Bunce, and Johnson (2006). An example of their organization using hypothetical data is shown in Table 23.1.

This codebook contains the name of the code, a brief definition and a more extended definition, instances that should and should not be categorized within the code, and one or more sample quotations to illustrate the type of evidence that would

TABLE 23.1 A Sample Codebook Organization Based on Guest, Bunce, and Johnson (2006)

Code	Brief Definition	Full Definition	When to Use	When Not to Use	Sample Quotations
Safety	Whether students felt safe after the incident	Safety as identified through possibility of the incident occurring again, safety in their dorm rooms or on campus	When students actually mention the word *safety* or a synonym	When it cannot be reasonably interpreted as the students' talking about safety or their security	"I was scared for my own safety." "The campus was no longer a safe environment for me or my friends."

be identified for the code. Often this codebook of codes is created by one person and then revised as the process proceeds ahead. The codebook is not a fixed document, but is continually reviewed and clarified for all of the coders.

Step 3

Choose a method for conducting intercoder agreement. Approaches run from an informal process of comparing codes for percentage agreement to a more systematic procedure that involves several steps and uses statistics. Selecting which method to use, a more informal process or a more formal procedure, depends on the norms for your discipline. It might also be decided with eventual publication in mind. For example, do the journals you intended to target describe a process or a specific coefficient of agreement? Later, I provide four examples of procedures used, including the one I used in the Department of Veterans Affairs project. A clear challenge in using intercoder agreement is noted in my passage on this procedure (Creswell, 2013): What unit is the basis for agreement among the coders? Are the coders agreeing on a passage with the exact same code word, a passage with "similar" code words for the same passage, a passage with the same text lines coded or different text lines, or a passage that relates to the same theme? Agreeing on the exact same code word for the same lines of text is a high standard. As you will see from the examples, qualitative researchers differ in how they go about seeking agreement from text passages. My approach is to encourage a procedure that fits the time and resources of the project, and a procedure that is flexible so that the overall intent of determining agreement among different coders can be reasonably obtained. As I will relate in my example below, I like the idea of having multiple coders code the text file, and then selecting several passages where coding occurs and see if the coders all code the passage using the same or a similar version of the code as found in the codebook. This procedure seems to give an agreement perspective between coders without setting the criteria so high that I cannot obtain a good sense of this agreement.

Step 4

Conduct the intercoder agreement using a procedure found in the examples below or some combination of procedures.

Step 5

The final step in the process is to determine if agreement exists. An informal procedure can be used to determine if there is agreement. Miles, Huberman, and Saldaña (2013) recommended striving for 85% to 90% intercoder agreement. Researchers might consider a procedural approach to discuss and resolve coding questions and differences that arise. Some refer to this as a consensual coding process. It does not necessarily mean calculating coefficients. Alternatively, you can use a more rigorous procedure and calculate the coefficient of reliability, the kappa statistic. Cohen's (1960) kappa coefficient is a way to statistically measure the agreement between two individuals. It requires two binary variables, say Individual A and Individual B, and whether they agree or disagree on the code for a particular text segment. A formula exists to determine their degree of agreement minus what could be expected due to chance, resulting in a coefficient that ranges from +1 to –1. Good agreement tends to be a coefficient .60 to .80 and very good agreement from .80 to 1.00 (perfect agreement). This coefficient is often calculated in the health science literature.

Examples of Intercoder Agreement From Informal to More Systematic Procedures

I have selected four examples of procedures qualitative researchers (including myself) have used for conducting intercoder agreement checks. Central to the differences among these approaches are procedures from more informal to formal, the extent to which the codes are discussed and negotiated, the nature of the codebook used in the process, what agreement is based on, and whether percentage agreement or a statistical difference in agreement (a kappa coefficient) was used in the study.

Here is an example of interrater agreement based on negotiating differences. Hopfer and Clippard (2011) studied vaccine decision narratives about human papillomavirus obtained from college women and health clinicians. Interrater agreement followed an informal process, as follows:

> **Step 1:** A second coder was trained to read all of the 38 transcripts and provide an initial response.

> **Step 2:** The two coders met to discuss and negotiate the interpretation of the emerging themes. In this process the second coder was instructed to verify that the data interpretation "rang true" from a college woman's point of view.

> **Step 3:** Both researchers coded the transcripts using a priori domains. The coders met to ensure consistent interpretation of the coding criteria.

> **Step 4:** Data were interpreted for whether the participants' narratives reflected acceptance or resistance.

> **Step 5:** Coder discrepancies on two transcripts were discussed and resolved.

> **Step 6:** Final coder agreement of decision narratives of vaccine acceptance and resistance resulted in a Cohen's kappa coefficient of .92.

In this example we see intercoder agreement using a detailed codebook. Intercoder agreement procedures were used in a study by Guest et al. (2006) examining perceptions of social desirability bias and accuracy of self-reported behavior in the context of reproductive health research in West Africa and Ghana.

Step 1: Two data analysts developed a codebook for six interviews. Each code had a brief definition, a full definition, a "when to use" section, a "when not to use" section, and an example section of quotations.

Step 2: Intercoder agreement was assessed for every third interview, and combined segment-based kappa scores were calculated on two double-coded transcripts.

Step 3: Coding discrepancies receiving kappa scores of .5 or less were discussed and resolved by the analysis team.

Step 4: The codebook was revised and recoding performed to ensure consistent application of codes.

Step 5: Kappa was recalculated, resulting in a score of .82.

This next example illustrates intercoder agreement procedures using mutually coded text segments. We conducted intercoder agreement with four coders in a project at the Veterans Affairs Healthcare System in Ann Arbor, Michigan (Creswell, 2013; L. J. Damschroder, personal communication, March 2006). This project related to the Health Insurance Portability and Accountability Act and how patients viewed the act as they sought health care from Veterans Affairs hospitals.

Step 1: All four coders analyzed three or four interview transcripts. We developed a preliminary codebook that contained a definition of each code and sample text segments that related to each code.

Step 2: We then coded three additional transcripts. We looked at the passages where we had all provided code labels. We were not interested in whether the text segments matched in terms of the lines in the segments (some of us would assign fewer lines or more lines to the text passage). We asked whether we all assigned the same code labels from the codebook for these passages. The decision would be either a "yes" or a "no."

Step 3: We calculated the percentage of agreement among the four of us on each of the text passages. We used an 80% agreement standard to determine our intercoder agreement percentage.

Step 4: We used this same procedure—using the same code label from the codebook to a text segment we all had coded—for several more transcripts. As we worked through more transcripts, our percentage of intercoder agreement grew until we had more than 80% agreement in coding that we could report in our study.

This final example illustrates intercoder agreement procedures using two different methods. Intercoder agreement was used in a study about tuberculosis among newly arrived Vietnamese refugees in two counties in New York State (Carey, Morgan, & Oxtoby, 1996). In this study two methods for calculating intercoder agreement were used. The first required that the coders use the same words and code the text passages the same way. This required some discussion on the coders' part. The second method had more "give": The coders were not asked to code the same passage using the same code word, but simply whether the belief was "present" or "absent." This second approach was less stringent and would probably be easier to administer. Both approaches relied on coders' viewing an a priori codebook for code names and their definitions. The following steps were used:

Step 1: The researchers drafted a codebook on the basis of what the respondents said. This codebook contained a list of mnemonic codes, along with their definitions. For example, the letter sequence "CAUSESMK" referred to the belief that tuberculosis could be caused by smoking.

Step 2: The researchers ensured that different coders could independently replicate each other's work using the same instructions. They selected 320 passages of text for the 32 questions for the first 10 individuals interviewed. They then used two methods to develop intercoder agreement.

Step 3: In Method 1, two coders independently coded the 320 text segments two times. For the first time, they compared the sets of codes that each coder assigned to each of the 320 text passages. Agreement consisted of having both coders use the identical set of codes. This led to 45% agreement. For the second time, the two coders first discussed the problems with the codebook (redundant codes, lack of mutual exclusivity, lack of shared understanding), and then recoded, attaining 88.1% agreement. Codebook clarifications made it possible to nearly double the final level of agreement.

Step 4: In method 2, agreement in how each separate code was used by the two coders was examined. They constructed a two-by-two contingency table showing the presence or absence of the belief as judged by both coders across the 320 text passages (Table 23.2). Kappa reliability values indicated that the two coders had 82.9% agreement on 152 codes in the 320 text passages. Kappa values of .90 or greater were achieved for 88.8% of the codes. These results indicated a high level of intercoder agreement.

TABLE 23.2	Contingency Table for Checking Interrater Agreement for 320 Text Passages

		Rater 1	
		Yes	No
Rater 2	Yes	Agreement—number of times both coders assigned the code to a text segment	Disagreement—code assigned by one coder but not the other to a text segment
	No	Disagreement—code assigned by one coder but not the other to a text segment	Agreement—number of times that both coders did not assign the code to a text segment

Source: Carey et al. (1996).

SUMMARY

Intercoder agreement provides a means for checking the consistency between two or more researchers as they code a qualitative database. The procedure calls for researchers to independently code a database and then compare their coding results. It is essentially a qualitative reliability check for consistency It is a practical, often recommended, and commonly used procedure in the health sciences. The degree of agreement can be hand calculated, or it can be derived using qualitative computer software programs.

The overall procedure involves engaging multiple coders, creating a codebook of codes, choosing a method for calculating intercoder agreement, using established procedures, and then determining and reporting on the extent to which agreement exists between the coders. Several procedures are available in the literature that range from informal to formal approaches. They differ in the extent of discussion and negotiation of the codes, the centrality of the codebook in the process, the basis for agreement, and the report of agreement on the basis of percentages or the kappa statistic.

ACTIVITY

The following activity provides qualitative researchers in a class with the opportunity to practice the procedure of intercoder agreement that I have used. This process can be used with a sample of transcripts or a single transcript.

1. Take the first paragraph of an interview and have everyone code the passage by assigning a one- or two-word code label to the paragraph.

2. Form into groups of twos or threes.

3. Have each individual in the group continue coding the transcript. Be sure to draw brackets around the passages. Perhaps consider an entire passage as a text segment.

4. After the entire transcript has been coded, look for passages in which the coders (all) have coded the same passage (with brackets).

5. Look for *similar* code words used to describe the passage (synonyms will do).

Passage 1	Code Label—Coder 1	Code Label—Coder 2	Code Label—Coder 3	Percentage Agreement
				Average agreement (>80%)

6. Calculate the overall average agreement for all passages that have multiple coders assigning codes. Miles et al. (2013) suggested aiming for 85% agreement.

7. As a final step, the coders can discuss disagreements and negotiate their differences.

FURTHER RESOURCES

For further information on a process for intercoder agreement, see:

Guest, G., MacQueen, K. M., & Namey, E. E. (2012). *Applied thematic analysis*. Thousand Oaks, CA: Sage.

Kuckartz, U. (2014). *Qualitative text analysis: A guide to methods, practice and using software*. London: Sage Ltd.

Richards, L., & Morse, J. M. (2013). *Readme first for a user's guide to qualitative methods* (3rd ed.). Thousand Oaks, CA: Sage.

For a detailed description of how to determine an intercoder agreement coefficient, see:

Carey, J. W, Morgan, M., & Oxtoby, M. J. (1996). Intercoder agreement in analysis of responses to open-ended interview questions: Examples from tuberculosis research. *Cultural Anthropology Methods, 8*(3), 1–5.

Visit study.sagepub.com/30skills for quizzes, eFlashcards, and more!

Writing and Publishing Qualitative Research

PART

VI

Writing in a Scholarly Way

Skill

Make your qualitative report scholarly.

Why the Skill Is Important

Qualitative researchers work hard at writing. The extensive time recording field notes, the choosing and shortening of quotations, the marshaling of evidence for themes, and the conceptually interesting way to write all require strong writing skills. Because qualitative studies tend to be long, there is considerable writing required. Writing challenges an ability to be sensitive to participants, such as sensitivity to gender, race, economic level, or personal politics. Qualitative writing needs to be shaped with an audience in mind. Richardson's (1990) study of women in affairs with married men illustrates how a writer can shape a work differently for a trade audience, an academic audience, or a moral or political audience. Harry Wolcott (2009), the late famous ethnographer, underscored the importance of writing:

> An honest claim that I can make is that I care about my writing. I work diligently at editing. What others read are always final drafts, not early ones. Pride and perseverance substitute for talent. Although I do not write with a natural ease, I have learned what it takes to produce (final) copy that may make you think I do. (p. 4)

Good scholarly writing begins with establishing a habit or routine of continuous writing, getting ideas out of your head and down on paper, staging your ideas so that they are scaffolded from easy-to-understand ideas to more complex ones, and using correct grammar.

My Writing Habit

Recently I picked up Stephen King's (2000) book *On Writing: A Memoir of the Craft.* It reminded me of the emphasis I have placed on writing during the writing phase of my career, which has now lasted since the late 1980s, some 25 years. I have always said that some people collect stamps while I collect books on writing, and I point to my long shelf of some 40 or so books on writing that I have bought and read over the years. I also say that when I am writing about research methods (in my books), I am also reading a book about writing that has helped inform my methods of writing. Sometimes these books emphasize structure, sometimes they convey the finer points of grammar, and sometimes they present the author's experiences with the process of writing. One of my favorites is a book about writers' desks, with pictures of the actual desks that distinguished writers have used over the years. Picturing writers at their desks helps me visualize myself at my table typing on the computer.

Over the years I have bought fewer and fewer books about writing, and I see that they now have found locations at different places on my bookshelf rather than tightly organized into one section. Right now I am reading *On Writing* by Stephen King (2000), a thoughtful memoir about King's development as a writer, his tips for good writing, and his suggestions for publishing. I have recently completed a memoir-writing workshop sponsored by the Nebraska Writers Conference, which was facilitated by a well-known essayist, Megan Daum. I routinely read books on the top 10 list of the *New York Times*, and popular books of fiction and nonfiction (I just completed a biography of the famous British novelist Penelope Fitzwater). I bring into my research methods classes segments from books to illustrate writing points. In short, I read books about writing, I read good literature, and I am always thinking about how the ideas writers share in their works might be applied in writing good research. My books span a wide spectrum, from professional trade books to academic writing books.

To write this chapter, I pulled out my first research methods book, *Research Design: Qualitative and Quantitative Approaches* (Creswell, 1994). Chapter 11, "Scholarly Writing," includes a discussion of my favorite books on writing that existed at that time, on my shelf around 1988 to 1990. My topics in that chapter included writing as thinking; the habit of writing; readability of the manuscript; voice, tense, and fat; and computer programs for writing. Since the late 1980s, my shelf of writing books has expanded considerably, and I thought that I would revisit these topics with what I know now about scholarly writing. This discussion will expand on these earlier topics and add some new ones. I should also mention that I have received throughout the years many comments on my "Scholarly Writing" chapter, mostly from readers who were delighted that I had given attention to scholarly writing, because most methods texts simply ignore it. I think that my fascination with writing, and scholarly writing, stems first from my interest in improving my own writing for publication and, more recently, from my continued interest in developing not only as a scholarly but as a literary writer as well. Good qualitative writing does border on literary writing, and qualitative approaches, such as narrative research and autoethnography, may, in many cases, simply be considered good creative nonfiction (Ellis, 2014). In the past few years, I have attended several summer writing workshops and have begun to "workshop" my short stories to see if I bridge academic and literary writing. While I need to stay with my day job of academic writing, I also hope that I can include fiction (such as good dialogue) and nonfiction (detailed description, a good story line) in my academic writing. In my qualitative classes, students know that I emphasize writing (or recommend that they secure the services of a good editor) and may see my approach to qualitative scholarly writing as overly picky. I often bring into my classes good fiction writing to study and to help students write with detail and expressiveness that will enliven their qualitative research reports.

Here, then, are the topics I discussed back in my first methods book and how I would expand on them today, after 25 years of writing. I will pose them as statements or rules, if you will, for good qualitative scholarly writing.

Writing to Think About Your Topic

The process of research begins when you first put your ideas down on paper and remove them from your head. Good research begins not with talking about ideas to others, but actually writing the ideas down for yourself and others to examine. As Natalie Goldberg has said, "keep your hand moving." In addition, at all stages of the writing process you need to approximate the "end product," which, of course, is a written qualitative research report. I routinely "work backward" from the image I have of the final product to how I will get to this product. Furthermore, new researchers believe that they need to have an absolute clean draft in the first rendering. Stephen King (2000) recommended writing down, quickly, the first draft, without much thinking. This idea of having a polished first draft immediately may be a result of viewing clean, fixed journal articles. The reader does not see the back story—the multiple drafts, the revisions, and, most important, the careful review and scrutiny of a technical editor or writer. Here is the process I follow to use writing as thinking:

- I write out my ideas rather than talking them over with others.

- I write out my first draft rapidly, not paying attention to complete sentences or complete ideas. You should see my first drafts—they resemble a stream-of-consciousness, loosely collected series of statements that are roughly held together by some overall shape.

- I do follow the idea of designing a general structure first, then moving the larger parts around to make them fit together, and then polishing the final copy through editing. Too many inexperienced researchers move quickly to the editing stage, and unfortunately, reviewers I engage after I have written a paper all too often simply "edit" and do not provide valuable feedback on the most important phase—the larger structure, and what parts need to again be moved around.

- I routinely write two or three drafts and keep reworking ideas. When I finally have a paper completed, I then entrust a friend or colleague to look it over and provide feedback.

Develop the Habit of Writing

You need to get into a routine of writing—typically at the same time each day, at the same location, with the same writing implements (whether a yellow legal pad, a computer, a fountain pen, a dictionary, or whatever). This calls for training yourself and self-discipline. Do not expect to sit at your desk and work on your qualitative project for 5 hours at a stretch initially. Build up to it. Make it a daily activity, as Boice (1990) suggested. Find a time of day that works best for you. Are you a morning person, and writing seems to flow early in the day? An evening person? I like to think about ending a session on writing (or thinking, or sketching) with something to start with the next day so that I do not begin the new day wondering what I should work on next. Some people recommend warm-up exercises (writing a letter, writing in a diary, and so forth). I do not do this, because I can generally work into my subject matter quickly if I leave a to-do note to myself (or a conscious reminder, like the last paper on my design) from the last session. I do feel that setting the physical stage for writing is important. For me, it typically begins by turning on classical music on my computer to set a relaxed tone, returning to my favorite desk, and working in a tranquil space.

Staging Your Thoughts

Over the years I have relied on Tarshis's (1982) approach to thinking about the large narrative thoughts in a qualitative study. He recommended that you consider your study to be made up of four types of thoughts. First, there are *umbrella thoughts*, the core ideas you are trying to get across in a study. It is often helpful to think about a single phenomenon to explore in a qualitative study. This would be the umbrella thought. At the end of a study, what is the one idea you would like your readers to better understand? The difficulty with much qualitative writing is that the reader is left with multiple big

> Qualitative research requires good writing, such as staging your thoughts from large umbrella thoughts to big thoughts, little thoughts, and attention thoughts.

ideas, each one distracting from the overall message you would like to deliver. In the health sciences, the umbrella thought is often referred to as the "take-home message."

Second, there are *big thoughts*. These thoughts provide reinforcement, clarification, or elaboration for the umbrella thoughts. These might be the major themes in your qualitative findings. Third, *little thoughts* provide reinforcement for the big thoughts. These are small details found in paragraphs and sentences in a qualitative study. An example would be a code that provides evidence for a theme. Fourth, and finally, *attention thoughts* represent organizational ideas that keep the reader on track. A qualitative example would be a summary statement about themes at the beginning of the findings section. This statement tells readers what they can expect to find in the section. All of these thoughts are important, but I would pay careful attention to using a limited number of *umbrella thoughts* and be sure to include *attention thoughts* to keep readers on track with where you are headed in your qualitative study. For attention thoughts you might ask yourself, "How am I keeping the reader on track with the discussion I am including?"

Use Principles of Good Writing

Good grammar books abound with specifics about voice, verbs and verb tense, and ways to tighten your writing. Here are some of the grammar ideas I constantly hold in my mind as I write:

- On verbs: I try to eliminate all passive verb constructions and replace them with active verbs. This way we know who is doing the action rather than leaving it to guesswork. In terms of verb tense, its use varies. Unquestionably the present tense represents strong writing in qualitative research, the past tense should be reserved for reviewing the literature and summarizing past studies, and the future tense is standard for proposals and plans for conducting a study. Also, I am on the lookout for unnecessary shifts in verb tense within paragraphs, as this causes the reader to pause and abruptly stop processing ideas (American Psychological Association, 2010).

- On word usage: I think that colloquial expressions and jargon have no place in good scholarly writing. In reporting qualitative themes, they do have a place when you are capturing the language of participants and the way they look at the world. First-person pronouns are quite acceptable in qualitative writing because of its literary quality. The pronoun *I* brings the interpretation back to yourself as the author and reflects how qualitative research is highly interpretive.

- On wordiness: I like to write my qualitative reports in a lean, concise way. I call my writing "plain speak." This means taking out of my writing the "fat" (Ross-Larson, 1982) such as unnecessary propositions, "the . . . of" constructions, and unnecessary adjective and adverb modifiers.

- On bias: Before writing a qualitative proposal or study, I would highly recommend that you consult the *Publication Manual of the American Psychological Association* (2010) for strategies for reducing bias in language in a qualitative study. Be specific when referring to a person or persons, be sensitive to the use of labels that may stereotype people, use descriptive terms that precisely mention the participants in your study, and use accepted terms for gender, sexual orientation, racial and ethnic identity, disabilities, and age.

Other Strategies for Good Writing

Here are additional tips on good scholarly writing that do not seem to fit under the above topics:

- Use computer tools for writing when necessary. Bibliographic computer software can help organize your references. Software is also available for you to dictate into a digital recorder and let the program transcribe it for you. With some software, you can have the computer read back to you a chapter or an article and make corrections as you listen.

- Read and study good qualitative research articles. In good writing, the eye does not pause and the mind does not stumble on a passage. In the qualitative area, good literature serves to illustrate clear prose and detailed passages. Individuals who teach qualitative research assign well-known books from literature, such as *Moby-Dick, The Scarlet Letter*, and *The Bonfire of the Vanities*, as reading assignments (Webb & Glesne, 1992). *Qualitative Inquiry, Qualitative Research, Qualitative Health Research, Qualitative Family Research*, and the *Journal of Contemporary Ethnography* represent good scholarly journals in qualitative research to examine.

- Work backward from your final product. I always visualize the final qualitative report that I want to write. I study articles from journals (or, in your case, dissertations or theses) to which

I will submit, and note length, style, tone, number of tables, number of figures, and so on. I then begin to visualize what this final product should be. I also complete each draft of my paper as if it is the *final copy*. All too often, inexperienced researchers work on "drafts," and the manuscript comes off that way to readers. Every time you work on a "draft," consider it the final copy, even the final product, and submit your best effort to reviewers. I discourage students from submitting "drafts" to me; only the "final product," I say.

SUMMARY

Being a good writer and continually working on your writing is part of the life of a qualitative researcher. A final qualitative report needs to be persuasive, to be realistic, and to draw the reader in. You can work on being a good writer by reading books on writing, as I have done over the years. Consider writing your ideas down and sharing them rather than simply talking about your qualitative research project. Develop the habit of writing at the same time each day, at the same location, and with the same writing tools. Stage your ideas in your writing and pay close attention to the one large idea that is found in your central phenomenon, and the sentences that help orient the reader as to the topics you are discussing. Use good grammar, and pay attention to your verb use, excessive words, and biased language that can creep into your scholarly writing. Consider using computer tools as an aid to your writing, reading good literature and good qualitative published studies as models, and working backward from your final product.

ACTIVITY

Select a popular novel. Think about the staging of ideas in the novel and develop a concept map of the flow of topics in the novel. Identify how the author uses umbrella thoughts and attention thoughts to guide the reader.

FURTHER RESOURCES

King, S. (2000). *On writing: A memoir of the craft.* New York: Scribner.

Wilkinson, A. M. (1991). *The scientist's handbook for writing papers and dissertations.* Englewood Cliffs, NJ: Prentice Hall.

Visit study.sagepub.com/30skills for quizzes, eFlashcards, and more!

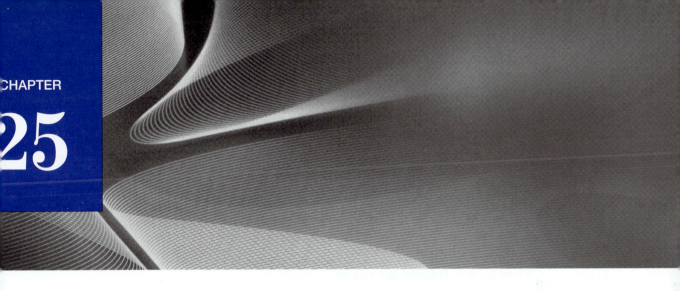

Writing in a Qualitative Way

Skill

Write your qualitative study using good description, the coherence of ideas, similes, and short quotations.

Why the Skill Is Important

The idea behind good qualitative writing is to develop a storyline or narrative that engages readers and draws them into the study. A detailed description will bring them in. So also will passages that coherently relate and flow. Writing techniques, such as similes, are often part of good qualitative writing because they can take an unfamiliar situation and relate it to a familiar situation. The use of quotations, especially short ones, also brings a qualitative narrative to life, and they can capture the essence of what many words might be used to describe a theme or to illustrate a theme. Another important part of qualitative research is to position yourself in the study by writing reflexively. I will cover this idea in Chapter 26. In short, there are several writing strategies in qualitative research that should become part of your approach to writing.

Use "Thick Description" When You Write

> A description is rich if it provides abundant, interconnected details, and possibly cultural complexity, but it becomes thick description if it offers direct connection to cultural theory and scientific knowledge. (Stake, 2010, p. 49)

Qualitative studies are written using detailed description, coherence of ideas, and literary techniques such as similes and good quotes.

Writing detail into a qualitative study is called "thick description." It means writing in a way to provide details about the setting, about people, and about events. The term comes from the anthropologist Clifford Geertz and his essay "Thick Description: Toward an Interpretive Theory of Culture" (Geertz, 1973). Qualitative books address how to write using "thick description," and these discussions are typically about comparing a "thin" description with a "thick" description. We can also view examples of "thick" description to see how it is written by authors.

Where to Place Detailed Description

Detail can go into many places in a qualitative study, but it is especially important in describing the setting, which typically goes into the "findings" section as the first passage. It is also important to place the detail into the theme passages to provide an element of realism to the discussions. Here are some examples of detailed description that you might place in your qualitative study:

- A place or physical description of the setting that might begin by circling outside of a place and then moving inside, such as we used in our study of the soup kitchen in a homeless shelter (Miller, Creswell, & Olander, 1998)

- An emotional description based on the faces of individuals (see the New York marathon example of studying the emotions on faces as presented in Chapter 19's activity)

- An artistic description, such as found in music or in comic books (see Millhauser's [2007] opening cartoon description, called "Cat 'n' Mouse")

- A taste description (or draw on all of the senses: sight, hearing, taste, smell, touch, or other senses, such as balance, temperature, pain, and others)

- An activity description, such as the description of adolescent students using tobacco (McVea, Harter, McEntarffer, & Creswell, 1999)

- A movement description, such as our assessment of the development of the mixed methods movement in South Africa (Creswell & Garrett, 2008)

- A description that goes from broad to narrow, such as the description in our "gunman" case study where we talked about the region of the country, the campus, the building, and then the classroom (Asmussen & Creswell, 1995)

- A description that educates the reader, such as the qualitative health account of the needs of AIDS-infected victims in rural China (Lu, Trout, Lu, & Creswell, 2005)

Examples of "Thick" Description

To best understand the use of "thick" description, it is helpful to see some examples where "thin" language has been changed to "thick" language, and how "thick" description has been used in qualitative projects.

Example 1: From Thin Description to Thick

- Thin: "I had trouble learning the piano keyboard." (Denzin, 1989, p. 85)

- Thick: "Sitting at the piano and moving into the production of a chord, the chord as a whole was prepared for as the hand moved toward the keyboard, and the terrain was seen as a field relative to the task. . . . There was chord A and chord B, separated from one another . . . A's production entailed a tightly compressed hand, and B's . . . an open and extended spread. . . . The beginner gets from A to B disjointly." (Sudnow, 1978, pp. 9–10)

Example 2: Activity and Setting Description

Daniel feels it is important to approach the experience of materials through aesthetics rather than explanation. He stresses the ordinariness of many of the things he uses: starch, soap bubbles, milk cartons. "You've got to get teachers confident enough to get the materials into the hands of students, and to tolerate them playing around with them." . . . Around the room are some samples of the work that is going on in Daniel's courses. A tray of starch has dried out to leave characteristic crack lines. In a plastic bucket is a water wheel made out of milk cartons. When the wheel turns, it winds up a winch. (cited in Stake, 2010, p. 50)

This passage includes a description of an activity, and it also includes a physical description of the setting.

Example 3: A Chronological Description

> George bought a broken clock at a tag sale. The owner gave him a reprint of an eighteenth-century repair manual for free. He began to poke around the guts of old clocks. As a machinist, he knew gear ratios, pistons and pinions, physics, the strength of materials. . . . He could replace the worn tooth on a strike wheel by hand. Lay the clock facedown. Unscrew the screws; maybe just pull them from the cedar or walnut case, the threads long since turned to wood dust dusted from mantels. Lift off the back of the clock like the lid of a treasure chest. Bring the long-armed jeweler's lamp closer, to just over your shoulder. Examine the dark brass. See the pinions gummed up with dirt and oil. Look at the blue and green and purple ripples of metal hammered, bent, torched. Poke your finger into the clock; fiddle the escape wheel (every part perfectly named—escape: the end of the machine, the place where the energy leads out, breaks free, beats time). Stick your nose closer; the metal smells of tannic. Read the names etched onto the works: *Ezra Bloxham-1794*; *Geo. E. Tiggs-1832*; *Thos. Flatchbart-1912*. Lift the darkened works from the case. Lower them into ammonia. Lift them out, hose burning, eyes watering, and see them shine and star through your tears. File the teeth. Punch the bushings. Load the springs. Fix the clock. Add your name. (Harding, 2009, pp. 14–15)

This passage, from Paul Harding's 2009 Pulitzer Prize–winning book *Tinkers*, includes a chronology of steps in fixing a clock and the use of documents to add depth, and it educates readers about a task they may not know.

Example 4: A Mixture of Details

> "One thing about life in New York: wherever you are, the neighborhood is always changing. An Italian enclave becomes Senegalese; a historically African-American corridor becomes a magnet for white professionals. The accents and rhythms shift; the aromas become spicy or vegetal. The transition is sometimes smooth, sometimes bumpy. But there is a sense of loss among the people left behind, wondering what happened to the neighborhood they once thought of as their own. (Leland, 2011)

This passage, from John Leland's 2011 *New York Times* article "A Community of Survivors Dwindles," shows good description of a geographical space: music, smell, geometry, and emotion.

Writing Coherently

"'A lot of critics,' Vonnegut would later say with some asperity, 'think I'm stupid because many sentences are so simple and my method is so direct; they think these are defects. No. The point is to write as much as you know as quickly as possible'" (Buckley, 2011).

You have probably read a journal article or a research report that is easy to read, and that flows smoothly so that you can quickly read through it. If so, this is because the author threads the parts together carefully, and one idea builds on another. The author is writing coherently with all parts closely tied together to make a logical whole. We need to write research articles and studies the same way. In short, we need to write coherently.

An Example of Good Coherence

Coherence means that the writing is seamless, and one thought flows to the next. The reader does not notice disjunctions between thoughts, and the reading proceeds effortlessly. Wilkinson (1991) wrote, "Coherence is the ordering of words into sentences, sentences into paragraphs, and so on, so that they develop a closely reasoned, logical, line of thought, both within and between units" (p. 66). How can a writer build in congruence? Wilkinson went on to state that "connectives," *externally* connected transitional words or phrases, can help build this unity. Also, she recommended *internal* connections in which one sentence is explicitly connected to the preceding sentence. So in your writing:

- Connect sentences—key words, phrases, synonyms

- Connect paragraphs—connect the first and last sentences of the paragraph

- Use transitional phrases and words, such as *therefore, moreover, hence, consequently, on the contrary, in spite of this*, and so forth

- Have an overall logic to your narrative

Look at the following example, called the "hook-and-eye exercise," in Figure 25.1. This was an approach to viewing coherence in a written passage first introduced by Wilkinson (1991) that I incorporated into my section on writing strategies in my text (Creswell, 2014). When you look closely at Figure 25.1, you will see that this qualitative passage has good coherence. The author stays focused on "students," and each hook and eye connect the word *student* or synonyms for *students* in each sentence. So the reader follows the central thread of students through a paragraph. Then each paragraph is connected as well, to keep the focus on "students." The writer

FIGURE 25.1   An Example of Coherence Using the Hook-and-Eye Technique

They sit in the back of the room not because they want to but because it was the place designated to them. Invisible barriers that exist in most classrooms divide the room and separate the students. At the front of the room are the "good" students who wait their hands poised ready to fly into the air at a moment's notice. Slouched down like gaint insects caught in educational traps, the athletes and their following occupy the center of the room. Those less sure of themselves and their position within the room sit in the back and around the edge of the student body.

The students seated in the other circle make up a population whom for a variety of reasons are not succeeding in the American public education system. They have always been part of the student population. In the past they have been called disadvantaged, low achieving, retards, impoverished, laggards and a variety of other titles (Cuban, 1989; Presselsen, 1988). Today they are called students-at-risk. Their faces are changing and in urban settings their numbers are growing (Hodgkinson, 1985).

In the past eight years there has been an unprecedented amount of research on the need for excellence in education and the at-risk student. In 1983, the government released a document entitled, A National At-Risk, that identified problems within the American education system and call for major reform.

intentionally included the word *students* in each sentence and across paragraphs to provide coherence to the writing. This is an example of good writing.

An Example of a Narrative Needing Better Congruence

Now look at another example, which illustrates how the author did not provide much congruence in the discussion:

> The complicated phenomena in health care require a multifaceted approach to develop understanding and insight (Andrew & Halcomb, 2006). Quantitative methods aimed at producing generalizable results have long dominated the health sciences, while the essence of qualitative research is to explore and understand complex dynamic phenomena. The methodologies for health science research should be diverse and selected to suit the problems being investigated. Neither a qualitative nor a quantitative approach can stand alone if the research aim is to understand the richness of the communities we study (Baum, 1995). Therefore, health science researchers need to apply research methods to address complex, multidisciplinary research problems. Mixed

methods research is such an approach, combining the strengths of quantitative and qualitative research. (From the introduction to a doctoral dissertation, Wanqing Zhang, "Mixed Methods Embedded Design in Medical Education, Mental Health, and Health Services Research: A Methodological Analysis," University of Nebraska–Lincoln, December 2011)

Look at this passage in terms of the transitional phrases—only one is provided, "therefore." Also see this passage in terms of the connection of ideas—what ideas are being connected? Finally, does the passage skip around from topic to topic? Build large ideas (often with a topic sentence) and draft sub-ideas under the large ideas.

Writing Using Similes

If you notice, many prose writers use similes to convey thoughts. They often find their way into qualitative projects. Similes make a comparison between two things using words such as *like* and *as*. They can be distinguished from metaphors that do not use these words but still make comparisons ("this room is a refrigerator") and from analogies that provide logical arguments comparing one thing with another. Here are some examples:

> Like children leaving home, the fragmentation of qualitative methods from overviews to discipline-specific books has showed both a breaking away and remaining within the family of qualitative methods. (Creswell, 2009)

> The realization was like that of a first-time mother who at last fully understands that only she can give birth to the new life within: I knew I was the only one who could rebirth myself. (Cameron Plagens, qualitative doctoral dissertation, Institute for Transpersonal Psychology, 2009)

Writing Using Quotations

Another aspect of good writing is to use quotations to provide evidence for the themes in the findings of a study. Quotations are not easy to use, and you need to consider whether you will use short, medium-length, or long quotations, and introduce them into the qualitative narrative.

In most of my qualitative studies I have used short quotations consisting of a few words or phrases. As mentioned in Chapter 21, I find the quotations in my qualitative database, and then tag with them a code called "quotation" during my analysis of a database using qualitative data analysis software. These short quotations do not take up much space, and they can be liberally used as evidence for each theme in a findings section. What might be quotable material may differ between your perspective and mine, but I consider phrases that seem to capture in a few words the key ideas of a theme and then tag them with a code ("quotation") in my data analysis.

Quotations of entire sentences or entire paragraphs are more difficult to use as evidence for themes. They take up much space in a manuscript, which may be a problem given the length requirements for some published articles of journals. For a dissertation or thesis project, they add to the overall length of the study, which already might be quite long. Most important, midsized or large quoted passages raise the difficult issue of focus—in a long passage, what should the reader focus on? The way around this is to lead readers into the passage ("here is what you should see . . .") and then lead the reader out of the passage ("here was the important point . . .") with words that focus their attention. Because long passages contain many ideas, this help for the reader is essential to work into your writing.

SUMMARY

Using writing conventions typically used in qualitative research is part of good writing. A qualitative study needs to convey detailed descriptions that provide a sense of place, an emotion, an artistic rendering, the senses, an activity, a movement, and an education for the reader, taking the reader from a broad perspective to a narrow one. A detailed, "thick" description will convey a sense of realism to a study. Writing coherently will help move the action along quickly, and sentences need to connect, as well as entire paragraphs. Similes are popular in good qualitative writing because they allow readers to make comparisons between two things using words such as *like* and *as*. Finally, short quotations help capture in a few words the central ideas of themes, and they provide important evidence to use in the theme passages.

ACTIVITY

Select a theme passage from a published qualitative journal article. Use the "hook-and-eye" exercise to connect the sentences. See if you can find words that make this connection. Next, see if the paragraphs connect with specific words. In this way, judge the overall coherence of the written theme passage.

FURTHER RESOURCES

See these excellent books on scholarly writing:

Wolcott, H. F. (1990). *Writing up qualitative research* (3rd ed.). Newbury Park, CA: Sage.

Meloy, J. M. (2002). *Writing the qualitative dissertation: Understanding by doing* (2nd ed.). Mahwah, NJ: Lawrence Erlbaum.

I would also recommend a book on qualitative writing and how it needs to be adjusted based on your audience:

Richardson, L. (1990). *Writing strategies: Reaching diverse audiences*. Newbury Park, CA: Sage.

Visit study.sagepub.com/30skills for quizzes, eFlashcards, and more!

Writing Reflexively

Skill

Write about reflexivity in your qualitative report.

Why the Skill Is Important

> Our readers have a right to know about us. And they do not
> want to know whether we played in the high school band. They
> want to know what prompts our interest in the topics we inves-
> tigate, to whom we are reporting, and what we personally stand
> to gain from our study. (Wolcott, 2010, p. 36)

Reflexivity is the engagement by researchers in self-understanding about the
background they bring to a research study and how it shapes their interpretations,
how the participants may be experiencing a study, and how readers may react to a
study. It is often considered the act of "positioning oneself" in a qualitative study.
It is an essential part of good qualitative research today. However, in the literature
on qualitative research, it is fraught with ambiguity, mainly because authors do not
understand what it means, its importance in a study, its placement in a project, and
its writing forms. Also, it is challenging to write. Some researchers are not used to
writing about themselves. They have kept themselves out of their research for many
years, and this approach has been reinforced by quantitative approaches to inquiry.
Furthermore, the topics studied by qualitative researchers are often of a sensitive
nature, and the researcher may not want to disclose personal information.

Qualitative researchers today are much more self-disclosing about their qualitative writings than they were a few years ago. No longer is it acceptable to be the omniscient, distanced qualitative writer remaining behind the scene (as in quantitative research). As Richardson and St. Pierre (2005) wrote, researchers "do not have to try to play God, writing as disembodied omniscient narrators claiming universal and a temporal general knowledge" (p. 961). Postmodern thinkers "deconstruct" the omniscient narratives, and challenge text as contested terrain that cannot be understood without references to ideas being concealed by the author and contexts framed within the author's life (Agger, 1991). Denzin (1989) espoused a similar theme in his "interpretive" approach to biographical writing. As a response, qualitative researchers today acknowledge that the writing of a qualitative text cannot be separated from the author, from the participants involved in the study, and from the readers of the text.

What Is Reflexivity?

In a good qualitative study, you should write about the biases, values, and experiences you bring to a study as well as how the study may affect participants and readers. In terms of how you need to write about your own experiences, you might convey two points. First, talk about your experiences with the phenomenon being explored. This involves relaying past experiences through work, schooling, family dynamics, and so forth. The second part is to discuss how these past experiences shape your interpretation of the phenomenon. This second point is often overlooked or left out. It is actually the heart of being reflexive in a study, because it is important not only that you detail your experiences with the phenomenon, but also that you be self-conscious about how these experiences may potentially have shaped the findings, the conclusions, and the interpretations drawn in a study.

> Write yourself into your qualitative study by reflexively commenting on your personal experiences with the phenomenon and how your experiences have shaped the development of your qualitative project.

Reflexivity for the Researcher

How we write is a reflection of our own interpretation based on the cultural, social, gender, class, and personal politics we bring to research. All writing is "positioned" and within a stance. All researchers shape the writing that emerges, and qualitative researchers need to accept this interpretation and be open about it in their writings. According to Richardson (1994), the best writing acknowledges its own "undecidability"—all writing has "subtexts" that "situate" or "position" the material within a particular historically and locally specific time and place. In this perspective, no writing has "privileged status" (Richardson, 1994, p. 518) or superiority over other writings. Indeed, writings are co-constructions, representations of interactive processes between researchers and the researched (Gilgun, 2005).

Weis and Fine (2000) discussed a "set of self-reflective points of critical conscious-ness around the questions of how to represent responsibility" in qualitative writings. Qualitative researchers need to reflect on the key questions (p. 33):

- Should I write about what people say or recognize that some-times they cannot remember or choose not to remember?

- What are my political reflexivities that need to come into my report?

- Has my writing connected the voices and stories of individuals back to the set of historic, structural, and economic relations in which they are situated?

- How far should I go in theorizing the words of participants?

- Have I considered how my words could be used for progres-sive, conservative, and repressive social policies?

- Have I backed into the passive voice and decoupled my respon-sibility from my interpretation?

- To what extent has my analysis (and writing) offered an alter-native to common sense or the dominant discourse?

Reflexivity for the Participants

There is increased concern about the impact of the writing on the participants. How will they see the write-up? Will they be marginalized because of it? Will they be offended? Will they hide their true feelings and perspectives? Have the participants reviewed the material, and interpreted, challenged, and dissented from the inter-pretation (Weis & Fine, 2000)? Perhaps when researchers write objectively, in a sci-entific way, they silence the participants, and they may silence themselves as well (Czarniawska, 2004). Gilgun (2005) made the point that this silence is contradictory to qualitative research that seeks to hear all voices and perspectives. Because of this, authors need to be concerned about the impact of their writing on their readers, and acknowledge its potential impact.

Reflexivity for the Readers

The writing has an impact on the reader, who also makes an interpretation of the account and may form an entirely different interpretation than the author or the participants. Should the researcher be afraid that certain people will see the final report? Can the researcher give any kind of definitive account, when it is the reader who makes the ultimate interpretation of the events? Indeed, the writing may be a performance, and the standard writing of qualitative research into text has expanded to include split-page writings, theater, poetry, photography, music, collage, drawing, sculpture, quilting, stained glass, and dance (Gilgun, 2005). Language may "kill" whatever it touches, and qualitative researchers understand that it is impossible to truly "say" something (van Maanen, 2006).

How to Facilitate Reflexive Writing

How can reflexive writing be encouraged during the qualitative research process (Probst, personal communication, June 2013)? As a study moves forward, the researcher needs to write reflexive comments about what is being experienced. These might be observations about the process of data collection, hunches about what one is finding, concerns about how a person's presence disturbs or does not disturb the research site being examined, and reactions of participants to phases of the project such as data collection or the final report. These reflexive comments can be posted to a memo file that is maintained throughout the study. In qualitative software programs, the memos reflecting on these points can be attached to particular parts of the study, such as the themes or codes.

How does one know if one is being sufficiently reflexive (Probst, personal communication, June 2013)? This is a hard question to answer, and my response would be only tentative. But I think that sufficient reflexivity exists when researchers record notes during the research process that reflect their own personal involvement (i.e., their backgrounds, how their backgrounds shape their interpretations of data), the likely impact the study will have on readers, and how the participants are reacting to the study. If *something* is written about each of these three areas, I might assess the reflexivity in the study as sufficient. Also, I think that there can be too much reflexivity, in which the personal comments of the author overshadow the overall story being told (the topic being studied, the data, the findings, and the interpretation). A qualitative project can become self-focused to the point where the centerpiece becomes the researcher and not the participants. This represents to me too much reflexivity in a study.

Where Do You Place Your Personal Reflexive Statements in a Study?

The placement of personal reflexive comments in a study also needs some consideration. They can be positioned in one or more places in a qualitative study. Here are some of the more popularly used placements:

Opening (or Closing) Passage

It is not unusual for a phenomenological qualitative study to begin with a personal statement. Similarly, in a case study, the researcher might begin with what Stake

(1995) called a "vignette." Here is an example of beginning a study with one of the authors' disclosing his background, which led to the study. It is drawn from the article "Waiting for a Liver Transplant" (Brown, Sorrell, McClaren, & Creswell, 2006):

> This study arose out of being ill at ease. One of the authors (J.S.) is a psychiatrist responsible for the assessment and selection of all patients with end-stage liver disease (ESLD) who present as candidates for liver transplantation at a large Midwestern transplant center. Out of the silences and repetitions of their time on the waiting list, an occasional voice was heard. It was at times an articulate plea for recognition of the uniqueness of their experience; more frequently, it was the moaning of a soul that we clinically recognize as depression. J.S. offered reassurance and medication but began to wonder about much more that was left unsaid and unexplored. (p. 119)

In this case, the senior author mentioned the background that brought him to the study, but we only have hints about how his sympathetic position toward these patients might have influenced his approach to and the writing of the study.

Thread Personal Comments Throughout the Study

In narrative research projects we often see the personal, reflexive comments flowing into the study at different points. They may be included in the introduction, in the literature review, in the methods, in the findings (and themes), and in the final discussion phase of the research. A couple of examples will illustrate how authors use this form of writing reflexively.

Angrosino (1994) published a qualitative journal article reporting on the life history of Vonnie Lee, an individual with a mental disability who found meaning for his life by traveling on a bus. It is interesting in this study to see where and how Angrosino talked about himself and his role in the study. After an initial opening segment on Vonnie, Angrosino then discussed extensively how he met Vonnie, his initial conversations with him, and then his collaboration with him as Vonnie recounted the story of his life. Angrosino did not stop there with his own involvement; he then described his role in helping Vonnie ride the bus and riding on the bus with him. Meanwhile, Angrosino was reflecting on what he saw in Vonnie's actions aboard the bus. After another passage talking about the meaning of the bus, Angrosino then ended the study with a discussion in which he once again brought himself into the picture as he talked about coming up with the framework of a metaphor to describe Vonnie's journey, and his own fieldwork experiences and what he learned personally from Vonnie. In terms of research process, Angrosino treated his role and involvement throughout the study as a researcher, as a collaborator, and as an interpreter of Vonnie's actions. We do not learn, as I would have liked, how this role and involvement shaped his interpretation of events and Vonnie. Reading this story, however, I do get a sense of the caring, supportive person whom Angrosino seemed to be in this situation.

Another narrative study—this one being my favorite narrative or autoethnography—by Ellis (1993) is about how the author lost her brother in an airplane accident. She began by positioning herself as coming from a small town and describing her family. In this segment she discussed her brother, who later died in the accident. During the passage about the actual plane crash, we read dialogue that Ellis created (re-created) in which we learn about her emotional state following the crash. She takes us through a personal chronology of events that happened after the crash and the family's reaction to it. We visit the funeral and both her own and her parents' reactions. Throughout this passage as well, we learn about Ellis's own personal reaction to events. We also learn about her dreams following the funeral. At the end of the article, she brings herself in again and discusses how the writing of this story was "a difficult passage" (p. 725). In short, Ellis appears through the article in many of the scenes. Her reflexivity flowed throughout the article, and we learned from her quite expected emotional response how her experiences shaped the telling of the story.

Write Yourself in the Methods Section

This form of reflexivity is sometimes called the "role of the researcher," in which the inquirer talks about his or her role in the study and perhaps about his or her background. I will draw on three examples from methods sections.

In a study of how individuals with AIDS image their disease (Anderson & Spencer, 2002):

> As a health care provider for and researcher with persons with HIV/
> AIDS, it was necessary for the interviewer to acknowledge and
> attempt to bracket those experiences. (Statement of experiences)

In a study about women coping with childhood sexual abuse (Morrow & Smith, 1995):

> A central feature of the analysis was Morrow's self-reflectivity
> .... Morrow's own subjective experiences were logged, exam-
> ined for tacit biases and assumptions, and subsequently analyzed.
> (Statement about researcher's notes used in analysis)

In a study about parents' roles in education for working-class families of color (Auerbach, 2007, p. 257):

> Given the centrality of the researcher as a qualitative research
> tool, it is essential to monitor the subjective factors I assume
> that parents and educators often differ in their views of parent
> involvement. Although my outsider position . . . may have blinded
> me . . . my experiences as a parent of a struggling student and

an activist . . . provided some common ground. (This is a good example of the author's mentioning personal experiences and how they shaped the interpretation)

Place Reflexivity Outside the Box

Here I am referring to unusual ways to write reflexivity into a study. One way would be to put reflexive comments into a footnote in a qualitative study. In footnotes, the researcher can describe his or her positionality, interactions, and other self-reflexive comments. In this way, the text can still flow, but the material is available to the reader who wishes to know more (Probst, personal communication, June 2013).

Another way would be to run reflexive comments in a parallel column to the text of the study. Another unusual way that I used in my study of the gunman who attempted to fire on students at a large university (Asmussen & Creswell, 1995) was to write an epilogue (written at the end of the study) in which I described my own, indirect experiences with a gunman on a campus. I wrote,

> Our involvement in this study was serendipitous, for one of us had been employed by a correctional facility and therefore had direct experience with gunmen such as the individual in our case; the other was a University of Iowa graduate and thus familiar with the setting and circumstances surrounding another violent incident there in 1972. (p. 591)

I then went on to say that these experiences affected our assessment by drawing attention to the campus response and the psychological reactions of fear and denial. Thus, in this epilogue, I covered both bases important in reflexivity: talking about our personal experiences and discussing how these experiences shaped our assessment of the campus situation. We did not speculate on how participants and readers might be influenced by our account.

SUMMARY

Reflexivity needs to go into all qualitative studies. As I define it, reflexivity involves authors' reflecting on their personal experiences with the subject under study and how their experiences might shape their interpretations of the data. Researchers need to be reflexive about their role in the study. They also need to be sensitive to the impact of their writing on participants and the potential readers of the qualitative study. During a study, the researcher can write reflexive notes to later be incorporated into a study. That incorporation can assume different forms, such as presented at the beginning or end of a study, threaded throughout the study, included in the methods discussion, or placed in footnotes, as parallel text to the discussion, or in an epilogue.

ACTIVITY

You might look at several articles to see how other authors incorporate reflexive comments into a qualitative project. I think that you will find reflexivity to be present in all qualitative studies. It will probably differ only in terms of what authors incorporate into the statements and where they place these statements in the study.

FURTHER RESOURCES

Here is a book that talks about the potential impact of qualitative writing on readers, audiences, and the participants studied:

Weis, L., & Fine, M. (2000). *Speed bumps: A student-friendly guide to qualitative research*. New York: Teachers College Press.

Visit study.sagepub.com/30skills for quizzes, eFlashcards, and more!

Writing a Good Conclusion Section

Skill

Write a conclusion (or discussion) section to your qualitative study

Why the Skill Is Important

The conclusion section is the final passage in a qualitative report. Sometimes it is called the "discussion." This section is important for reviewing how your research questions were answered with the findings. The conclusion focuses the reader's attention on the most important aspects of your study, and it shares the unique contribution of your study. As the end point of a project, it can also serve as a "jumping off" point for additional research or practice for other researchers or practitioners. It can raise important questions for further research, and signal to others the limitations you encountered in your project and those that other researchers will need to take into consideration. Finally, writing a conclusion section to a research study is an accepted part of the process of reporting research, and it needs to be written so that it covers important elements in concluding a study.

How Do You Conclude a Qualitative Study?

"You must conclude. What choices do you have?" asked Bogdan and Biklen (1998, p. 198). These questions have occupied my thinking for years. I think that I began thinking about the answers back in 1998, when I asked Harry Wolcott to help me fashion an ending for my ethnographic rendering of five ways to conduct research on my campus gunman story (Asmussen & Creswell, 1995). This study was about a 43-year-old graduate student, enrolled in a senior-level actuarial science class, who arrived a few minutes before class, armed with a vintage Korean War semiautomatic rifle, and pointed the rifle at the students and tried to fire it. It jammed, the gunman panicked, and he ran out of the building. In my book, *Qualitative Inquiry and Research Design: Choosing Among Five Traditions* (Creswell, 1998), I reconstructed this case study, and "turned" the case through five iterations to reflect different approaches to qualitative research

> Include the elements of a summary of findings, an interpretation of the findings as compared to the literature, your personal interpretation of findings, limitations, and future research in a conclusion section of your study. Also end the section commenting on the significance of your study.

(this same "turning" occurs in Chapter 30, where I use a different scenario). Harry Wolcott helped me shape my ethnographic description of the gunman case. Wolcott suggested two possible endings: the first he called the "canoe into the sunset" approach. I wrote this approach to end the study:

> For the ethnographer working "at home," one has to find ways in which to make the familiar seem strange. An upsetting event can make ordinary role behavior easier to discern as people respond in predictable ways to unpredictable circumstances. Those predictable patterns are the stuff of culture. (Creswell, 1998, p. 226)

From predictability, Wolcott moved me over into uncertainty. In the second version, the writing conveyed more of an interpretive quality and pondered the complexity of the situation:

> Some of my "facts" or hypotheses may need (and be amenable to) checking or testing if I have carried my analysis in that direction. If I have tried to be more interpretive, then perhaps I can "try out" the account on some of the people described, and the cautions and exceptions they express can be included in my final account to suggest that things are more complex than the way I have presented them. (Creswell, 1998, pp. 226–227)

From these different writings I learned that there are multiple ways to conclude a study. In the larger literature, I found little mention of writing a conclusion section and what it would contain.

Perspectives on Elements of a Conclusion Section

Unfortunately, authors writing about qualitative research have given little attention to the content of a "conclusion" or a "discussion" section for a qualitative study. They also have not talked about how authors are to conclude and the choices available to them. What I have found is a piecemeal approach to writing about concluding a qualitative study. Some of the perspectives are to include:

- A summary of the findings (Mayan, 2001)

- A discussion about the implications of the study (Bogdan & Biklen, 1998)

- A call for further research or further actions (Bogdan & Biklen, 1998)

- Commentary on the personal stance of the author (values, style, ethics) (Hesse-Biber & Leavy, 2006; Weis & Fine, 2000)

- Limitations of the study (Marshall & Rossman, 2011)

- The conclusions that result from using a specific qualitative design (see Chapter 30 and Creswell, 2013)

- Information that appropriately fits the "type of research tale" being told (Hatch, 2002; Shank, 2006; van Maanen, 1988)

- The unique contribution of the study

As I look through all of these different perspectives, the unfortunate part is that they are not combined into an overall discussion about the elements of or the writing of a good qualitative conclusion section. They all seem important.

A Summary of the Findings

The conclusion section needs to move beyond the detail of the codes and themes in the findings and summarize the major elements found in the study. As Mayan (2001) stated, "In the conclusion, the researcher should summarize the findings clearly and concisely" (p. 35). This summary might provide specific answers to the research questions, and you could restate the research questions and then show how the participants (or what you observed or the information from documents or images) answered the questions. Alternatively, you can summarize the major themes of the study and focus in on the general evidence of the themes. I would not simply repeat the themes, but provide an overview of each theme in the conclusion section.

Implications of the Study

Sometimes this is referred to as the "interpretation" of the findings. It often takes the form of relating the summary or themes to the broader literature. This section is a point where the citations and references come back into a qualitative study.

To write this section requires asking yourself how your themes are consistent with those derived by other authors and how they are inconsistent. Moreover, once this assessment is made, you can then reflect on "why" a consistency or an inconsistency exists. This approach to grounding the findings in the literature parallels what we often find in quantitative research studies.

Call for Further Research

It is standard practice to make suggestions for future research that will build on the current findings in a conclusion section. This practice cannot be underestimated. When new scholars look for topics to study, they often reflect on the "further research" implications of studies. In this passage I would enumerate several potential directions for future studies that directly build on the themes I have reported in my findings section. I am specific about these recommendations, and may cite other authors who have also talked about the need for further study. Sometimes this further study is to develop new practices, to add to the literature, or simply to repeat a study within a new context. Sometimes this further study aims to improve on the research practices used in the present study.

Commentary on Personal Views

The personal interpretation that a qualitative researcher forms during a study is also useful information for a conclusion section. This aspect sets qualitative research apart from quantitative research. Perhaps a section of your study already provides a perspective on reflexivity, as mentioned in Chapter 26. Interpretation cannot be separated from your personal values, beliefs, and ethics, and it relates to your standpoint, as postmodern writers would say (Weis & Fine, 2000). Thus, it is acceptable in qualitative research to convey the meaning you would draw from your themes and your reflections on the overall findings in a qualitative project.

Limitations

Although Marshall and Rossman (2011) talked about identifying limitations in the introduction to a qualitative proposal, it is standard procedure to identify limitations also at the conclusion of a study. Here a balance is required between acknowledging potential limitations in a study and creating a list that might be seen as too overwhelming and indicative of a weak study. Furthermore, the limitations can be related to many aspects of a study, such as elements of the methods (e.g., the sampling, the size of the sample, restrictions on data collection), the theoretical orientation used in the project, the lack of substantial evidence in the themes, or the constant need to change the questions to best fit an understanding of the central phenomenon. What is not helpful is to construct limitations that relate to quantitative research, such as limits to generalizability or the lack of a large sample. Researchers should remember that a qualitative study has different purposes and strengths (see Chapter 1) (Marshall & Rossman, 2011).

Conclusions Within a Specific Design

As will be discussed in Chapter 30, the end points in conclusion sections for qualitative studies that are framed within specific designs (e.g., a case study, a grounded theory project) differ. In a narrative project, the conclusion might include a discussion that ties together a personal story. In a phenomenological study, a discussion paragraph can advance how the participants experienced the phenomenon and the context in which they discussed it. In a grounded theory project, it might include a diagram of a theoretical model generated during the project, and in an ethnography, a description as to how the culture-sharing group works. In a case study, it may include a summary of a description of the case and the themes that emerged.

Type of Research Tale

Finally, a conclusion section might reflect the overall type of research tale being told in the qualitative project (Hatch, 2002; Shank, 2006; van Maanen, 1998). In short, as we conclude a study, we cannot separate it out from the overall macrostructure being used in the project, a macrostructure that I discussed in Chapter 9 and that has framed how we write up qualitative projects. Van Maanen (1998) authored a guide to the types of research tales—ethnographic genres—that qualitative researchers use. His forms of ethnographic representation have been popular and highly cited as ways to tell the qualitative story. The three popular types of tales are the realist tale, the confessional tale, and the impressionist tale. Although others exist, these are the three most important types (Shank, 2006). In a realist tale, the author's voice is submerged and absent, the focus is on mundane details of everyday life, and the perspectives shared are those of the participants, not the researcher. In a confessional tale, the style is highly personalized and self-absorbed in the views of the researcher (fieldworker), and this account is accurate and natural. In an impressionist tale, the researcher draws the reader into a dramatic situation, the writing takes on a storytelling approach, the researcher conveys a high level of detail about characters in the story, and the story moves along toward a dramatic resolution (dramatic control). This overall structure of the type of tale told, it seems to me, influences how conclusions are drawn in the final passages of a study, from a focus on participants and their ideas to a focus on the researcher, or on a summary of the resolution of a dramatic event. In short, the type of tale shapes how the conclusion unfolds.

End With the Unique Contribution of the Study

I always suggest that the final sentence in the conclusion address the unique contribution of the study. Hopefully, in this way you will reinforce what readers have already learned. If they have not learned it, you have now made it explicit and told the readers about the uniqueness of your project. This ends the study on a positive note. Just as the first sentence in a study is important, the final sentence is also significant.

Two Approaches to Concluding a Qualitative Study

All of these elements could be used in concluding a study or writing a conclusion section into a qualitative study. In any given conclusion, not all of them frequently appear, although in a more scientifically oriented study (see Chapter 9 on the macrostructure of a qualitative project), more elements appear than in a literary-oriented study. We can see this by studying two different conclusions in published journal articles.

A Scientific Approach

This first article illustrates the inclusion of many of the elements that could go into a conclusion section of a qualitative study. This article sought to understand the motivation and the personal, organizational, and communal aspects that drive firefighters (both paid and volunteer) to engage in additional voluntary community work (Haski-Leventhal & McLeigh, 2009). In this section, I highlight the final sections of this study: "Discussion," the implications ("Fire Departments as Community Assets"), and the final section, "Further Suggested Study" (pp. 88–90).

The "Discussion" begins with restating the *research questions*:

> Why do firefighters volunteer above and beyond volunteering as firefighters? They seem to already have the recognition and the satisfaction, so why go the extra mile to further help the community they are already protecting?

Then the authors summarize the *key findings*:

> The most important aspect seems to be their high commitment to their leader (the chief), their workplace (the first department), and to their work group (feeling of brotherhood; Lee & Olshfski, 2002).

Next, the authors *relate these key findings to the literature*:

> This strong commitment was already mentioned in the literature. Lee and Olshfski (2002) studied the commitment of firefighters and showed that they had high attitudinal commitment (identification with the goals and values of the job and exertion of extra effort).

They add to this an *explanation*:

> This exploratory study shows how this commitment can be used for enhancing volunteering and creating an important community asset.

They then discuss the *implications for practice*:

> Community practitioners should be aware of the potential within
> fire departments to serve the community and include them in
> their maps. One of the primary obstacles for asset-based com-
> munity developers is to continually build and rebuild the asso-
> ciations between and among residents, organizations, and
> institutions (Kretzmann & McKnight, 1993).

Finally, the authors suggest *further research*:

> Collective volunteering such as this needs a further explana-
> tion . . . perception and position in the community are all new
> aspects of motivation to volunteer yet to be explored . . . focus-
> group findings may be further studied through a national sur-
> vey . . . another interesting aspect would be to further explore
> the differences between volunteer and career firefighters.

Thus, this article includes many of the elements I have discussed for inclusion
within a conclusion section. The personal stance of the authors was not mentioned,
nor were the limitations. The type of tale told in this conclusion reflected what van
Maanen (1988) would call a realist tale.

A Literary Approach

Contrast this example of concluding sections with a second one that illustrates a more
literary approach of storytelling. One of my favorite qualitative studies is the story
about an individual with retardation, Vonnie Lee, told by Angrosino (1994). This is
the story of Vonnie Lee, who found meaning for his life in riding the bus each day.
Angrosino rode the bus with Vonnie Lee to his workplace and gained insight through
observing him during his ordinary round of activities. This moved Angrosino away
from viewing Vonnie Lee as an "exotic" participant, and as a "typical" person who
learned how to use elements of the common culture (the bus) to serve his needs.

The "Discussion" begins with a discussion about Angrosino's *research project*:

> Vonnie Lee's autobiography, and the story of my interaction with
> him, is part of a long-term research project whose methodology
> and conceptual framework were described in some detail in ear-
> lier writings. . . .

Angrosino then talked about how he used *literary theory* in the long-term project,
and how he used rhetorical devices to profile his participants:

> . . . they adopted clearly defined social roles . . . and the roles
> became a dominating metaphor for the stigmatization . . . .

And then Angrosino talked about the *participant*, Vonnie Lee, specifically:

> The dominating metaphor of Vonnie Lee's life, then emerges not out of retrospective narrative but out of the action he is currently taking . . .

Then, an *interpretation* is made of Vonnie Lee's story:

> Vonnie lee's story goes one step further: It demonstrates the desirability of contextualizing the autobiographical interview within the ongoing life experiences . . .

Next, he brings in the *literature*:

> There is a great deal of published material based on the life histories of people with mental retardation, but, as Whittemore, Langness, and Koegel (1986) point out in their critical survey of that literature, those materials are almost entirely lacking in any sense of an insider's perspective.

Then, he returns to what he learned from Vonnie Lee in another *interpretive* segment:

> My encounter with Vonnie Lee taught me that his worldview was not a failed approximation of how a "normal" person would cope, nor was it, when taken on its own terms, intrinsically disordered. . . . Once we start looking for evidence of "disorder," then "disorder" is almost certainly what we find. If anything, Vonnie Lee's logic more clearly worked out and better integrated than that of more sophisticated people . . .

Then, Angrosino moves into a *limitation* and he asks a *question*:

> It is certainly true that Vonnie Lee's is only one story. I have been asked by several people who have read drafts of this article, "But is he typical of retarded people in his ability to concentrate and integrate his life experiences?" The honest answer is that I don't know.

Finally, the author speaks to the *significance* of the study:

> What this fragment of a research project demonstrates is that for at least some people with mental retardation, it is possible to do what anthropological ethnographers have long done: get away from asking retrospective questions that only emphasize

the "exoticism" of the subjects and instead, allow questions to flow naturally out of observations of the subjects in their ordinary round of activities.

A concept map, as shown in Figure 27.1, can help explain how this literary approach veers backward and forward through important elements of a description of the participant, theory, literature, interpretation, limitations, and unique contribution often found in concluding sections of a qualitative study.

FIGURE 27.1   Concept Map of the Discussion Section

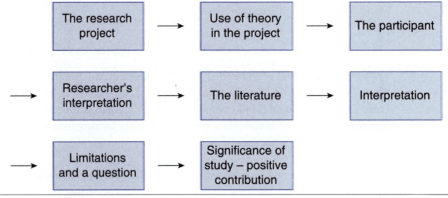

Source: Adapted from Angrosino (1994).

SUMMARY

How do you conclude a qualitative study and write the conclusion section? This discussion provides an analysis of a topic not often addressed in qualitative methods books. The conclusion section can include a summary of the findings, implications of the study, a call for further research, the personal stance of the researcher, limitations of the study, commentary that relates to the "outcomes" of using a design, and "outcomes" that reflect the type of research tale being told. These elements can flow into a conclusion section, and you might examine several conclusion or discussion sections to see how authors incorporate them into a scientifically oriented or a literary-oriented conclusion of a qualitative journal article.

ACTIVITY

Find a published qualitative research journal article. Develop a concept map (such as found in Figure 27.1) of the "discussion" or "conclusion" of the study. Evaluate its contents in terms of the elements that could go into a conclusion section: a summary, implications, future research, personal stance of author, limitations, end point of the qualitative design (e.g., how the culture works in ethnography), the type of tale told, and the unique contribution of the study.

FURTHER RESOURCES

One of the most interesting aspects about concluding a qualitative study is to frame it within the type of tale being told. For this I would direct you to a classic in the field on writing ethnography:

van Maanen, J. (1988). *Tales of the field: On writing ethnography*. Chicago: University of Chicago Press.

On what to include in a postmodern ending to a qualitative study, I would direct you to:

Weis, L., & Fine, M. (2000). *Speed bumps: A student-friendly guide to qualitative research*. New York: Teachers College Press.

Visit study.sagepub.com/30skills for quizzes, eFlashcards, and more!

Publishing a Qualitative Journal Article

Skill

Learn how to publish your qualitative journal article.

Why the Skill Is Important

I encourage all of my students to publish their qualitative projects. This applies especially to those going into academic positions, but it is useful, too, for those working outside of academia in that by writing up and publishing their studies, they learn about how research is composed, a skill useful when they need to read research articles. Most people feel that publishing a study is difficult, and it indeed may be for some who are less experienced in writing up articles for publication. Often individuals select journals that have low acceptance rates. They may not give enough attention to how they should present their studies to maximize the potential for publication. Some people simply do not understand the publication process. This chapter will review this process and how to organize your manuscript so that it will receive the best review possible.

Publishing During an Academic Career

As you think about publishing from your qualitative study, you might consider how publication relates to the unfolding of an academic publishing career. Here are the stages I have found helpful (realizing that the exact order of these stages may vary and that they may, at times, overlap).

Stage 1: Publishing in Journals From a Dissertation or Thesis

Typically students emerge with doctoral dissertations or theses as the research products of their graduate programs. In the first few years of their academic careers, they need to spend time publishing from their dissertations or theses because it is the research they have just completed. Often they publish with the chairs of their committees or with established faculty who have name recognition and can be easily published. In these early years, they also start developing conference papers from their dissertations or from research they have had time to collect during their early academic careers.

Stage 2: Publishing Conference Papers or Posters

As faculty move on with their careers, they begin to present their research at conferences. Many conferences are open to new faculty or recently graduated students who need to disseminate their research. Regional conferences would be the easiest to be accepted for, and these conferences require that an abstract or a short summary of the research be presented. Typically these abstracts or summaries are reviewed by individuals in the field for acceptance of presentation at the conferences. One form of conference presentation is to share a poster of your research, and there are good models for how to organize your information for a poster. At a more sophisticated level, your conference research paper may be selected for a research panel, in which three or four people share their research studies, and these studies are organized under a common theme. Sometimes there will be a discussant at the research panel who critiques the papers and provides helpful feedback. Some individuals take this feedback role seriously; others do not. Also available at conferences would be an invited panel of individuals who have all completed research on the same topic, and the invitation may bypass the formal review process and be organized by one or more individuals who have written on the topic. Finally, at a conference, papers may be further reviewed for inclusion in a published proceeding, and authors may need to decide whether they want proceeding publication or publication in a recognized journal.

Stage 3: Publishing Journal Articles

I always field-test my manuscript first at a conference before I submit it to a journal. When I look at the résumés of colleagues in the academy, I am suspicious of those résumés where individuals have long lists of conference presentations and short lists of published journal articles. Those individuals obviously do not subscribe to my field-test idea. There should be a one-to-one ratio (roughly) of conference papers to journal articles. This is my first step for publishing in journals. Journals stand at a more advanced level of publication than conference papers. My next step is to locate two or three appropriate journals for my qualitative research. How to select and "research" those journals as appropriate for my study is the subject of the next section of this chapter. But for now, I look for national, refereed journals to publish in, and I may start, as an early-career faculty member, in a "third tier" journal that has a lenient acceptance rate (say 20%).

Stage 4: Publishing Book Chapters and Books

At the next level of rigor in my career would be to publish book chapters in edited volumes. At this point I hope that editors will invite me to compile a chapter. Sometimes these chapters are thoroughly reviewed, and often only the editors of the volume review them. I certainly look at this point for distinguished publishing houses, either university presses or large commercial publishers. When choosing a large commercial publishing house, I am most concerned about whether it has a large marketing list that spans a substantial geographic region. For example, I can look to see if a publisher has offices around the world and a catalogue of publications that goes out to faculty and students at many campuses. A related topic is writing a book in your career. This is a substantial undertaking and is probably reserved for midcareer phases of your work life. Again, finding a publisher with a large marketing list and a fair review process is central to publishing books. Often books come about from compiling multiple journal article studies in a field, from developing a conceptual framework or idea that is widely used, or from the need for a textbook for classroom purposes.

All of my books (except one) have been written to address a pedagogical need in the classroom. My books have started from rough outlines of ideas that I share with students in class, and then they develop into PowerPoint presentations, and then into distinct chapters that I share as the final copy emerges. This book resulted from this process. When I use material from students, I seek their approval and have them sign a consent form to use their material. From student questions and comments, I have been the beneficiary of many fantastic ideas about writing research over the years.

Stage 5: Writing Proposals for Funding

From conference papers to journal articles and book chapters, the next development in publishing for a qualitative scholar becomes writing proposals for extramural funding. These proposals may go to private foundations or to public federal or state agencies. The way to write a proposal for funding is a topic in its own right and beyond the scope of this book. However, workshops exist on developing expertise in proposal writing. As with finding the right journal for your qualitative manuscript, you need to research the appropriate funding agency for your work.

How I Study a Journal Before Submission

One aspect of this research publication trajectory is to publish in journals. In order to maximize the possibility of acceptance of your qualitative study in a journal, you need to conduct your research on the nature of the journal. Here are the steps I have used repeatedly to find the right journal and increase my chances of publication.

> Do your research on the format and structure of journal articles published in your selected journal before you submit your article. This will maximize the possibility of acceptance.

Step 1: Identify Two or Three Journals

I search the large databases (e.g., EBSCO, FirstSearch) and begin by identifying two or three journals that might be interested in the content of my qualitative study. I look for national journals with boards that review manuscripts for quality before they are published. There is no definitive list of journals friendly to qualitative research, but more and more journals are opening up to this form of inquiry. However, you can find a list of qualitative-friendly journals that has been updated over the years at http://www.slu .edu/organizations/qrc/QRjournals.html.

Step 2: Study the Editorial Board

Once I have found these journals, I study the backgrounds of the editorial board members and editors of the journal. At the front of most issues of journals, you can find the names of the editors (typically one editor and several associate editors). The list of editorial board members can also be found on these front pages. I look through the list of editorial board members and search for individuals who may have published qualitative studies. I especially want my qualitative project to receive a fair hearing. I may also write a letter to the editor in which I briefly describe my qualitative study and ask whether the study would be a suitable topic for the journal.

Step 3: Examine Guidelines for Submission

I next look for guidelines for submission that will provide information that I will need to submit, such as information as to what style manual to use (i.e., the *Publication Manual of the American Psychological Association* [American Psychological Association, 2010] is probably the most popular one for social and behavioral science research), the maximum number of words permitted, the information necessary for the title page, and the proper formatting for tables, figures, and bibliographic references. Many journals now require electronic submission, so I am interested in how I will need to submit my manuscript for review.

Step 4: Dealing With Feedback From the Review

I recognize the various acceptance categories and how I need to react to them. The review process for my submitted manuscript may take several months, and I will receive detailed reviews about my study. I look for what I call "pearls of wisdom" in the detailed feedback from the reviewers, and consider what points are legitimate and what points are outside the bounds of normal review. To make this determination I may call in my coauthors or someone experienced in publishing in the journal to examine the reviews and help me find the "pearls" to include in my revision.

Journals typically have three categories of acceptance: accept, resubmit, and reject. A "reject" means that my manuscript was not suitable for the journal or was considered too low quality to be published. A "resubmit" means that I need to revise the manuscript carefully on the basis of the reviewers' and the editor's feedback. I typically view a "resubmit" as an acceptance, and I take the reviewers' comments seriously. An "accept" it seems is rare, and it means that there may still be some minor points to adjust before a manuscript will be published. If I receive a "resubmit" decision on my qualitative manuscript, I then make changes in the draft of the paper, and develop a detailed letter to send back to the editor when I return the manuscript. This letter takes each one of the critical points raised in the reviews, and point by point I discuss how each concern was addressed and where in the manuscript the editor can find my changes. It is typically then up to the editor to determine if the revised manuscript should be sent out for additional reviews.

Step 5: Study the Structure of Articles Published in the Journal

I study the overall structure of articles published in the journal. This means that I will find two or three published articles in each of the one to three journals I have selected as possible outlets for my qualitative study and look closely at the organization and structure of the articles. I will look at the types of headings and the flow of topics to determine the extent to which they are written in a more scientific way or a literary way. A scientific way would include the standard headings of introduction, literature, methods, results or findings, and conclusions or discussion. A literary way would contain headings or topics that essentially tell a narrative story. Regardless of which structure prevails, I want to compose my qualitative article to look identical to what has been published in prior issues of the journal. To see the difference between a scientifically structured qualitative article and a literary one, I provide two concept maps.

The first map, in Figure 28.1, illustrates a scientifically structured article by Shivy et al. (2007). In this project the authors used qualitative methods to understand the reentry-related personal experiences of offenders (six men and nine women) at 1- to 3-day reporting centers, a nonresident form of community corrections. As you can see in Figure 28.1, a concept map of the flow of ideas in the article illustrates the progression of topics from the purpose, through the sample and the results, and then on to the discussion.

An alternative concept map or flow of ideas using a literary structure can be seen in Figure 28.2, from a study by Dutro, Kazemi, and Balf (2006). This qualitative study presented a case analysis of a fourth grade boy's experiences (before, during, and after) writing a story about a boy whose struggles in writing led directly to his death. The flow of ideas is quite different from the structure of the scientific article illustrated in Figure 28.1. As shown in Figure 28.2, the authors began with personal experiences and moved on to a description of the boy, a theoretical framework, the methods, the story of the boy's experiences, and then the discussion and implications. The concept map of Figure 28.2 portrays this flow of ideas.

FIGURE 28.1   **A Concept Map of a Scientific Structure Based on Shivy et al. (2007)**

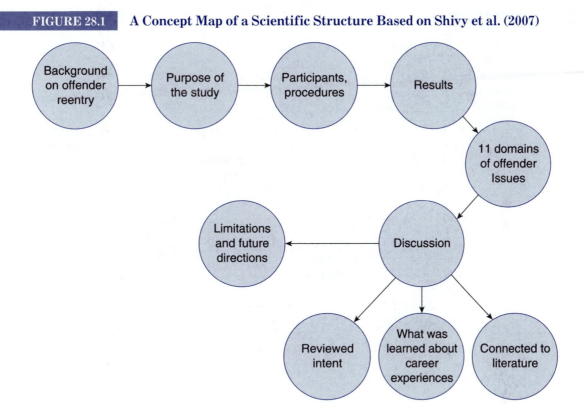

Step 6: Consider the Length, Details Included, and Impact Factor

Other elements of the content of published articles must be considered. Some other factors I look at include the overall length of the manuscript; its use of quotations, figures, and tables (how many, how often); the extent to which some quantitative features are included (see Chapter 25, on writing in a qualitative way); and the overall Impact Factor, a score that indicates the rating of the journal. The Impact Factor reflects the average number of citations to recent articles published in the journal. Higher impact scores indicate a higher quality journal, and these are compiled in *Journal Citation Reports*, an annual publication of the Science and Scholarly Research Division of the Thomson Reuters Corporation.

Step 7: Look at the Qualitative Designs Used

I am also curious about whether qualitative research designs are used in publications in the journal or whether the authors take more of a basic, thematic approach to their study. These designs are discussed in some detail in Chapter 30, and they include such designs as narrative research, phenomenology, grounded theory, ethnography, and case study.

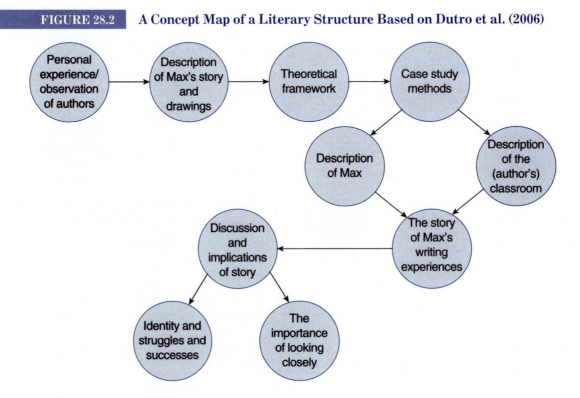

SUMMARY

Publishing is not easy regardless of methodology used. I believe that the type of publication generally relates to the stage of an individual's career and proceeds from early publications related to graduate student research and on to conference presentations, journal articles, books, and then proposals for funding. Because publishing in journals is such a prized award during this trajectory, I have given thought to how I would research finding an appropriate journal for my qualitative publications. This process involves identifying potential journals for my content area, and studying many aspects of the journals using current issues. This study includes looking at the overall writing structure—scientific or literary; appropriate length; style; use of quotations, figures, and tables; and the level of sophistication of the qualitative methods, from a basic thematic approach to a more advanced use of a qualitative research design.

ACTIVITY

Find a qualitative research journal article that has been published in a national refereed journal. Scan the article for the following elements, and note each element:

- Is the study scientific or more literary in its structure? Create a concept map of the flow of ideas.

- What approximate number of pages were typeset? (And if the typeset page equates to 70% of a double-spaced manuscript page, how many pages would the typed manuscript be?)

- What style manual was used for the article?

- How frequently were quotations, tables, and figures used?

- Was the article written reporting themes in the findings, or did the authors use a specific research design (e.g., ethnography, case study) and identify this specific design in the methods section?

FURTHER RESOURCES

For help with writing qualitative reports in general, see:

Merriam, S. B. (2009). *Qualitative research: A guide to design and implementation.* San Francisco, CA: Jossey-Bass.

Visit study.sagepub.com/30skills for quizzes, eFlashcards, and more!

Evaluating a Study and Using Qualitative Designs

PART

VII

Selecting Quality Criteria for a Qualitative Study

Skill

Choose your standard for assessing the quality of your qualitative project.

Why the Skill Is Important

Certainly not all qualitative researchers are in agreement about the use of qualitative standards or even whether there should be standards applied widely across qualitative research (Freeman, deMarrais, Preissle, Roulston, & St. Pierre, 2007). Qualitative research represents a heterogeneity of practices and a diverse community. What expectations do we hold for high-quality qualitative work? Some answers to this question appear in this chapter. The answers reflect multiple views from those taking a data interpretation stance, a quantitative validity stance, and a rigor and transparency stance. In the end, we must each identify how we judge the quality of a qualitative work, and we come at it from our own philosophies, work experience, and disciplines.

I will first discuss whether we should use standards of quality to assess our projects. Then, I will review some of the perspective on using quality standards in qualitative research. I will then suggest my own standards and how I view standards in my qualitative writing. You can choose how to proceed, but you must realize that research is closely scrutinized, and that others will be using some standard to evaluate the quality of your study.

Are Standards Important in Qualitative Research?

Different answers exist in the large qualitative community in the United States and around the world. The *conventional view* in qualitative research holds that the use of standards limits creativity and is difficult to achieve because of the diversity of approaches within the qualitative community. This diversity exists in theoretical orientations, methodological aims (e.g., ethnography vs. grounded theory), and philosophical differences (e.g., a more postpositivist orientation vs. a constructivist orientation). Thus, Freeman et al. (2007) wrote that quality standards are neither desirable nor possible from a consensus standpoint. Still, others would argue that from a *practice standpoint*, standards are important and are in wide use. Some qualitative books end with lists of questions that could be asked to determine a high-standard qualitative study (e.g., Hatch, 2002). Even those unwilling to talk about standards or quality indicators often make suggestions as to what to include and what not to include in a qualitative report (Silverman, 2007). The practice of qualitative research requires that some standards be applied, such as during the process of journal manuscript review, the assessment of an application for federal funding, the review of a qualitative book prospectus, and the assessment of student projects. Standards are being used. *My own perspective* is that I like to advance some standards for judging the quality of a qualitative study. My orientation is from a methods perspective, where I want rigorous and well-documented methods. This perspective comes from my extensive work in the social and health sciences in the past 20 years, my initial training in quantitative research, and, most important, my stance of always keeping the graduate student foremost in mind when I consider methods. Graduate students need some guidance about qualitative research (after all, they are new to this methodology), they are open to learning about how to proceed, and, in the initial stage of their development as researchers, they profit from having a structure to their work. Numerous examples of a structured approach to qualitative research exist in this book, and this is intentional as a way to reach beginning qualitative researchers. After these researchers gain some experience, they can innovate on their own and be creative with processes that better fit who they are. In many fields, it is my belief, beginners need to master the basic skills first, so that later they can wander outside the box and create new structures and new innovations. But first come the basic skills and the structure often needed in teaching these skills.

There is no consensus on how to judge the quality of qualitative research, but several approaches exist for you to review and decide for yourself what criteria would be best.

Some Perspective on the Standards Question

Despite many different approaches and traditions within qualitative and evaluative research, there are widespread concerns about quality. There is also shared interest in issues such as "rigour";

the need for principles of practice to be made manifest; the importance of sound or "robust" qualitative research evidence; and in the relevance and utility of research. (Spencer, Ritchie, Lewis, & Dillon, 2003)

In book after book and report after report, authors have advanced different perspectives on the use of quality standards in qualitative research (e.g., Creswell, 2013; Kuckartz, 2014). An eye-opening experience was to view the Robert Wood Johnson Foundation's Qualitative Research Guidelines Project (http://www.qualres.org) Web site, developed by Cohen and Crabtree in 2008. In this project the authors talk about the criteria for rigorous qualitative research. They first acknowledge that one's epistemological standpoint or research paradigm shapes how one views "good" research, and that a broad range of criteria exist. They emphatically do not commit to a particular set of criteria, and proceed to identify 13 different studies suggesting diverse perspectives on the criteria for a rigorous qualitative study. I will not attempt to summarize all of the perspectives here, but I will highlight studies that provide different perspectives.

Common Concerns About Standards

Several educators have written about the lack of consensus in standards and the diversity of the qualitative community that will discourage consensus building (Freeman et al., 2007). At the same time, they say that qualitative researchers have accomplished high-quality studies and have demonstrated quality in their reports. They suggest that discussions of quality come from studying what researchers say they are doing, and then encouraging excellence in that research. The common ground for qualitative researchers has been the use of theory and validity. Quality also comes from data and the evidence with those they study, and their analyses, interpretations, and representations of data. Researchers also make claims, statements that connect the data with interpretations of those data. In the end, they do not advocate for a set of standards, but discuss common concerns that have shaped the dialogue and debate on the issue of quality.

Standards Based on Validity

In many discussions, the standard of quality discussed for qualitative research is the question of the validity or "the trustworthiness of inferences drawn from data" (Eisenhart & Howe, 1992, p. 644). Validity certainly has a role in qualitative research (see Chapter 22), but whether it is the central—perhaps only—feature of the standard to be used in qualitative research might be questioned. Lincoln and Guba (1985) used parallel terms for the quality of data analysis and interpretations, such as *trustworthiness, credibility, transferability, verisimilitude, relevance, plausibility,* and *confirmability*. In an informative discussion about quality standards, Kuckartz (2014) discussed quality using parallel ideas to internal and external validity: internal quality and external quality. Internal quality refers to the procedures used in data collection and analysis, while external quality includes a variety of strategies, such as member checking, peer debriefing, and extended stay in the field.

Standards Based on the Research Community

Kuckartz (2014) also commented on subtle realism as one perspective on quality in qualitative research. Subtle realism, a philosophical approach, as applied to qualitative research means that while we have subjective judgments, there is also a reality outside our individual perspectives. This perspective provides support that the research community has agreed upon standards of judgment for the plausibility, credibility, and relevance of research reports. Thus, the research community looks for the strongest evidence for claims or interpretations and asks all readers to scrutinize the methods according to the community of critical peers.

Standards Based on Impact

Richardson (2000) has written about scholarly writing and qualitative research and identified questions for judging the writing on the basis of the impact of the work on the reader. I find these standards quite unusual and taken from the perspective of how a reader might be affected by a qualitative project. These points are:

- Substantive contribution: Does this piece contribute to our understanding of social life?

- Aesthetic merit: Does this piece succeed aesthetically? Does the use of practices open up the text and invite interpretive responses? Is the text artistically shaped, satisfying, complex, and not boring?

- Reflexivity: How did the author come to write this text? Are there adequate self-awareness and self-exposure for the reader to make judgments about the point of view?

- Impact: Does this affect me? Emotionally? Intellectually? Move me to write? Move me to try new research practices? Move me to action?

- Expression of a reality: Does this text embody a fleshed out sense of lived experiences? Does it seem true?

Standards Based on Research Methods

Morse and Richards (2002) discussed the rigor of a qualitative study and how you can ensure that your project is "solid" (p. 179). They took a methods orientation and asked that you pose the right question (e.g., bracketing past information, revisiting your questions), ensure the use of the appropriate design (e.g., sensitive to the type of data collected, collect data that relate to your questions), make trustworthy data (e.g., establish trust with participants, carefully code and categorize data), build solid theory (e.g., check developing relationships in the data, compare your findings with the literature), and verify your findings (e.g., use a peer review process, implement results in subsequent projects).

Standards Based on Rigor

Mayan (2009) reviewed 15 different sets of rigor for a qualitative study advanced by authors. After this extensive analysis, she concluded with her own criteria for what constitutes rigor in a qualitative study:

- It does not mean that you cook up findings in your head. There is logic to them, you can provide a reasonable explanation for them, they tell a story.

- She is involved in her research, and how she constructs research, generates data, and represents and writes the report.

- She is reflexive.

- She likes to work with images and people stories that help explain, in the context of the literature, why our world works the way it does.

- She wants to open up people's minds.

- She revisits what she is trying to do in her research and makes decisions in consultation with interested and supportive others.

- She writes her research so that its integrity and rigor are apparent.

Rigorous and Systematic Methods

Mayan's (2009) self-disclosure of her own personal standards has emboldened me to suggest my own standards. I do like that research should be *transparent* of all relevant research processes and should be *systematic* or use regular or set data collection and analytical procedures (Meyrick, 2006). Beginning researchers need some standard of quality they can apply to their projects. These standards do not need to be rigid and complex. When I review qualitative projects of students in my classes, I look for the following:

- Include a clear *central phenomenon* being explored (see Chapter 12). This is a centerpiece of writing good purpose statements and research questions. Although a study can begin with one phenomenon, after all of the various data collection is complete, it becomes quite complex, and that complexity shines through in a well-written qualitative report.

- Comment about your *reflexivity* (see Chapter 26). I like to see researchers tell me about their past experiences with the phenomenon they are exploring and how their experiences have shaped their approach to research and their interpretation of the data.

- Gather *extensive data* of multiple forms. In Chapter 13, I tried to convey the wide array of sources of qualitative information and to encourage you to collect multiple forms and to be creative about selecting unusual forms.

- Conduct multilayered *data analysis* using computer programs to assist you in this process. I have suggested rigorous approaches to qualitative data analysis that have layers going broader and broader from the raw data to themes and their relationships (Chapters 19 and 20). Qualitative data analysis programs can help store, organize, and find important passages for your qualitative report (Chapter 21).

- Engage in multiple forms of *validity* checks. The accuracy of your interpretation is of paramount importance in a qualitative project. In Chapter 22, I suggested multiple strategies of conduct validity checks in qualitative research.

- Report themes and interrelate them, but also consider how the process of research can be enhanced through the use of a specific type of *qualitative research design* (see Chapter 30). These designs will take you beyond the basic skills introduced in this book and provide a more advanced approach to your qualitative project.

What Standards Should You Use?

You now know my perspective, that I would recommend using standards to assess your qualitative study. You also know that there is no consensus about standards, but that different perspectives exist in the literature. Choose one of the perspectives that seems most comfortable to you and the significant audience that will receive your qualitative project. Consider also the standards of your qualitative research community. Read through the perspectives I have mentioned and understand the stances taken by the authors. Finally, convey in your written project the standards you are using and why you chose them. In this way, you will be transparent in your writing and systematic about how you have selected specific standards to use.

SUMMARY

Qualitative researchers are not in agreement about the use of standards of quality or even whether there should be such standards. The question of the importance of standards also leads to diverse perspectives. Standards may limit creativity, may not be suitable for the diverse qualitative community, and may vary depending on one's theoretical orientation, methodology, and philosophy. However, within the practice of research, we find that standards exist in such forms as used by faculty committees, journal editorial boards, review panels for funding, and book prospectuses. In addition, I believe that beginning qualitative researchers are well served by having some standards to apply to their own projects. Beginning researchers can choose from among several perspectives about quality: shaped by common concerns today, based on validity, based on scholarly communities, the impact of research, research methods, and rigor. I personally suggest that students use a standard of quality to assess their projects on the basis of transparent processes and rigorous procedures.

ACTIVITY

Find a published qualitative article or a journal article of your academic interest. Review the criteria you have used to evaluate a qualitative study. Evaluate the selected article with the criteria proposed in this chapter, comparing the similarities and differences in evaluation process.

FURTHER RESOURCES

In this chapter I have drawn on several perspectives about quality standards in qualitative research. These perspectives can be found in the following works:

Hatch, J. A. (2002). *Doing qualitative research in education settings*. Albany: State University of New York Press.

Kuckartz, U. (2014). *Qualitative text analysis: A guide to methods, practice and using software*. London: Sage Ltd.

Mayan, M. J. (2009). *Essentials of qualitative inquiry*. Walnut Creek, CA: Left Coast.

Meyrick, J. (2006). What is good qualitative research? A first step toward a comprehensive approach to judging rigour/quality. *Journal of Health Psychology, 11*(5), 799–808.

Morse, J. M., & Richards, L. (2002). *README FIRST for a user's guide to qualitative methods*. Thousand Oaks, CA: Sage.

Richardson, L. (2000). Writing: A method of inquiry. In N. K. Denzin & Y. S. Lincoln (Eds.), *Handbook of qualitative research* (2nd ed., pp. 923–948). Thousand Oaks, CA: Sage.

Seale, C. (1999). Quality in qualitative research. *Qualitative Inquiry, 5*(4), 465–478.

Silverman, D. (2007). *A very short, fairly interesting and reasonably cheap book about qualitative research*. London: Sage Ltd.

Spencer, L., Ritchie, J., Lewis, J., & Dillon, L. (2003). *Quality in qualitative evaluation: A framework for assessing research evidence*. London: Cabinet Office.

Visit study.sagepub.com/30skills for quizzes, eFlashcards, and more!

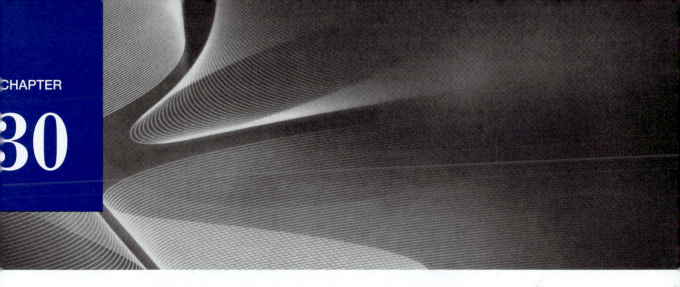

Introducing Qualitative Designs

Skill

As you proceed ahead with your qualitative study, include a qualitative design.

Why the Skill Is Important

For publications, for sophisticated qualitative studies, and for proposals or applications for funded projects, you need to go beyond the basic skills addressed in this book and start to incorporate more advanced thinking through specific qualitative research designs. Although we see in many published studies a thematic analysis of data and no mention of a specific design, the use of designs that inform many aspects of the process of qualitative research has become much more frequent (Creswell, 2014). The first time I became aware of the specific types of qualitative designs available to the researcher was in work by Jacob in 1987. She essentially came up with a categorization of qualitative research into "traditions," such as ecological psychology, symbolic interactionism, and holistic ethnography. Looking back a couple of years earlier, I could now see that different ways of conducting qualitative research were emerging, and that the classic text on qualitative research by Lincoln and Guba (1985) embraced a specific procedure—case study research. My favorite classification from this period was the tree diagram from the famous educational ethnographer Harry Wolcott. As shown in Figure 30.1, the trunk of the tree consisted of nonparticipant observation strategies, participant observation strategies, interview strategies, and archival strategies. On the branches of this trunk hung 20 types of qualitative approaches. The trunk and branches were then grounded into dimensions of everyday life.

FIGURE 30.1   **Qualitative Strategies in Educational Research**

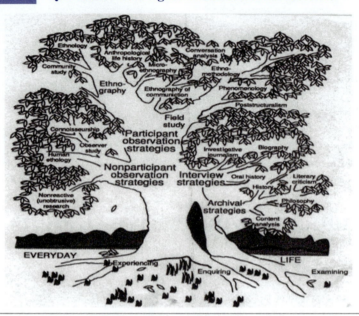

Source: Wolcott (1992). Used with permission from Academic Press.

I also knew that *quantitative research* had unfolded as specific designs, emerging from the correlational and group comparison experiments to an elaboration of different types of quasi-experimental and experimental designs and their accompanying threats to validity announced by Campbell and Stanley (1963). *Quantitative research* then expanded into the diverse approaches that we know today, including surveys, single-subject research, and the multiple experimental research forms. I felt that it was a matter of time until qualitative research did the same. By the early 1990s, it had done just that, and multiple authors came forward with their qualitative designs in specific books. For example, Strauss and Corbin (1990) announced a specific grounded theory approach, Moustakas (1994) described phenomenology, and Stake (1995) wrote about his case study design. The discussions about different types of qualitative research and these specific books on procedures led me to write *Qualitative Inquiry & Research Design: Choosing Among Five Approaches* (Creswell, 1998) to place side by side five different approaches to qualitative design so that inquirers might be able to select which approach might be best for their particular studies. So, today we have multiple approaches for how to design a qualitative study, and this design can be added to the skill base introduced in the chapters in this book to yield a more advanced design. A design is how to plan and conduct a research study, and the topics in this book have threaded throughout this process from philosophy, through methods, to conclusions and interpretations. Using a qualitative design helps reviewers identify the type of qualitative study you employ, adds to the rigor and sophistication of a study, and provides useful techniques for framing your project.

Moving From Generic to Types of Qualitative Designs

What exactly changes from the basic design of qualitative research as we move toward the incorporation of a specific type of research design? We can find clues about whether a qualitative study is more basic or incorporates a specific qualitative design. We must look into the methods section of a study and first see what types of qualitative data collection and analysis are used, and then examine how the inquirer reports the findings or results of a study.

> After you have mastered the basic skills in this book, explore the types of qualitative designs available to researchers and select one that addresses the intent of your study.

- In a basic study, the authors do not identify a specific *design type*. Instead of reporting that the study used a design such as phenomenology or grounded theory, the authors typically report that they collected interviews, observations, or documents. In short, the data collection is not grounded in a specific design.

- Turning to the *findings* in a study, in a basic approach, the authors report only themes and seldom do much else (perhaps they might interrelate the themes). When a qualitative design is used, the research follows the approach to reporting findings that is consistent with the design, such as the phenomenological procedures of significant statements, meaning units and the essence, or the grounded theory procedures of different types of coding (open, axial, or selective). In short, the findings section looks different between a generic approach and the use of a design.

- The *outcome* of a study will look different between a basic approach and a type of design. In the basic approach, the author often advances a diagram or picture of the overall findings. When the author uses a design, a distinct outcome emerges consistent with the design, such as a theory in grounded theory, a narrative story in narrative research, or a discussion of the essence of the phenomenon in phenomenology.

- The framing of the *research questions* will also differ. Although all qualitative questions need to be open ended to allow the participants to express their diverse views, the wording of the questions will differ between a basic design and a study that uses a specific research design. For example, contrast these two statements:

  o Basic: What does it mean to "bully" another person?

  o Grounded theory: What theory emerges about the process that occurs when one person "bullies" another?

- The second statement illustrates how the specific language changes when a design is used. Consistent with good grounded theory practice, we learn that the focus will be on a "process" and that the outcome of the study will be the identification of a "theory." This language labels the research question as a grounded theory statement (see Creswell, 2013).

- Many *aspects of the study* are also framed differently between a basic design and the specific use of a qualitative design. For example, the author titles the study differently, as well as the use of theory, the writing structure, and the evaluation criteria used to assess the quality of the study.

The Choice of Five Designs to Emphasize

Taking our cue from the Wolcott's (1992) tree, we have many types of qualitative designs (or what he called strategies) from which to select. When I decided to write about the various types (Creswell, 1998), I considered what types were most prevalent in the social and health sciences. I then conferred with my publisher, SAGE Publications, and I looked across a number of journals to see what types were being identified. Remember, this was in the late 1990s, and I wanted to reflect different disciplinary perspectives as well as popular approaches at that time. I also wanted to be able to point the reader toward at least one book that laid out the design type in a systematic manner. The beginning researcher, I felt, needed some concrete guidance for conducting qualitative research. I also wanted to include in the book recent journal publications so that the reader could see at least one good example of a published study using the design. Finally, I had engaged in a number of these designs in my own research, and I needed to try out each approach before I could recommend it. Now, writing about 15 years later, I understand that the field of qualitative research has moved forward. More and more individuals, for example, are using participatory action research designs as well as discourse analysis designs. I could certainly add more approaches, but ultimately I chose five approaches to emphasize:

- Narrative research

- Phenomenology

- Grounded theory

- Ethnography

- Case study

Narrative Research

A narrative research study would report an interesting story about the personal experiences of an individual. In it, the author would:

- Focus on a *single individual* (or two or three individuals). In many narrative projects, there is a focus on a single individual that the researcher selects on the basis of criteria, such as an ordinary person, a person of strong conceptual interest, or a well-known individual. The characteristics of individuals studied in narrative research vary. Sometimes qualitative researchers select more than one individual, but the intent is the same: to report stories about the individual's life that illuminates a specific issue. This focus may be in the form of an autoethnography or autobiography that features the stories of the author, a biography of another person, or stories of individuals in a classroom or specific situation.

- Collect stories about the *individual's experiences* (Clandinin & Connelly, 2000). These stories result from diverse types of data from interviews, observations, and documents. These stories often have a narrative arc with a beginning, a middle, and an end.

- Develop a *chronology* that connects different phases or aspects of a story. It is not necessary, but these stories may be told chronologically, over time, punctuated by events. Sometimes these stories can begin at the end, or at the middle, rather than being told in a linear, timeline fashion. Because individuals do not typically tell stories in a linear fashion, it is up to the researcher to "restory" the story, to place it within a chronological story line (Ollerenshaw & Creswell, 2002).

- Analyze the stories for *themes*. From the overall story, the qualitative researcher can identify themes that emerge from the story as well as report the overall story. Typically, the writing structure is to first report the story and then highlight several themes to emerge from the story.

- Highlight an *epiphany* or *significant turning point* in the life of the individual. At these points, the story takes a decided turn or new development that shapes the outcome of the story.

- Place the story and themes within a specific *context* or *situations*. The narrative researcher discusses to some extent the context or setting of the stories and the themes. This helps develop the context in which the stories are told. This context may be the workplace, the home, friends, or any other setting in which the stories take place. This provides necessary detail for the stories.

Phenomenological Research

In a phenomenological study, I would want to see a detailed description of how a number of individuals experience a specific phenomenon. Such a study would be one in which the author:

- Focuses on a single *phenomenon* to explore. The researcher identifies a specific concept or phenomenon to study. This concept may be something like "loneliness," "developing a professional identity," or "being a charismatic leader." It is a single concept and is the centerpiece of the phenomenological study.

- Collects data from *individuals who have experienced the phenomenon*. This is an important idea in phenomenology. Individuals studied must have had experience with the phenomenon. The size of the group may vary from 3 to 15 individuals. The forms of data collected in a phenomenological study, however, are diverse, and can range from the typical form of one-on-one interviews to an eclectic array of data sources such as observations, documents such as poems and written letters, and music and sounds. The key question to be answered is "How are individuals experiencing the phenomenon?"

- Explores the *context* in which the individuals experience the phenomenon. Besides an understanding of how the individuals experience the phenomenon, the researcher is also interested in the question "What is the context in which the individuals are experiencing the phenomenon?" This context may be the specific setting, individuals, conversations, the workplace, or the home.

- Frames the study within a broad *philosophy*. Phenomenology has strong philosophical roots and is based on the key idea that the lived experiences of individuals involve both the subjective experiences of people as well as an objective experience of sharing something with others.

- *Brackets out* personal experiences. Phenomenologists discuss how they set aside their personal experiences in order to learn how the individuals they study experience the phenomenon of interest. Of course, this is impossible to do completely, but we find in good phenomenology a discussion about the author's personal experience with the phenomenon so that he or she can best report on the experiences of others.

- Reports on the *essence* of the experience. The essence is simply the common experiences of individuals—what they have in common about the phenomenon (e.g., loneliness). This essence is reported as a discussion toward the end of the study. A phenomenologist gets to this essence through a series of steps, such as locating significant statements in the interview transcripts, developing meaning units that aggregate these statements, and then developing a description of what the individuals have experienced and the context of their experiences (Moustakas, 1994). In the end, the phenomenologist reports a detailed description of how several individuals commonly experience the phenomenon—the essence of the phenomenon.

Grounded Theory

In a grounded theory study, the intent of the researcher is to generate a theory that explains a process, an action, or an interaction. Specifically, the author:

- Seeks a *general explanation,* a *theory,* of a process, or how people act or interact (e.g., how a committee decides to implement a new program). This qualitative design requires knowing about the nature of a theory, especially as traditionally viewed within the social and behavioral sciences. A theory is an explanation that helps predict what will occur, how people will behave, or how events will unfold in many situations. We say that a theory can be generalized to many situations and can range from a narrow theory (e.g., how one committee at one school implements a new program) to a broad theory (e.g., how the implementation of a new program works in many settings, such as the YMCA, the Girl Scouts, the Congregational church, the elementary school, and so forth).

- Reports how the *process* of the theory unfolds. The qualitative researcher reports on how the process unfolds in steps—what occurs first, what occurs second, and so forth. A process is something that unfolds over time in somewhat distinct steps that can be identified.

- Documents this process with evidence from *interviews* and from *memos*. Interviews are the typical form of data collection for grounded theory. From these interviews, the grounded theorist documents how the process unfolds over time. While these interviews are being conducted, the researcher writes memos of what the process might look like. So data collection in grounded theory is an interactive process of collecting data, writing memos about the process, and forging the final picture of the process.

- Advances a theory. The grounded theory project culminates in the *identification of a theory*, a general explanation of a process (or an action or interaction). The researcher may develop this theory on the basis of a series of analytic steps that include coding the data in several ways, such as open coding, axial coding, and selective coding (Strauss & Corbin, 1990). The theory may appear as a description of the explanation of the process, or, more likely, it may appear as a diagram that highlights the major steps in the theory and the process that was involved. Accompanying the diagram may be hypotheses or research questions that the theory raises for future testing.

Ethnographic Research

The basic idea of an ethnographic study is to describe how a cultural group develops patterns of action, talking, and behavior from interacting together over time. The author:

- Identifies a *culture-sharing group* and what is of interest to study about this group. This group is an intact one that has been interacting for some time (e.g., a punk rock group). In their process of interaction, they have begun to develop shared ways about how they talk, how they behave, their rituals, their ways of communicating, their patterns of dress, and many other aspects of what we would call "culture." The ethnographer may focus on one aspect of the culture for close inspection (i.e., cultural concepts or theory), such as their communication, or may more broadly seek to describe many aspects of their culture (e.g., their dress, their interaction). This culture-sharing group can be quite large, such as Native Americans who belong to the Cherokee tribe, or quite small, such as a single elementary school classroom of 20 people.

- Records beliefs, ideas, behaviors, language, and rituals primarily through conducting *interviews* and *observations*. A cultural theme is specified that will be examined in light of this culture-sharing group.

- Spends *considerable time* with the group to learn about the culture they share. A hallmark of good ethnography is that the researcher spends extended periods of time "in the field" with the culture-sharing group. This time may be 6 months or longer. The idea is that patterns of behavior, language, and ideas evolve over time, and the ethnographer needs to examine how these patterns develop and become established within a group. This all takes time.

- Develops a detailed *description* and *themes* of how the group works. The end product of an ethnography is a detailed description about the culture sharing, followed by themes that describe the patterns of beliefs, ideas, behaviors, and language that have emerged over time with the group. On the basis of this description and themes, the ethnographer then writes a description about how the culture-sharing group works. Often this description is one that members of the group may not realize or consciously reflect. It may also not be one that an "outsider" to the group knows about. Good ethnographies, for example, have been written about inner-city gangs and how they operate—certainly workings that are not usually familiar to people or consciously reflected by members of the gang. Sometimes this description is written as a set of "rules" for how the culture-sharing group works (see Creswell, 2013).

Case Study Research

The basic idea in case study research is to select a case (or several cases, a multiple case study) and describe how the case illustrates a problem or an issue. This leads to an in-depth analysis of the case. The author would:

- Clearly *identify the case* being described in the study. A case could be a concrete entity such as a group, an individual, an organization, a community, a relationship, a decision process, or a specific project. Case studies are often used to study or evaluate programs. A case study could encompass many people or a few people or span a long period of time or a short period. In other words, it is bounded by time and place, and its borders can clearly be separated from the larger context of which it is a part. The research could involve a single case or multiple cases. The researcher therefore identifies the case and describes its bounding.

- Describe the case of interest (and it may be an unusual case and of intrinsic interest), but the researcher chooses the case in order to provide insight into an *issue* or a *problem*. A study of adolescent pregnancy (an issue) may be understood by examining one specific center (the case) that provides support for pregnant adolescent girls. The issue may be broad in scope, or confined to a small geographical area. The case bounds where the issue is studied.

- Collect *multiple sources of data* to provide an in-depth perspective about the issue within the case. A hallmark of good case study work is the collection and analysis of multiple sources of qualitative data, such as interviews, observations, documents, and visual materials. In many case studies, we see a table that organizes various sources of data and reports on the expansive extent of the data collection to develop the in-depth description of the case.

- Develop the case. The end product of a case study is a case. The *analysis* of the multiple sources of information results in this detailed description of the case, followed by the themes that emerge from the data, and generalizations (or assertions) about the case (Stake, 1995). Generalizations are ways in which the issue being explored is now better understood by learning about the case. In the end, the reader should emerge with an in-depth analysis of the issue being explored by the case study.

How Do You Choose What Design Is Appropriate for Your Project?

Certainly several factors contribute to your choice of one of these five types of qualitative designs. At the top of my list would be the overall intent of your project. Each of these five designs leads to different "products" at the end of your qualitative study. Examine Figure 30.2, a decision tree that might be useful to help you select the best type of qualitative design for a project.

As shown in this figure, if your research question focuses on developing a portrait of an individual, then narrative research would be the best qualitative design. Also,

FIGURE 30.2   **Five Types of Qualitative Designs Differing by Intent of the Research Question**

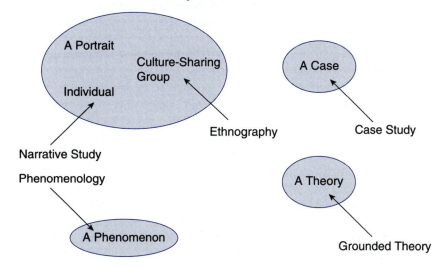

developing a portrait of a culture-sharing group would lead to an ethnography. A case study emerges when the question relates to describing a case, and a phenomenological study results from exploring the experiences of individuals about a phenomenon. In grounded theory, the outcome of the study leads to the development of a theory, a general explanation for a process. Beyond the intent to be accomplished by your question, other factors will play a role in the selection of your qualitative design: the audience for your study and their knowledge of qualitative designs, your training in learning specific types of designs, the needs in your scholarly literature, and your personal preference for a more structured approach (e.g., grounded theory) or a more literary approach (e.g., narrative research).

An Example, "Turning the Story"

To illustrate these five types, I will create a simple qualitative research project and then discuss how each design would be crafted differently given the type of design used. Assume that we are interested in this question: How do students learn qualitative research in the graduate school classroom? This question is broad enough so that any of the five approaches could be used. But as I have just discussed, the intent or outcome of the study will differ widely depending on your design. This "turning of the story" way of highlighting differences among the five types of qualitative designs was used in the last chapter of my qualitative inquiry book (Creswell, 2013), as I mentioned in Chapter 27 when I talked about designing different types of conclusions.

Using a *narrative* design, I would select an individual in the class to tell the story of learning qualitative research. It might be the student who has tested best in the class so far, or it might be someone who is available and willing to participate in my study. I would interview the person as well as his or her friends and perhaps look at the notes they have taken in class. As I go over this information I am thinking about the storyline I would like to write, preferably a story with a beginning, a middle, and an end. During the interview, of course, the participant will not tell me the story in the way I will tell it (I will be restorying the participant's story). I will look for "a-ha" moments in the story (a turning point) where the participant changed direction during the class or had a sudden insight about qualitative research. I would highlight this turning point. I might also emphasize themes that emerge from the data, such as learning through books in the class or through interacting with other students. In the end, I would write an interesting story about this individual's personal experiences and wrap the story around the turning point of his or her interest in qualitative research.

In my *phenomenological* design, I would be interested in knowing how several people in the class (say, 10 of them) all have common experiences with learning qualitative research. I would try to set aside my own experiences with the class and conduct interviews with the 10 students. I would then ask them, "What did you experience in this class?" and "What was the context in which you experienced qualitative research?" I would then analyze the data and describe what all of my participants had in common (the essence) about the experience and the various contexts (e.g., through the books, in conversations out in the hall, through the PowerPoint lectures) in which they best learned about qualitative research.

In my *grounded theory* design I would be interested in developing a theory about *how* the students learned qualitative research. What were the steps in this process? I would conduct interviews with several students in the class (maybe 10 again) and begin to develop a theory that explains their processes of learning. It might be that they learned best through visual diagrams of various aspects of qualitative research (e.g., a diagram of the theory) or through their own notes (memos) that they wrote during the class sessions. They might tell me that diagrams are a good method for learning. I would try to identify why diagrams are good methods, how diagrams were used in the class, what strategies the instructor employed in using the diagrams, and what their overall impact might be. These aspects would provide information about the process of learning qualitative research, and I would end by drawing a diagram (myself) of the process with all of the parts identified. In short, I would generate an explanation about the process of learning qualitative research through diagrams.

In my *ethnographic* study, I would view the class as a culture-sharing group. I would observe them through the semester-long class and conduct interviews with a few of them. From these sources of data I would be interested in the culture-sharing patterns that emerged—how they talked about qualitative research, what they believed qualitative research to be, and how they typically engaged in learning the content (e.g., by sitting in the same seats each week). In my ethnographic report at the end of the semester I would describe the classroom context—how the content unfolded, where the students sat, how the delivery of content emerged during the semester, and other aspects to provide a good understanding of the culture-sharing classroom group. I would then identify several themes related to "learning qualitative research," such as the types of words they used to explain it that emerged during the semester. Through this report, I would be able to provide someone who was not in the class or not familiar with learning qualitative research a good description of how these students learned the subject and what patterns of experiences emerged during the semester.

In my *case study*, I would need to first identify my case. I might select the entire class as my case, and seek to develop a detailed description of the class as well as themes that emerged about an issue in the class, such as the "grading practices" used by the instructor. I would collect different sources of data, such as interviews, observation, and the syllabus (a document) that provides and understanding of grading. My case study would then first describe the case (e.g., the content, the sessions, when grading occurred, what was graded) and then identify themes that the data yielded about grading, such as students' reactions to the grading practices, how students felt about the fairness of grading, the types of grades actually given to the students by the instructor, and other themes. In the end, my case study report would be an in-depth understanding of grading using one case (the class) as a site where qualitative grading practices were implemented. My case study would first describe the case and then go into the themes of the case. I would end with some generalizations about what I learned about grading through this case.

SUMMARY

This book has emphasized a large set of skills for engaging in qualitative research. It provides a basic understanding of the topic and the skills that will be useful in conducting a qualitative research study. It does not go into a more advanced level of understanding qualitative research, which can be obtained by studying the various types of qualitative designs. This advanced level is available in other books. In those books you will learn about specific designs, and plans for conducting qualitative research within those designs. In this chapter I have emphasized five types: narrative research, phenomenology, grounded theory, ethnography, and case studies. They differ in what they attempt to accomplish: to present a good story of an individual's experiences (narrative research); to describe what a number of people experience about a phenomenon (phenomenological research); to develop a theoretical understanding of a process (grounded theory); to describe the patterns of ideas, behaviors, and language of a culture-sharing group of people (ethnography); or to provide an in-depth understanding of a case that is used to illuminate a specific issue (case study). From this basic skill orientation of this book, I would recommend now that you proceed on to a specific qualitative research design and select an appropriate design based on your research question and what you intend to accomplish with the design.

ACTIVITY

From the skills introduced in this book, identify those that would be most useful for you to use as you proceed to learn about a specific qualitative design for a project.

Identify the skills and then discuss how you would use them in one of the five types of designs in this chapter—a narrative study, a phenomenological study, a grounded theory study, an ethnography, or a case study.

FURTHER RESOURCES

Examine these references for specific approaches to narrative research, phenomenology, grounded theory, ethnography, and case studies:

Clandinin, D. J., & Connelly, E. M. (2000). *Narrative inquiry: Experience and story in qualitative research.* San Francisco, CA: Jossey-Bass.

Corbin, J., & Strauss, A. (2007). *Basics of qualitative research: Techniques and procedures for developing grounded theory* (3rd ed.). Thousand Oaks, CA: Sage.

Corbin, J., & Strauss, A. (2014). *Basics of qualitative research: Techniques and procedures for developing grounded theory* (4th ed.). Thousand Oaks, CA: Sage.

Creswell, J. W. (2013). *Qualitative inquiry & research design: Choosing among five approaches* (3rd ed.). Thousand Oaks, CA: Sage.

Moustakas, C. (1994). *Phenomenological research methods.* Thousand Oaks, CA: Sage.

Stake, R. (1995). *The art of case study research.* Thousand Oaks, CA: Sage.

Wolcott, H. F. (1999). *Ethnography: A way of seeing.* Walnut Creek, CA: Altamira.

Wolcott, H. F. (2010). *Ethnography lessons: A primer.* Walnut Creek, CA: Left Coast.

Visit study.sagepub.com/30skills for quizzes, eFlashcards, and more!

REFERENCES

Adams, V., Burke, N. J., & Whitmarsh, I. (2014). Slow research: Thoughts for a movement in global health. *Medical Anthropology*, *33*(3), 179–197.

Agency for Healthcare Research and Quality. (2009, September). *The AHRQ informed consent and authorization toolkit for minimal risk research*. Retrieved from http://www.ahrq.gov/funding/policies/informedconsent/icform1.html

Agger, B. (1991). Critical theory, poststructuralism, postmodernism: Their sociological relevance. *Annual Review of Sociology*, *17*, 105–131.

American Psychological Association. (2010). *Publication manual of the American Psychological Association* (6th ed.). Washington, DC: Author.

Anderson, E. H., & Spencer, M. H. (2002). Cognitive representations of AIDS: A phenomenological study. *Qualitative Health Research*, *12*(10), 1338–1352.

Angrosino, M. (2007). *Doing ethnographic and observational research*. London: Sage Ltd.

Angrosino, M. V. (1994). On the bus with Vonnie Lee: Explorations in life history and metaphor. *Journal of Contemporary Ethnography*, *23*(1), 14–28. doi:10.1177/089124194023001002

Asmussen, K. J., & Creswell, J. W. (1995). Campus response to a student gunman. *Journal of Higher Education*, *66*, 575–591.

Auerbach, S. (2007). From moral supporters to struggling advocates reconceptualizing parent roles in education through the experience of working-class families of color. *Urban Education*, *42*, 250–283.

Badiee, M. (2011). *Portraits of empowerment exhibited by One Million Signatures Campaign activists* (Doctoral dissertation). Lincoln: University of Nebraska-Lincoln.

Bananuka, T., & John, V. M. (2015). Picturing community development work in Uganda: Fostering dialogue through photovoice. *Community Development Journal*, *50*(20), 196–212. doi:10.1093/cdj/bsu036

Bazeley, P. (2013). *Qualitative data analysis: Practical strategies*. London: Sage Ltd.

Bazeley, P., & Jackson, K. (2013). *Qualitative data analysis with NVivo* (2nd ed.). London: Sage Ltd.

Benoit, C., Jansson, M., Millar, A., & Phillips, R. (2005). Community-academic research on hard-to-reach populations: Benefits and challenges. *Qualitative Health Research*, *15*, 263–282.

Berg, B. L. (2004). *Qualitative research methods for the social sciences* (5th ed.). Boston: Allyn & Bacon.

Bhattacharya, K. (2013). Border crossing: Bridging empirical practices with de/colonizing epistemologies. In N. K. Denzin & M. D. Giardina (Eds.), *Global dimensions of qualitative inquiry* (pp. 115–134). Walnut Creek, CA: Left Coast.

Bogdan, R., & Biklen, S. K. (1992). *Qualitative research for education. An introduction to theory and methods* (2nd ed.). Needham Heights, MA: Allyn & Bacon.

Bogdan, R. C., & Biklen, S. K. (1998). *Qualitative research for education: An introduction to theory and methods* (3rd ed.). Needham Heights, MA: Allyn & Bacon.

Bogdan, R., & Biklen, S. K. (2006). *Qualitative research for education: An introduction to theories and methods* (5th ed.). Upper Saddle River, NJ: Pearson Education.

Boice, R. (1990). *Professors as writers: A self-help guide to productive writing*. Stillwater, OK: New Forums.

Boyle, M., & McKay, J. (1995). "You leave your troubles at the gate": A case study of the exploitation of older women's labor and "leisure" in sport. *Gender & Society*, *9*(5), 556–575.

Brinkmann, S., & Kvale, S. (2015). *Interviews: Learning the craft of qualitative research* (3rd ed.). Thousand Oaks, CA: Sage.

Brown, J., Sorrell, J. H., McClaren, J., & Creswell, J. W. (2006). Waiting for a liver transplant. *Qualitative Health Research*, *16*(1), 119–136. doi:10.1177/1049732305284011

Buckley, C. (2011, November 25). How it went. *The New York Times*. Retrieved from http://www.nytimes.com/2011/11/27/books/review/and-so-it-goes-kurt-vonnegut-a-life-by-charles-j-shields-book-review.html

Campbell, D., & Stanley, J. (1963). Experimental and quasi-experimental designs for research. In N. L. Gage (Ed.), *Handbook of research on teaching* (pp. 1–76). Chicago: Rand McNally.

Carey, J. W., Morgan, M., & Oxtoby, M. J. (1996). Intercoder agreement in analysis of responses to open-ended interview questions: Examples from tuberculosis research. *Cultural Anthropology Methods, 8*(3), 1–5.

Chambers, R. (2007). *Poverty research: Methodologies, mindsets and multidimensionality*. Brighton, UK: Institute of Development Studies at the University of Sussex.

Churchill, S. L., Plano Clark, V. L., Prochaska-Cue, K., Creswell, J. W., & Ontai-Grzebik, L. (2007). How rural low-income families have fun: A grounded theory study. *Journal of Leisure Research, 39*, 271–294.

Clandinin, D. J., & Connelly, E. M. (2000). *Narrative inquiry: Experience and story in qualitative research*. San Francisco, CA: Jossey-Bass.

Cohen, D., & Crabtree, B. (2008). *Qualitative Research Guidelines Project*. Retrieved February 3, 2015, from http://www.qualres.org

Cohen, J. (1960). A coefficient of agreement for nominal scales. *Educational and Psychological Measurement, 20*, 37–46.

Constantine, M. G., Wallace, B. C., & Kindaichi, M. M. (2005). Examining contextual factors in the career decision status of African American adolescents. *Journal of Career Assessment, 13*(3), 307–319. doi:10.1177/1069072705274960

Cook, K. (2008). Marginalized populations. In L. Given (Ed.), *The SAGE encyclopedia of qualitative research methods* (pp. 496–497). Thousand Oaks, CA: Sage.

Corbin, J., & Strauss, A. (2007). *Basics of qualitative research: Techniques and procedures for developing grounded theory* (3rd ed.). Thousand Oaks, CA: Sage.

Corbin, J., & Strauss, A. (2014). *Basics of qualitative research: Techniques and procedures for developing grounded theory* (4th ed.). Thousand Oaks, CA: Sage.

Creswell, J. W. (1994). *Research design: Qualitative and quantitative approaches*. Thousand Oaks, CA: Sage.

Creswell, J. W. (1998). *Qualitative inquiry & research design: Choosing among five approaches* (2nd ed.). Thousand Oaks, CA: Sage.

Creswell, J. W. (2009). *How SAGE has shaped research methods: A 40-year history*. Retrieved from http://www.sagepub.com/repository/binaries/pdfs/HistoryofMethods.pdf

Creswell, J. W. (2013). *Qualitative inquiry & research design: Choosing among five approaches* (3rd ed.). Thousand Oaks, CA: Sage.

Creswell, J. W. (2014). *Research design: Qualitative, quantitative, and mixed methods approaches* (4th ed.). Thousand Oaks, CA: Sage.

Creswell, J. W. (2015). *Educational research: Planning, conducting, and evaluating quantitative and qualitative research* (5th ed.). Boston: Pearson.

Creswell, J. W., & Garrett, A. L. (2008). The "movement" of mixed methods research and the role of educators. *South African Journal of Education, 28*(3), 321–333.

Creswell, J. W., & Maietta, R. C. (2002). Qualitative research. In D. C. Miller & N. J. Salkind (Eds.), *Handbook of research design and social measurement* (6th ed., pp. 143–184). Thousand Oaks, CA: Sage.

Creswell, J. W., & Miller, D. L. (2000). Determining validity in qualitative inquiry. *Theory Into Practice, 39*(3), 124–130. doi:10.1207/s15430421tip3903_2

Crotty, M. (1998). *The foundations of social research: Meaning and perspective in the research process*. London: Sage Ltd.

Czarniawska, B. (2004). *Narratives in social science research*. London: Sage Ltd.

Davidson, P., & Page, K. (2012). Research participation as work: Comparing the perspectives of researchers and economically marginalized populations. *American Journal of Public Health, 102*(7), 1254–1259.

Deardorff, D. K. (2006). Identification and assessment of intercultural competence as a student outcome of internationalization. *Journal of Studies in International Education, 10*, 241–266.

Denzin, N. K. (1978). *The research act: A theoretical introduction to sociological methods* (2nd ed.). New York: McGraw-Hill.

Denzin, N. K. (1989). *Interpretive biography*. Newbury Park, CA: Sage.

Denzin, N. K., & Giardina, M. D. (Eds.). (2013). *Global dimensions of qualitative inquiry*. Walnut Creek, CA: Left Coast.

Denzin, N. K., & Lincoln, Y. S. (Eds.). (1994). *Handbook of qualitative research*. Thousand Oaks, CA: Sage.

Denzin, N. K., & Lincoln, Y. S. (Eds.). (2011). *The SAGE handbook of qualitative research* (4th ed.). Thousand Oaks, CA: Sage.

Dower, N. (2002). Global ethics and global citizenship. In N. Dower & J. Williams (Eds.), *Global citizenship: A critical introduction* (pp. 146–157). New York: Routledge.

Dutro, E., Kazemi, E., & Balf, R. (2006). Making sense of "The Boy Who Died": Tales of a struggling successful writer. *Reading & Writing Quarterly, 22*(4), 325–356.

Eisenhart, M. A., & Howe, K. R. (1992). Validity in educational research. In M. D. LeCompte, W. L. Millroy, & J. Preissle (Eds.), *The handbook of qualitative research in education* (pp. 643–680). San Diego, CA: Academic Press.

Ellis, C. (1993). "There are survivors": Telling a story of sudden death. *Sociological Quarterly, 34*(4), 711–730.

Fielding, N. G. (2013). Qualitative research in a globalizing world. In N. K. Denzin & M. D. Giardina (Eds.), *Global dimensions of qualitative inquiry* (pp. 47–62). Walnut Creek, CA: Left Coast.

Fish, S. E. (2011). *How to write a sentence and how to read one.* New York: HarperCollins.

Fisher, C. B., Oransky, M., Mahadevan, M., Singer, M., Mirhej, G., & Hodge, D. (2008). Marginalized populations and drug addiction research: Realism, mistrust, and misconception. *IRB: Ethics and Human Research, 30*(3), 1–9.

Freeman, M., deMarrais, K., Preissle, J., Roulston, K., & St. Pierre, E. A. (2007). Standards of evidence in qualitative research: An incitement to discourse. *Educational Researcher, 36*(1), 25–32.

Freshwater, D., Cahill, J., Walsh, E., Muncey, T., & Esterhuizen, P.

(2012). Art and science in health care research: Pushing at open doors or locked in institutions? *Qualitative Health Research, 22,* 1176–1183.

Geertz, C. (1973). Thick description: Toward an interpretive theory of culture. In C. Geertz, *The interpretation of cultures: Selected essays* (pp. 3–30). New York: Basic Books.

Gilbert, K. R. (Ed.). (2001). *The emotional nature of qualitative research.* Boca Raton, FL: CRC.

Gilgun, J. F. (2005). Qualitative research and family psychology. *Journal of Family Psychology, 19*(1), 40.

Glesne, C., & Peshkin, A. (1992). *Becoming qualitative researchers: An introduction.* White Plains, NY: Longman.

Goldberg, N. (1993). *Long quiet highway: Waking up in America.* New York: Bantam.

Guest, G., Bunce, A., & Johnson, L. (2006). How many interviews are enough? An experiment with data saturation and variability. *Field Methods, 18*(1), 59–82.

Guest, G., MacQueen, K. M., & Namey, E. E. (2012). *Applied thematic analysis.* Thousand Oaks, CA: Sage.

Hall, S. (2015). Financial networks and the globalization of transnational corporations: The case of educational services. *Journal of Economic Geography, 15*(3), 539–559. doi:10.1093/jeg/lbu024

Hammersley, M., & Atkinson, P. (1995). *Ethnography: Principles in practice* (2nd ed.). London, UK: Routledge.

Harding, P. (2009). *Tinkers.* New York: Bellevue Literary Press.

Haski-Leventhal, D., & McLeigh, J. D. (2009). Firefighters volunteering beyond their duty: An essential asset in rural communities. *Journal of Rural and Community Development, 4*(2), 80–92.

Hatch, J. A. (2002). *Doing qualitative research in education settings.* Albany: State University of New York Press.

Hesse-Biber, S. N., & Leavy, P. (2006). *Emergent methods in social research.* Thousand Oaks, CA: Sage.

Holstein, J., & Gubrium, J. F. (Eds.). (2003). *Inside interviewing: New lenses, new concerns.* Thousand Oaks, CA: Sage.

Hopfer, S., & Clippard, J. R. (2011). College women's HPV vaccine decision narratives. *Qualitative Health Research, 21,* 262–277. doi:10.1177/1049732310383868

Hsieh, H.-F., & Shannon, S. E. (2005). Three approaches to qualitative content analysis. *Qualitative Health Research, 15*(9), 1277–1288.

Hudson, P., & Taylor-Henley, S. (2001). Beyond the rhetoric: Implementing a culturally appropriate research project in First Nations communities. *American Indian Culture and Research Journal, 25,* 93–105.

Jacob, E. (1987). Qualitative research traditions: A review. *Review of Educational Research, 57,* 1–50.

James, D.C.S., Pobee, J. W., Oxidine, D., Brown, L., & Joshi, G. (2012). Using the Health Belief Model to develop culturally appropriate weight-management materials for African-American women. *Journal of the Academy of Nutrition and Dietetics, 112*(5), 664–670.

James, N., & Busher, H. (2009). *Online interviewing*. London: Sage Ltd.

Jones, R. T., Hadder, J., Carvajal, F., Chapman, S., & Alexander, A. (in press). Conducting research in diverse, minority, and marginalized communities. In F. Norris, S. Galea, M. Friedman, & P. Watson (Eds.), *Research methods for studying mental health after disasters and terrorism*. New York: Guilford.

King, S. (2000). *On writing: A memoir of the craft*. New York: Simon & Schuster.

Knoblauch, H., Tuma, R., & Schnettler, B. (2014). Video analysis and videography. In U. Flick (Ed.), *The SAGE handbook of qualitative data analysis* (pp. 435–449). London: Sage Ltd.

Kretzmann, J., & McKnight, J. (1993). *Building communities from the inside out: A path toward finding and mobilizing a community's assets*. Evanston, IL: The Asset-Based Community Development Institute, Institute for Policy Research, Northwestern University

Krueger, R. A., & Casey, M. A. (2009). *Focus groups: A practical guide for applied research* (4th ed.). Thousand Oaks: Sage.

Kuckartz, U. (2014). *Qualitative text analysis: A guide to methods, practice and using software*. London: Sage Ltd.

Kuhn, T. S. (1962). *The structure of scientific revolutions*. Chicago: University of Chicago Press.

Kvale, S., & Brinkmann, S. (2009). *Interviews: Learning the craft of qualitative research interviewing* (2nd ed.). Thousand Oaks, CA: Sage.

Lacroix, N. (1999). Macrostructure construction and organization in the processing of multiple text passages. *Instructional Science, 27*, 221–233.

Lather, P. (1993). Fertile obsession: Validity after poststructuralism. *Sociological Quarterly, 34*(4), 673–693.

Lee, S. H., & Olshfski, D. (2002). Employee commitment and firefighters: It's my job. *Public Administration Review, 62*(s1), 108–114.

Leland, J. (2011, November 25). A community of survivors dwindles. *The New York Times*. Retrieved from http://www.nytimes.com/2011/11/27/nyregion/community-of-holocaust-survivors-dwindles-in-queens.html?_r=0

Lincoln, Y. S., & Guba, E. G. (1985). *Naturalistic inquiry*. Beverly Hills, CA: Sage.

Lincoln, Y. S., Lynham, S. A., & Guba, E. G. (2011). Paradigmatic controversies, contradictions, and emerging confluences, revisited. In N. K. Denzin & Y. S. Lincoln (Eds.), *The SAGE handbook of qualitative research* (4th ed., pp. 97–128). Thousand Oaks, CA: Sage.

Lu, Y. L., Trout, S. K., Lu, K., & Creswell, J. W. (2005). The needs of AIDS-infected individuals in rural China. *Qualitative Health Research, 15*(9), 1149–1163.

Maiter, S., Alaggia, R., & Trocmé, N. (2004). Perceptions of child maltreatment by parents from the Indian subcontinent: Challenging myths about culturally based abusive parenting practices. *Child Maltreatment, 9*, 309–324.

Marshall, C., & Rossman, G. B. (2011). *Designing qualitative research* (5th ed.). Thousand Oaks, CA: Sage.

Maxwell, J. A. (2013). *Qualitative research design: An interactive approach* (3rd ed.). Thousand Oaks, CA: Sage.

Mayan, M. J. (2001). *An introduction to qualitative methods: A training module for students and professionals*. Edmonton, Canada: International Institute for Qualitative Methodology.

Mayan, M. J. (2009). *Essentials of qualitative inquiry*. Walnut Creek, CA: Left Coast.

McVea, K., Harter, L., McEntarffer, R., & Creswell, J. W. (1999). A phenomenological study of student experiences with tobacco use at City High School. *High School Journal, 82*, 209–222.

Meloy, J. M. (2002). *Writing the qualitative dissertation: Understanding by doing* (2nd ed.). Mahwah, NJ: Lawrence Erlbaum.

Merriam, S. B. (1998). *Qualitative research and case study applications in education*. San Francisco, CA: Jossey-Bass.

Merriam, S. B. (2009). *Qualitative research: A guide to design and implementation*. San Francisco, CA: Jossey-Bass.

Mertens, D. M., & Ginsberg, P. E. (Eds.). (2009). *The handbook of social research ethics*. Thousand Oaks, CA: Sage.

Meyrick, J. (2006). What is good qualitative research? A first step towards a comprehensive approach to judging rigour/quality. *Journal of Health Psychology, 11*(5), 799–808.

Miles, M. B., & Huberman, A. M. (1994). *Qualitative data analysis: An expanded sourcebook* (2nd ed.). Thousand Oaks, CA: Sage.

Miles, M. B., Huberman, A. M., & Saldaña, J. (2014). *Qualitative data analysis: A methods sourcebook*

(3rd ed.). Thousand Oaks, CA: Sage.

Miller, D. L., Creswell, J. W., & Olander, L. S. (1998). Writing and retelling multiple ethnographic tales of a soup kitchen for the homeless. *Qualitative Inquiry, 4*(4), 469–491.

Millhauser, S. (2008). *Dangerous laughter*. New York: Knopf.

Morrow, S. L., & Smith, M. L. (1995). Constructions of survival and coping by women who have survived childhood sexual abuse. *Journal of Counseling Psychology, 42*, 24–33.

Morse, J. M., & Richards, L. (2002). *Readme first for a user's guide to qualitative methods*. Thousand Oaks, CA: Sage.

Moustakas, C. (1994). *Phenomenological research methods*. Thousand Oaks, CA: Sage.

Ollerenshaw, J. A., & Creswell, J. W. (2002). Narrative research: A comparison of two restorying data analysis approaches. *Qualitative Inquiry, 8*, 329–347.

Olson, C. L., & Kroeger, K. R. (2001). Global competency and intercultural sensitivity. *Journal of Studies in International Education, 5*(2), 116–137.

Patton, M. Q. (2002). *Qualitative research and evaluation methods*. Thousand Oaks, CA: Sage.

Penn, G. (2000). Semiotic analysis of still images. In M. W. Bauer & G. Gaskell (Eds.), *Qualitative research with text, image and sound: A practical handbook* (pp. 227–245). London: Sage Ltd.

Plano Clark, V. L., Miller, D. L., Creswell, J. W., McVea, K., McEntarffer, R., Harter, L. M.,

& Mickelson, W. T. (2002). In conversation: High school students talk to students about tobacco use and prevention strategies. *Qualitative Health Research, 12*, 1264–1283.

Pohl, S. L., Borrie, W. T., & Patterson, M. E. (2000). Women, wilderness, and everyday life: A documentation of the connection between wilderness recreation and women's everyday lives. *Journal of Leisure Research, 32*, 415–434.

Prosser, J. (2011). Visual methodology: Toward a more seeing research. In N. K. Denzin & Y. S. Lincoln (Eds.), *The SAGE handbook of qualitative research* (4th ed., pp. 479–496). Thousand Oaks, CA: Sage.

Reid, C. (2004). *The wounds of exclusion: Poverty, women's health, and social justice*. Edmonton, Canada: Qualitative Institute Press.

Richards, L., & Morse, J. M. (2013). *Readme first for a user's guide to qualitative methods* (3rd ed.). Thousand Oaks, CA: Sage.

Richardson, L. (1985). *The new other woman: Contemporary single women in affairs with married men*. New York: Free Press.

Richardson, L. (1990). *Writing strategies: Reaching diverse audiences*. Newbury Park, CA: Sage.

Richardson, L. (1994). Writing: A method of inquiry. In N. Denzin & Y. Lincoln (Eds.), *Handbook of qualitative research* (pp. 516–529). Thousand Oaks, CA: Sage.

Richardson, L. (2000). Writing: A method of inquiry. In N. K. Denzin & Y. S. Lincoln (Eds.), *Handbook of qualitative research* (2nd ed., pp. 923–948). Thousand Oaks, CA: Sage.

Richardson, L., & St. Pierre, E. A. (2005). Writing: A method of inquiry. In N. K. Denzin & Y. S. Lincoln (Eds.), *The SAGE handbook of qualitative research* (3rd ed., pp. 959–978). Thousand Oaks, CA: Sage.

Rogers, E. B., Stanford, M. S., Dolan, S. L., Clark, J., Martindale, S. L., Lake, S. L., . . . Sejud, L. R. (2012). Helping people without homes: Simple steps for psychologists seeking to change lives. *Professional Psychology: Research and Practice, 43*(2), 86–93.

Rose, D. (2000). Analysis of moving images. In M. W. Bauer & G. Gaskell (Eds.), *Qualitative researching with text, image and sound: A practical handbook* (pp. 246–262). London: Sage Ltd.

Rosenblatt, P. C. (2001). Qualitative research as a spiritual experience. In K. R. Gilbert (Ed.), *The emotional nature of qualitative research* (pp. 111–128). Boca Raton, FL: CRC.

Ross-Larson, B. (1995). *Edit yourself: A manual for everyone who works with words*. New York: W. W. Norton.

Rossman, G. B., & Rallis, S. F. (2011). *Learning in the field: An introduction to qualitative research* (3rd ed.). Thousand Oaks, CA: Sage.

Rubin, H. J., & Rubin, I. S. (2012). *Qualitative interviewing: The art of hearing data* (3rd ed.). Thousand Oaks, CA: Sage.

Schwandt, T. A. (2007). *The SAGE dictionary of qualitative inquiry* (3rd ed.). Thousand Oaks, CA: Sage.

Seale, C. (1999). Quality in qualitative research. *Qualitative Inquiry, 5*(4), 465–478.

Shamoo, A. E., & Resnik, D. B. (2009). *Responsible conduct* of research. New York: Oxford University Press.

Shank, G. D. (2006). *Qualitative research: A personal skills approach* (2nd ed.). Upper Saddle River, NJ: Pearson.

Shaver, F. M. (2005). Sex work research: Methodological and ethical challenges. *Journal of Interpersonal Violence, 20,* 296–319.

Shenton, A. K. (2004). Strategies for ensuring trustworthiness in qualitative research projects. *Education for Information, 22*(2), 63–75.

Shivy, V. A., Wu, J. J., Moon, A. E., Mann, S. C., Holland, J. G., & Eacho, C. (2007). Ex-offenders reentering the workforce. *Journal of Counseling Psychology, 54,* 466–473.

Silver, C., & Lewins, A. (2014). *Using software in qualitative research: A step-by-step guide* (2nd ed.). London: Sage Ltd.

Silverman, D. (2007). *A very short, fairly interesting and reasonably cheap book about qualitative research*. London: Sage Ltd.

Smith-Miller, C. A., Leak, A., Harlan, C. A., Dieckmann, J., & Sherwood, G. (2010). "Leaving the comfort of the familiar": Fostering workplace cultural awareness through short-term global experiences. *Nursing Forum, 45*(1), 18–28.

Spencer, L., Ritchie, J., Lewis, J., & Dillon, L. (2003). *Quality in qualitative evaluation: A framework for assessing research evidence*. London: Cabinet Office.

Spencer, S. (2011). *Visual research methods in the social sciences: Awakening visions*. New York: Routledge.

Stake, R. (1995). *The art of case study research*. Thousand Oaks, CA: Sage.

Stake, R. E. (2010). *Qualitative research: Studying how things work*. New York: Guilford.

Strauss, A., & Corbin, J. (1990). *Basics of qualitative research: Grounded theory procedures and techniques*. Newbury Park, CA: Sage.

Sudnow, D. (1978). *Ways of the hand: The organization of improvised conduct*. Cambridge, MA: MIT Press.

Tarshis, B. (1985). *How to write without pain*. New York: Plume.

Terenzini, P., Pascarella, E., & Lorang, W. (1982). An assessment of the academic and social influences on freshman year educational outcomes. *Review of Higher Education, 5*(1), 86–109.

Terenzini, P. T., Cabrera, A. F., Colbeck, C. L., Parente, J. M., & Bjorklund, S. A. (2001). Collaborative learning vs. lecture/discussion: Students' reported learning gains. *Journal of Engineering Education, 90*(1), 123–130.

Thomas, J. A. & Pedersen, J. E. (2003). Reforming elementary science teachers preparation: What about extant teaching beliefs? *School Science and Mathematics, 103*(7), 319–330.

Thomas, J. A., Pedersen, J. E., & Finson, K. (2001). Validating the Draw-a-Science-Teacher-Test Checklist (DASTT-C): Negotiating mental models and teacher beliefs. *Journal of Science Teacher Education, 12*(4), 295–310.

Thornton, R. (2014, Second Quarter). Globalization in

market research holds many considerations for the industry. *ALERT!*, pp. 18–20.

Trostle, J. (1992). Research capacity building in international health: Definitions, evaluations and strategies for success. *Social Science & Medicine, 35,* 1321–1324.

van Maanen, J. (1988). *Tales of the field: On writing ethnography*. Chicago: University of Chicago Press.

Wang, C., & Burris, M. A. (1997). Photovoice: Concept, methodology, and use for participatory needs assessment. *Health Education & Behavior, 24*(3), 369–387.

Wang, C. C., & Redwood-Jones, Y. A. (2001). Photovoice ethics: Perspectives from Flint photovoice. *Health Education & Behavior, 28,* 560–572.

Webb, R. B., & Glesne, C. (1992). Teaching qualitative research. In M. D. LeCompte, W. L. Millroy, & J. Preissle (Eds.), *The handbook of qualitative research in education* (pp. 771–814). San Diego, CA: Academic Press.

Weis, L., & Fine, M. (2000). *Speed bumps: A student-friendly guide to qualitative research*. New York: Teachers College Press.

Wheeldon, J., & Ahlberg, M. K. (2012). *Visualizing social science research: Maps, methods, & meaning*. Thousand Oaks, CA: Sage.

Whitehead, C. (2012, July 26). How to write. *The New York Times Sunday Book Review*. Retrieved from http://www.nytimes.com/2012/07/29/books/review/colson-whiteheads-rules-for-writing.html?_r=0.

Whittemore, R. D., Langness, L. L., & Koegel, P. (1986). The life history approach to mental retardation. In L. L. Langness & H. G. Levine (Eds.), *Culture and retardation*. Dordrecht, the Netherlands: D. Reidel.

Wilkinson, A. M. (1991). *The scientist's handbook for writing papers and dissertations*. Edgewood Cliffs, NJ: Prentice Hall.

Wolcott, H. F. (1992). Posturing in qualitative research. In M. D. LeCompte, W. L. Millroy, & J. Preissle (Eds.), *The handbook of qualitative research in education* (pp. 3–52). San Diego, CA: Academic Press.

Wolcott, H. F. (1999). *Ethnography: A way of seeing*. Walnut Creek, CA: Altamira.

Wolcott, H. F. (2009). *Writing up qualitative research* (3rd ed.). Thousand Oaks, CA: Sage.

Wolcott, H. F. (2010). *Ethnography lessons: A primer*. Walnut Creek, CA: Left Coast.

Wolcott, H. F. (2010). Overdetermined behavior, unforeseen consequences. *Qualitative Inquiry, 16*(1), 10–20. doi:10.1177/1077800409349755

Yakaboski, T. (2010). Going at it alone: Single-mother undergraduate's experiences. *Journal of Student Affairs Research and Practice, 47*, 456–474.

Yang, K. S. (2000). Monocultural and cross-cultural indigenous approaches: The royal road to the development of a balanced global psychology. *Asian Journal of Social Psychology, 3*, 241–263.

GLOSSARY OF TERMS

Abstract: a brief summary of the contents of the qualitative study that allows readers to quickly survey the contents of an article

Advocacy theory: threaded throughout a project to inform the entire research process; ends with advocating for change or improvements for individuals or groups that have been oppressed

Axiology: the worldview belief in the use of values and bias in a study and how these differ from paradigm to paradigm

Case study research: a qualitative design with the intent to identify a case and describe how the case illustrates a problem or an issue

Central phenomenon: the one central idea you would like to learn about or study in your project; it is a concise (usually two- or three-word) label that is neither too broad nor too narrow

Central question: narrows the purpose down to a general question that will be addressed through the data collection

Coding: the process of analyzing qualitative text data by taking it apart to see what it yields before putting it back together in a meaningful way

Collaboration with participants: a validation strategy in which investigators check in with participants and involve them in key decisions in the research process to help establish accuracy

Community-based participatory research: an action-oriented research method in which members of the population of interest are engaged in all phases of the research

Conclusion section: the final section or discussion in a qualitative report; it includes a summary of findings, an interpretation of the findings as compared with the literature, your personal interpretation of findings, the limitations, future research suggestions, and the significance of the study

Constructivism: a paradigm worldview of beliefs that individuals form their own realities, subjective participant views are important, researcher values should be made explicit, methodology is inductive, and a personal type of language should be used in writing

Critical theory: a paradigm worldview of beliefs in reality shaped by social, political, and cultural events; subjective opinions within the context; values of the researcher; methods negotiated with participants; and rhetoric that addresses power

Design: a guide for how to plan and conduct a research study

Disconfirming evidence: a validation strategy to look through all of the evidence for exceptions to a particular theme and present an alternative explanation

Emotional journey: qualitative research is especially emotional because of at least three factors: the subject matter being explored, the lack of definite structure for conducting this form of inquiry, and the labor-intensive aspects of conducting this form of inquiry

Epistemology: the worldview belief in the relationship between what we know and what we see (i.e., between the researcher and that being researched)

Ethnographic research: a qualitative design with the intent to describe how a cultural group develops patterns of action, talking, and behavior from interacting together over time

External audit: a validation strategy that consists of someone outside of the project looking closely at it to help to determine that the information is accurate and the study is done in a rigorous way

Field notes: a record of what you are observing on your observational protocol; consider both descriptive and reflective field notes

Focus groups: conducting interviews in groups that typically include about six individuals; the synergy of the group encourages people to speak up, and ideas can expand because multiple individuals weigh in on topics

Gerund: an "-ing" word to convey action in the study; a qualitative gerund word is a good way to begin a qualitative title

Global cultural awareness: requires building country-level expertise, understanding methodological orientations in a country, and becoming knowledgeable about preferred data collection methods used by researchers in the location where research is to be conducted

Going native: an idea drawn from ethnography in which the researcher identifies closely with the people being studied

Grounded theory: a qualitative design with the intent to generate a theory that explains a process, an action, or an interaction

In vivo: the words of the actual participants

Inductive: the research process of gathering data and then making sense of them by grouping data segments into codes, themes, and larger perspectives

Institutional review board (IRB): a board that reviews your project to ensure that you have protected the rights of your human subjects; before collecting qualitative data, you need to receive approval from your IRB

Intercoder agreement: a process whereby one or more additional coders analyze the qualitative database, provide codes for the database, and compare the results of coders for the amount of agreement on the codes

Interviewing: asking open-ended questions of participants

Lean coding: analyzing qualitative data by coding to come up with a small number of codes, such as 20 to 25, regardless of the size of your database

Literature map: a visual summary of the literature that allows the reader (and author) to understand how the proposed qualitative study adds to, extends, or replicates the existing research

Marginalized groups: any group that is excluded from mainstream social, economic, cultural, or political life; they are often labeled as sensitive, underresearched, or hidden populations

Maximal variation sampling: a sampling strategy that consists of determining in advance some criterion that differentiates the sites or participants, and then selecting sites or participants that are quite different on the criterion

Member checking: a validation strategy in which the researcher takes back to participants their themes or entire stories and asks the participants whether the themes or stories are an accurate representation of what they said

Methodology: the worldview beliefs related to the research process, and how this process varies from a more set process to one that emerges throughout the project

Mistrust: lack of trust for researchers and the research process that may lead participants to give unreliable responses to questions about themselves and the community to which they belong

Multiple perspectives: qualitative research shares information about themes drawn from many different perspectives; it reports "the good, bad, and the ugly"

Narrative research: a qualitative design with the intent to report an interesting story about the personal experiences of an individual

Observer role: the role the researcher assumes when conducing an observation; this role can range from that of a complete participant (going native) to that of a complete observer

Observing: involves locating a site, developing a protocol for recording information, focusing in on events, looking for events and activities that help inform the central phenomenon, determining the appropriate role as an observer, and recording "descriptive" and "reflective" field notes on the observation protocol

Ontology: the worldview belief that qualitative researchers differ in terms of how they see what is real or what exists

Paradigm: a belief or attitude that shapes our research approach

Participatory: a paradigm worldview of beliefs that reality is political and constructed among the lines of race, class, and gender; research is collaborative and political with groups representing their interests; researchers advance their own values as well as those being researched; methodology involves participants to empower them and bring about change; and writing uses the language of the participants

Peer debriefing: a validation strategy that consists of the review of the project by someone who is familiar with the research or the central phenomenon being explored

Phenomenology: a qualitative design with the intent to develop a detailed description of how a number of individuals experience a specific phenomenon

Postpositivism: a paradigm worldview of beliefs in a singular reality, interdependence between the researcher and that being researched, objective values, deductive research, and scientific language when writing

Probes: in an interview protocol, reminders to the researcher to ask for more information and to ask for an explanation of ideas

Process of research: identify a research problem, frame the problem as questions, create a research plan, carry out the research plan, and report the findings

Prolonged engagement in the field: a validation strategy whereby the more time the researcher

spends in the field, the more accurate will be the inquirer's account

Protocol: the means for recording qualitative data and for asking questions; types of protocols include observational and interview

Purpose statement: the overall objective or intent of the study; includes the central phenomenon being explored, the participants who will be studied, and the site where the research will take place

Purposeful sampling: the process of selecting participants for a qualitative project based on recruiting individuals who can help inform the central phenomenon in a study

Qualitative data analysis (QDA) programs: computer applications that assist researchers to store data and to analyze, report, and visualize the codes and themes

Qualitative validity: findings are accurate; may be assessed through the eyes of the researcher, through the views of participants, and through readers and reviewers of studies

Quality criteria: expectations to judge the quality of a qualitative study

Reciprocity: involves the researcher's giving back to participants in some form, from a minor token of appreciation to a major form of support

Reflexivity: researchers reflect on and share how their experiences and backgrounds have an impact on shaping their accounts

Research problem: the issue leading to a need for the study and to be addressed by the study

Research site: the location studied or place where the qualitative research takes place

Rhetoric: the worldview belief in the use of language that varies from more formal to informal (e.g., use of first-person pronouns)

Rich description: details about the setting, the people, and the themes in a qualitative report

Semiotic analysis: an interpretive framework for image coding that divides coding into what the image denotes and what it connotes

Sensitive topics: qualitative research involves the study of emotionally charged topics that are hard to research

Shadow side: reversing the perspective on a topic to take an angle or perspective that may not be expected

Skill: a particular ability or form of expertise that can be developed and, once it is acquired, can help a person conduct a thorough, rigorous qualitative study

Social science theory: a theory from the social sciences that serves as a broad explanation for what you hope to find in your qualitative project; it often informs the research questions in a study

Sub-questions: research questions that subdivide the central question into parts or topics

Themes: broader categories of information composed of a group of similar codes to build evidence of support

Thick description: writing in a way to provide details about the setting, about people, and about events; offers connections to theory and science

Triangulation: building evidence from different sources to establish the themes in a study

Visual elicitation: an approach to participatory visual research in which the researcher uses a visual image, such as a photograph, in a research interview to stimulate (i.e., elicit) a response, generating dialogue

Voices of participants: qualitative research involves reporting how people talk about things, how they describe things, and how they see the world, including quotations

Worldview: the philosophical assumptions behind qualitative research, also referred to as a "paradigm"

NAME INDEX

SUBJECT INDEX

literary structure and,
244, 246 (figure)
qualitative approach and,
13–14, 14 (table)
qualitative research designs,
use of, 245
quantitative approach and,
12–13, 12 (table)
quotations, use of, 245
rejection category and, 244
resubmit category, 244
reviewer feedback and,
243–244
scientific structure and,
244, 245 (figure)
structure, concept map
of, 71–72, 72 (figure)
submission guidelines
and, 243
target journal, selection
of, 242–245
See also Abstracts;
Qualitative reports;
Titles
Journal Citation Reports, 235

Lean coding, 155–156, 158,
161 (figure)
Literature maps, 58
central phenomenon and, 64
design of, 61, 62–64,
63 (figure)
guidelines for, 64
narrative description of, 64–65
nature of, 62
subtopics and, 64
See also Literature reviews
Literature reviews:
challenges in, 59
prioritization of literature
resources and, 61–62
steps in, 60–62
use of, 59–60, 61 (table)
See also Literature maps

Marginalized groups, 7–8, 137
advocacy theory and,
43, 44–46
community advisory boards,
role of, 142

community-based
participatory research
and, 141
cultural/language barriers
and, 139 (table), 140, 142
data collection process and,
137, 138–142, 139 (table)
description of, 138
ethics issues and,
139 (table), 140, 142
indigenous methodologies
and, 146
informed consent and, 142
mistrust issue and,
139–140, 139 (table)
protocols, development of, 142
researcher reflexivity
and, 141
sampling/access challenges
and, 138–139,
139 (table), 141
transparency and, 142
See also Global cultural
awareness
Maximal variation sampling,
110, 111 (table)
MAXQDA 11 software,
185 (table), 186
Member checking, 192–193
Methodology, 41
Mistrust issue,
139–140, 139 (table)
Mixed methods research, 3
Multiple perspectives,
7, 8, 16, 178, 191

Narrative research,
234, 261–262, 268
NVivo 10 software, 186 (table)

Observation, 117
challenges in, 123–124
checklist for, 124, 124 (figure)
data collection and, 112,
112 (table), 114 (figure),
117, 118
deception and, 123–124
descriptive notes and,
119, 119–120 (figures),
121–122

field notes and, 118, 119,
121–123
guidelines for, 122–123
image data coding process
and, 169–170
nature of, 118
observational skills,
development of, 118
protocol for, 114, 118, 119,
119–120 (figures)
public spaces and, 123
reflective notes and, 119,
119–120 (figures), 122
sample observation,
120 (figure)
sensory experience of, 118
steps in, 119, 121–122
sub-questions, role of, 94, 122
triangulated data and, 117
See also Interviewing;
Observer role
Observer role, 118, 121
One Million Signatures
Campaign, 45
Ontology, 41
Open-ended exploration,
7, 14, 16
Opening sentences. *See*
Introduction section

Paradigms, 39
basic beliefs of, 41
constructivist paradigm,
40, 41 (table), 42
critical theory paradigm,
40, 41 (table), 42
definition of, 39
participatory paradigm,
40, 41 (table), 42
postpositivist paradigm,
40–42, 41 (table)
qualitative research, shaping
of, 39–40, 40 (figure)
worldviews and, 39
Participatory paradigm,
40, 41 (table), 42
Participatory research:
collaboration with
participants and, 193
reciprocity and, 110–111

research committee meetings, guidelines for, 33–34
See also Qualitative reports; Qualitative research
Research problems, 16, 18, 86 (figure), 88–89
Research questions, 94
central phenomenon and, 94, 100–101
central question and, 94, 97–100
sub-questions and, 94, 99, 100 (figure)
See also Purpose statements
Research sites, 19–20, 78–79, 106, 119
Rhetoric, 41
Rich description, 194

Sampling process:
marginalized groups and, 138–139, 139 (table), 141
maximal variation sampling, 110, 111 (table)
purposeful sampling, 109–110, 111 (table)
sample size, determination of, 110
typology of sampling strategies and, 110, 111 (table)
See also Data collection
Scholarly writing, 206–207
attention thoughts and, 210
bias, reduction of, 211
big thoughts and, 210
computer tools and, 211
guidelines for, 211–212
habit of writing, development of, 209
little thoughts and, 210
model literature examples and, 211–212
practices of writing and, 207–208
principles of effective writing and, 210–211
thoughts, types of, 209–210
topic exploration through writing and, 208–209

umbrella thoughts and, 209–210
verb constructions and, 210
word usage and, 210
wordiness, avoidance of, 211
See also Journal articles; Qualitative reports
Scientific process of research, 68, 69 (figure)
Semiotic analysis, 170–171
Sensitive topics, 8, 30
Shadow side, 20
Silenced voices, 7–8, 224
Skype, 127
Social science theory, 43–44
Sociological Abstracts, 60
Software. *See* Electronic resources; Qualitative data analysis (QDA) software
Standards. *See* Quality criteria
Statistical analysis, 3, 198–199
Sub-questions, 45, 94, 99, 100 (figure), 122
Surveys, 3, 258

Technology. *See* Electronic resources; Qualitative data analysis (QDA) software
Theme passage development, 174
evidence, levels of, 175, 175 (figure)
multiple codes, multiple perspectives and, 178, 180 (table)
multiple information sources and, 178
quotations, incorporation of, 178–179, 180 (table)
raw data-to-themes process and, 155–156, 155 (figure)
theme labels and, 176, 178, 180 (table)
theme passage-to-coding analysis and, 156–157, 157 (figure)
theme passage, writing of, 157 (figure), 162, 175–179, 177 (figure)

themes, conceptual mapping of, 162–163, 163 (figure)
See also Coding textual data; Themes
Themes:
conceptual mapping of, 162–163, 163 (figure)
multiple themes, development of, 7, 14
open-ended questioning and, 14
raw data-to-themes process and, 155–156, 155 (figure)
See also Coding textual data; Theme passage development
Theory in qualitative research, 42
advocacy theory and, 43, 44–46
social science theory and, 43–44
Thesis/dissertation structure, 67–68
arguments for dissertation projects and, 68–69
general structural elements and, 69–71
journal article structure, concept map of, 71–72, 72 (figure)
macrostructural factors and, 67
process of research and, 68, 69 (figure)
quotations, use of, 220
varying forms of, 69
See also Abstracts; Qualitative reports; Titles
Thick description, 213–214
detailed description, placement of, 214–215
examples of, 215–216
See also Description; Qualitative reports
Thomson Reuters Corporation, 245
Titles, 76
central phenomenon and, 78
gerunds and, 78

guidelines for, 21–23
length of, 77
literary forms for, 77–78
open-ended language for, 77
participants, identification
of, 78
research site, mention
of, 78–79
revision/improvement
of, 77, 79
See also Abstracts; Journal
articles; Qualitative
reports; Thesis/
dissertation structure
Topic of research, 86 (figure),
87–88
Transcription process, 28
Tree diagram, 257, 258 (figure)
Triangulation, 117, 191

Validity checks, 190
collaboration with
participants and, 193
construct validity and, 191
disconfirming evidence
and, 192
external audits and, 193–194
external validity and, 191, 252

internal validity and, 252
ironic validity and, 191
member checking and,
192–193
multiple perspective on
validity and, 191
participants' lens and,
192–193, 192 (table)
peer debriefing strategy
and, 194
prolonged engagement in the
field and, 193
qualitative research, validity
in, 190–194
readers'/reviewers' lens and,
192 (table), 193–194
researcher reflexivity
and, 192
researcher's lens and,
191–192, 192 (table)
rich description of settings
and, 194
standards and, 252–253
statistical conclusion validity
and, 190–191
triangulation and, 191
validity strategies, selection
of, 194

worldview/paradigm
assumptions and,
191, 192 (table)
See also Qualitative validity
Video data. *See* Coding image
data
Visual elicitation approach,
167, 171–172
See also Coding image data
Voices of participants, 6, 7
qualitative journal articles
and, 13
silenced voices and, 7–8
in vivo language and, 156, 160
See also Participatory
research

Worldviews, 39–42, 41 (table)
Writing skills. *See* Abstracts;
Conclusion section;
Introduction section;
Journal articles; Proposal
writing; Purpose
statements; Qualitative
reports; Reflexive writing;
Scholarly writing; Thesis/
dissertation structure;
Titles